HISTORY OF HALIFAX COUNTY

HISTORY
OF
HALIFAX COUNTY

W. C. ALLEN
Superintendent Weldon Public Schools

AUTHOR OF NORTH CAROLINA HISTORY STORIES
A CHILD'S HISTORY OF NORTH CAROLINA
CENTENNIAL HISTORY OF HAYWOOD COUNTY
WHIGS AND TORIES

ILLUSTRATED

THE CORNHILL COMPANY
BOSTON

Notice

In many older books, foxing (or discoloration) occurs and, in some instances, print lightens with wear and age. Reprinted books, such as this, often duplicate these flaws, notwithstanding efforts to reduce or eliminate them. The pages of this reprint have been digitally enhanced and, where possible, the flaws eliminated in order to provide clarity of content and a pleasant reading experience.

Copyright © 1918, The Cornhill Company

Reprinted by:

Janaway Publishing, Inc.
732 Kelsey Ct.
Santa Maria, California 93454
(805) 925-1038
www.janawaygenealogy.com

2012

ISBN: 978-1-59641-262-0

Made in the United States of America

PREFACE

In September, 1915, Mrs. W. C. Allen, at the time, President of the Junius Daniel Chapter of the United Daughters of the Confederacy, of Weldon, suggested to the chapter the idea of writing the history of Halifax County as the year's work. The membership responded enthusiastically to the suggestion and unanimously decided to begin the task.

An outline of the county's history was made and topics assigned for investigation. The following members contributed papers: Mesdames Ida Wilkins, W. E. Daniel, J. W. Sledge, J. A. Johnston, Lee Johnson, J. A. Musgrove, W. A. Pierce, O. W. Pierce, J. W. Pierce, T. C. Harrison, J. S. Turner, L. C. Draper, R. S. Travis, John Zollicoffer, W. L. Knight, Ashby Dunn, H. D. Allen, W. T. Shaw, and Misses Mary Sledge, Julia Rhem, Laura Powers, and Annie Musgrove. These papers, together with notes and additions by the editor, constitute the story as it appears in this volume. In order to secure harmony of expression the editor has had to rewrite most of the material that was handed in. He has had also to verify the facts in order to be sure that there should be no misstatements. It is believed that a true story of the county is herein given.

Halifax is one of the real historic counties of the state, for within its borders some of the most important events in the making of North Carolina have taken place. Many of the men who have had much to do with the shaping of the State have either been natives of the county or have resided here at different periods of their lives. Throughout the colonial and Revolutionary periods, as well as the years since, Halifax County has played a conspicious part in the stirring events that have made North Carolina history so interesting and in the development of the State's resources.

With the hope that this little volume will help to introduce Halifax County more intimately to its own people and serve to make it better known to people of other counties and states, the authors and editor now send it forth upon its mission.

CONTENTS

PART ONE

CHAPTER		PAGE
I.	THE ORIGINAL INHABITANTS	3
II.	THE EVOLUTION OF THE COUNTY	6
III.	EARLY SETTLEMENTS	9
IV.	FORMATION OF THE COUNTY	14
V.	FORERUNNERS OF THE REGULATOR MOVEMENT	18
VI.	MUTTERINGS OF THE COMING STORM	21
VII.	LEADING UP TO THE REVOLUTION	26
VIII.	HALIFAX COUNTY AND NATIONAL INDEPENDENCE	30
IX.	NATIONAL INDEPENDENCE PROCLAIMED IN HALIFAX	36
X.	THE BIRTHPLACE OF THE STATE CONSTITUTION	40
XI.	EARLY DAYS OF THE REVOLUTION	44
XII.	HALIFAX COUNTY AND THE AMERICAN NAVY	48
XIII.	PASSING EVENTS	52
XIV.	THE BRITISH OCCUPATION OF HALIFAX	56
XV.	YEARS SUCCEEDING THE REVOLUTION	62
XVI.	HALIFAX COUNTY AND THE NATIONAL CONSTITUTION	65
XVII.	FIRST TWO DECADES OF THE NINETEENTH CENTURY	69
XVIII.	THE VISIT OF LAFAYETTE	73
XIX.	INTELLECTUAL DEVELOPMENT	76
XX.	SOCIAL AND ECONOMIC DEVELOPMENT	80
XXI.	COMING OF THE RAILROADS	86

CONTENTS

CHAPTER		PAGE
XXII.	"Royal White Hart Lodge"	92
XXIII.	Events Leading to the Civil War	99
XXIV.	In the Legislative Halls of the State	102
XXV.	The Call to Arms	106
XXVI.	War's Alarms	110
XXVII.	The Construction and Service of the Albemarle	115
XXVIII.	Closing Incidents of the War	121
XXIX.	Reconstruction Days	128
XXX.	Since Reconstruction Days	132
XXXI.	Some Odds and Ends of History	136
XXXII.	Summary	143

PART TWO

Builders of the County

I.	Joseph Montford	149
II.	John Baptista Ashe	151
III.	Willie Jones	153
IV.	William R. Davie	156
V.	James Hogan	162
VI.	Samuel Weldon	165
VII.	John Haywood	165
VIII.	Willis Alston	168
IX.	Willis Alston, Jr.	169
X.	Nicholas Long	170
XI.	Orondates Davis	171
XII.	John Bradford	172
XIII.	John Paul Jones	173
XIV.	Abraham Hodge	176
XV.	John Branch	177
XVI.	Hutchings G. Burton	181
XVII.	Joseph J. Daniel	183

CONTENTS

CHAPTER		PAGE
XVIII.	John R. J. Daniel	185
XIX.	Bynum and Potter	186
XX.	Bartholomew F. Moore	188
XXI.	Andrew Joyner	190
XXII.	Lawrence O'Bryan Branch	192
XXIII.	Edward Conigland	194
XXIV.	Junius Daniel	196
XXV.	Francis M. Parker	201
XXVI.	Spier Whitaker	202
XXVII.	Walter N. Allen	204
XXVIII.	Thomas L. Emry	206
XXIX.	Richard H. Smith	209
XXX.	George Green Lynch	212
XXXI.	Thomas N. Hill	215
XXXII.	Peter Evans Smith	218
XXXIII.	Robert O. Burton, D. D.	220
XXXIV.	Robert O. Burton, Jr.	223
XXXV.	William T. Shaw, Jr.	227
Others Who Have Wrought		229

LIST OF ILLUSTRATIONS

MAP OF HALIFAX COUNTY	Facing Page	8
WHITFIELD AVENUE, ENFIELD, N. C.	" "	16
GRAVE OF JOSEPH MONTFORD	" "	24
CONTINENTAL CURRENCY	" "	32
GEORGE WASHINGTON	" "	40
JOHN PAUL JONES	" "	48
BATTLE BETWEEN THE SERAPIS AND BONHOMME RICHARD	" "	56
WILLIAM R. DAVIE	" "	64
JOHN HAYWOOD	" "	72
LAFAYETTE'S RETURN	" "	80
THE ROANOKE RIVER, NEAR WELDON, N. C.	" "	88
ROYAL WHITE HART LODGE	" "	96
B. F. MOORE	" "	104
CONFEDERATE MONUMENT, WELDON, N. C.	" "	112
WILLIAM R. COX	" "	120
THE GENERAL DAVIS HOME, HALIFAX, N. C.	" "	128
OLD TRINITY CHURCH, SCOTLAND NECK, N. C.	" "	136
THE GROVE HOUSE	" "	144
RECEPTION TO WASHINGTON	" "	152
THE ROANOKE MILLS, ROANOKE RAPIDS, N. C.	" "	160
A TYPICAL SOUTHERN SCENE	" "	168
WASHINGTON AVENUE, WELDON, N. C.	" "	176
COLONIAL CEMETERY, HALIFAX, N. C.	" "	184
MAIN STREET, ROANOKE RAPIDS, N. C.	" "	192

One of the Good Roads, Halifax County,
 N. C. . . . . *Facing Page* 200
Court House, Halifax, N. C. . . . . " " 208
M. W. Ransom . . . . " " 216
Main Street, Littleton, N. C. . . . " " 224

INTRODUCTION

GEOGRAPHICAL SKETCH

Halifax County is situated in the northern portion of North Carolina, the most northerly point of the county lacking only about six miles of touching the Virginia State line. The Roanoke river skirts its northeastern border and Fishing Creek, a tributary of the Tar river, bounds it on the southwest. A strip of Martin County joins Halifax on the south. Warren County is on the northwest.

The county is slightly triangular in shape, the narrow part of the triangle being the southwestern portion and broadening toward the northeast. It is about sixty miles long and averages about twenty miles wide, and contains nearly 681 square miles of land surface.

In the southeastern section of the county, along the banks of the Roanoke river, the surface is level and the soil is exceedingly fertile. In the northwestern division, particularly west of the Wilmington and Weldon Railroad, the surface is rolling, resembling very much the Piedmont section of the state. Near the larger water courses, miniature canyons are frequent, through which the smaller streams flow in their ceaseless journey to the larger ones. At frequent intervals, along the Roanoke, "guts" pour their muddy volume of water into the giant stream.

On account of a curious topography, more than three-fourths of the drainage is south and southwest into Fishing Creek, the water shed lying quite close to the south bank of the Roanoke.

Besides the Roanoke river and Fishing Creek, which are not wholly within the county, there are a number of other water ways that give form and character to the surface. Flowing into the Roanoke, are Kehukee, Looking Glass, Quanky, Chockayotte, and Deep Creeks, and Conocanara and Cypress Swamps. Into Fishing Creek the following streams find their way: Deep, Powells, Butterwood, and Little Fishing Creeks and Marsh, Beech, Beaver Dam, Burnt Coat, Rocky, Jack Horse, and Bear swamps. Besides these, numerous rivulets and "branches" wind hither and thither in meadows and valleys. There are two Deep Creeks, one in the northern and another in the southern end of the county.

The climate is mild, highly suitable either for summer or winter residence and free from the extremes of either season. Out-door work is seldom interrupted by excessive heat or cold, or violent storms. The ground is seldom covered with snow for more than a few hours at the time. The mean annual temperature is about 58 degrees.

In the eastern and southern portions of the county, the soil is a gray sandy loam with a brown or red subsoil. In the western and northern section, a red clay subsoil and sandy loam predominate. Along the water ways, the soil is, in many places, made up of rich vegetable deposits and is very fertile.

The chief crops are cotton, corn, tobacco, potatoes, peanuts, hay, and oats. Many a farmer averages more than one hundred dollars an acre for his money crops.

The water power, supplied by the Roanoke river, is a source of present as well as future prosperity. From a point five miles above Roanoke Rapids, the river makes a fall of eighty-five feet to Weldon, thus furnishing a source of almost unlimited power. Numerous factories at Roanoke Rapids, Rosemary, and Weldon are supplied from this source, and those towns are also furnished with electric lights thereby.

In the eastern division of the county, the forest growth belongs to the normal type of upland piney woods, mixed with red cedar. Pine is the most important timber product. Oak predominates in the western portion with an intermixture of hickory, sweetgum, and dogwood. Near the river banks, the willow, ash, sycamore, maple, and cypress flourish.

Roanoke river, in the last few years, has been stocked with rockfish. Abundant also are shad, carp, catfish, and several other varieties. At certain seasons of the year the fishing interests are valuable.

For many years, both before and after the War between the States, the county was well supplied with deer, but the vigilance of the hunter has rendered that kind of game scarce. Squirrels and quails are found in large numbers in all parts of the county. Wild turkeys are found in certain sections. Wild geese and ducks are hunted on the Roanoke during the winter months.

Agriculture is the chief occupation of the people. Manufacturing cotton goods, hosiery, damask, pulp, and lumber form another important line of business. Peanut factories, cotton seed oil mills, fertilizer factories, and box factories also give employment to hundreds of men and women.

In 1916, the aggregate value of real and personal property in the county was over ten million dollars.

There are six towns of considerable importance, namely, Enfield, Halifax, Roanoke Rapids, Rosemary, Scotland Neck, and Weldon. Besides these, there are Hobgood, Tillery, Palmyra, Hollister, Ringwood, and Thelma. Littleton, a town of much importance, is partly in Halifax and partly in Warren County. Halifax has the distinction of having been at different times the seat of government of the province and afterwards of the new State. It also has the higher distinction of being the birthplace of the State Constitution and where the famous Independence Resolutions were passed April 12, 1776. Enfield is the oldest town in the county and was for several years the seat of Edgecombe county when it included Halifax. Enfield was also for a number of years the site of the district court of the counties of Edgecombe, Granville, Bute, and Northampton.

INTRODUCTION

Weldon, Roanoke Rapids, and Rosemary are extensively engaged in manufacturing. Scotland Neck is in the centre of the peanut industry, and is one of the largest markets in the world for that product. Hollister is a new town near the Warren County line where extensive lumber manufacturing is done. Hobgood is the junction of two branches of the Atlantic Coast Line Railroad.

There are twelve townships in the county as follows: Brinkleyville, Butterwood, Conocanara, Enfield, Faucetts, Halifax, Littleton, Palmyra, Roanoke Rapids, Roseneath, Scotland Neck, and Weldon.

Two trunk lines of railroads traverse the county. The Atlantic Coast Line, the highway from New York to Florida, crosses the central section of the county. The Seaboard Air Line passes through the northern portion and makes connection at Weldon with the Atlantic Coast Line. The Kinston Branch extends from Weldon to Kinston in Lenoir County through one of the finest sections of Halifax County.

There are extensive cotton and knitting mills at Roanoke Rapids, Rosemary, Weldon, and Scotland Neck. There is also a large pulp mill at Roanoke Rapids. A large lumber plant at Weldon exports large quantities of lumber. Peanut factories at Weldon and Scotland Neck prepare immense quantities of peanuts for the northern and western markets. There is at Weldon, also, an ice plant that supplies a large section of country.

Great improvements are constantly being made in building and equipping school houses, in the standardizing of the teaching force, in the enrichment of the course of study, and in the attendance of pupils. Besides the rural public schools that are found in every neighborhood, there are successfully operated city graded schools in Weldon, Enfield, Littleton, Roanoke Rapids, Rosemary, and Scotland Neck. At Littleton, there is a college for the education of girls. At Enfield is the School of Technology for the colored race.

HISTORY OF HALIFAX COUNTY

HISTORY
OF
HALIFAX COUNTY

PART ONE.

CHAPTER ONE.

THE ORIGINAL INHABITANTS.

Previous to the coming of white people, the Tuscarora tribe, or nation, of Indians held sway over the whole of Halifax County. They were the dominant peoples in Eastern North Carolina before the Albemarle country was settled. It is difficult to make an estimate as to the numbers of Indians that occupied the territory of the county at the time of the first settlements in the State. Excavations in various sections have brought to light many remains of that extinct race, which lead to the opinion that they were numerous along the banks of the Roanoke river and Fishing creek, but few and scattered in other places. Perhaps there were never more than a thousand in the county.

The country possessed by the Tuscaroras lay mostly along the Roanoke river, on both sides, and on the Neuse and the Tar. Other tribes in Eastern North Carolina were under the control to a large extent of the Tuscaroras and acknowledged their sway. Among these smaller tribes may be mentioned the Meherrins and the Yeopins, who lived in what is now Currituck, Camden, Pasquotank, Gates, and Northampton counties; the Pungos, the Chowanokes, and Croatans in what is now embraced in the counties of Perquimans, Chowan, Washington, Tyrrell, Dare, and Hertford; and the Corees, the Matchepungos, and the Mattamusketts in Hyde, Beaufort, Carteret, and Pamlico. Besides these, there were several other smaller and less important tribes; but none of them lived in Halifax County.

It is remarkable that for more than fifty years after the first settlements of white people in North Carolina there was complete peace between the races. While there were dreadful Indian wars and massacres in Virginia and the New England colonies, peace reigned in North Carolina between the white man and his red skin brother. This condition may be accounted for on the ground that the early settlers were regardful of the rights of the Indian, careful not to take their lands without recompense, paying them honestly for their furs, and abstaining from all acts of violence and hasty vengeance.

As in other parts of North Carolina, the Indians of Halifax County were living in a savage state. Their cultivation of the soil was of the rudest kind. Hardly any agricultural products were raised. Only a little Indian corn and a few potatoes, pumpkins, and melons were grown. The entire county with few exceptions was an unbroken wilderness. The women did what little agricultural work was done. The men hunted the deer, the raccoon, the buffalo, and the wild turkey. The dress of both men and women was of the simplest sort, consisting of skins and gorgeous headgear. Their homes were the wigwam made in the easiest way of poles covered with bark or skins of beasts that had been killed in the chase. In religion, they were pagan, believing in a Great Spirit that presided over the happy hunting ground of the beyond.

Nothwithstanding the fact that these Indians were few and in the lowest savage state, they have left some impression upon the county. Besides the relics that have been found in various localities, consisting of arrow heads and tomahawks of stone and specimens of pottery, they have left some names, such as Quanky, Chockayotte, Kehukee, and Conocanara.

THE ORIGINAL INHABITANTS

It is not known how soon the Indians vanished from the history of the county, but it is fairly well conjectured that nearly all of them had departed before 1720. At the close of the Indian War in 1713, the remaining Tuscaroras left the State and went to New York except the friendly Indians under "King Blunt," who were given lands in what is now Bertie County. It is thought that the last of the tribe in Halifax County left a few years later and joined their brethren in New York, where they united with the Iroquois, making the sixth nation of that powerful confederacy. Halifax County was thus clear of Indians at the time the white settlers began to come.

An incident is related of those early times that shows some of the traits of the red men of that day. While the Tuscaroras were occupying the "Indian Woods" in Bertie County, some of them often came to Halifax. On one of these trips, an Indian chief became desperately anxious for a bearskin blanket that belonged to Willie Jones, a prominent resident of Halifax. To make it known that he wanted the blanket, the chief told Mr. Jones that he had dreamed that the blanket was his. Indians then thought that dreams must come true. Mr. Jones readily made the chief a present of the blanket. Shortly afterwards the chief came again to Halifax. Mr. Jones called the Indian to him and said, "I dreamed last night that you gave me a tract of land of 500 acres in the Indian Woods."

"Ah! Willie, you beat me. You may have the land, but let's not dream any more," replied the chief.

It is not known whether or not Mr. Jones took advantage of this gift.

CHAPTER TWO.

THE EVOLUTION OF THE COUNTY.

About 1656, the first permanent settlements in what is now North Carolina were made on the eastern side of the Chowan river by emigrants from Virginia. By 1663, the population had increased to such an extent that the Lords Proprietors, to whom Charles II., king of England, had granted the territory of North and South Carolina, commissioned William Berkley, one of the Proprietors and, at the time, governor of Virginia, to appoint a governor for the colony of Albemarle. Berkley probably did not exercise his authority except by advice, for from a letter of the Proprietors to the new governor, William Drummond, it is very clear that they themselves commissioned him. In this letter of instruction to Governor Drummond the country is called the county of Albemarle, named in honor of the Duke of Albemarle, one of the Proprietors, the famous George Monk, who was one of the Parliamentary generals under Cromwell, and, after the collapse of the commonwealth, was the chief instrument in the restoration of Charles II. to the throne, and was rewarded for his services by being appointed to the peerage.

In 1722, on account of the increase of population west of the Chowan river, the Colonial Assembly with the sanction of the governor and his council organized Bertie precinct, which is described in the act of the Assembly as follows: "That that part of Albemarle County lying on the west side of Chowan river, being part of Chowan precinct, bounded to the northward by the line dividing this government from Virginia, and to the southward by Albemarle sound and Morotuck river, as far up as Welch's Creek, and then including both sides of said river

THE EVOLUTION OF THE COUNTY 7

and the branches thereof, as far as the limits of this government, be, and the same is hereby declared to be erected into a precinct by the name of Bertie precinct in Albemarle County."

"Morotuck" river as given in the wording of the act will be readily recognized as the Roanoke, the ancient Indian name being used instead of the modern one. Welch's Creek is a few miles up the Roanoke from Plymouth. So it is easily concluded that the present county of Halifax was included in this early precinct of Bertie.

In May, 1732, Governor Burrington and his council sitting at Edenton heard a "Petition of the south side of Roanoke river, Fishing Creek, and places adjacent," praying to have a new precinct erected on the south side of Roanoke river extending as far up as the mouth of Conocanara Creek. The petition was favorably acted on and the precinct formed and named Edgecombe. In October of the same year, the limits of Edgecombe precinct were more clearly defined so far as the portion bordering the Roanoke river was concerned. The eastern point was to be the Rainbow Banks, which is about two miles below the town of Hamilton, and the northern and western to be the southern line of Virginia.

Two members of the governor's council, Nathaniel Rice and John Baptista Ashe, protested against the formation of new precincts by the governor and his council without the concurrence of the popular branch of the Assembly as being in derogation of its rights. The governor and the other members were equally as determined as those two for the formation of the new precinct. So two memorials went to the Board of Trade in London, one from Ashe and Rice and another from the governor and his council, each memorial setting forth the reasons for and against the erection of the precinct, and each referring to the other in no complimentary terms. From that time, for about ten years, the contention was kept up as to the legality of the act of the council, and Edgecombe precinct was a name only, its representatives being denied seats in the Assembly. Finally at the session of the Colonial Assembly in 1741, under the administration of Gabriel Johnston, the act was confirmed and ratified, and the precinct of Edgecombe was thus established and allowed two representatives in the Assembly.

Many of the deeds recorded in Book I in the office of the Register of Deeds at Halifax, bearing dates between 1732 and 1741, locate the lands either in Bertie or Edgecombe precinct as the views of the draughtsman dictated. The deeds also, whenever the county is mentioned, locate the lands in Albemarle County, which shows that what is now Halifax County, in 1732 was either Bertie or Edgecombe precinct in the county of Albemarle. In 1738, an act of the Assembly changed the precincts into counties and so Edgecombe precinct became Edgecombe County.

In 1746, the northern portion of Edgecombe, that is the portion north and west of the present Warren County line, was cut off and converted into the county of Granville, which remained intact until 1764 when a portion of it was formed into Bute County, and later in 1779 Bute ceased to be a county and Warren and Franklin were formed from its territory.

Soon after the formation of Edgecombe County, the territory embraced in it was divided into two parishes for the convenience of the Episcopal clergy and the administration of the affairs of the established church. The parish of St. Mary included all that portion of the county south of Fishing Creek and Kehukee swamp. North of Fishing Creek to the Virginia line and west to the Granville County line was called Edgecombe Parish. Upon the formation of Halifax County a few years later, as will be seen, the parish of Edgecombe became the county of Halifax.

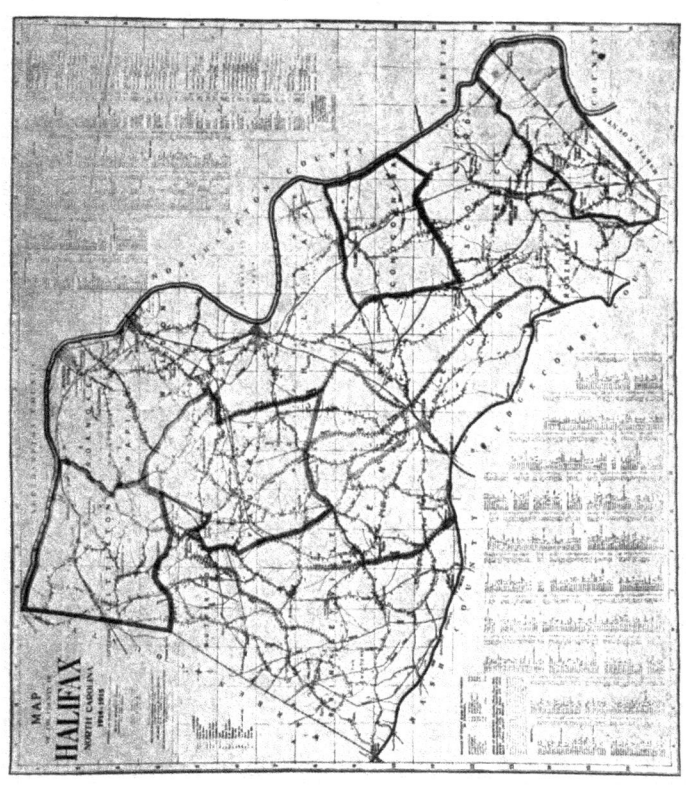

CHAPTER THREE.

EARLY SETTLEMENTS.

All of the early settlers of the northern portion of North Carolina came from or through Virginia. The reason for this is obvious. The coast of North Carolina being destitute of good harbors and known to be dangerous to shipping, all immigrants for the colony of Albemarle landed in Virginia and came to their destination by an overland route. It is also well known that many of the residents of the Old Dominion came to the southern colony as soon as the way was opened. At first the settlers clung to the shores of the sounds, the route being across the Albemarle sound to Mackey's Ferry about ten miles east of Plymouth, thence to Bath and across the Pamlico to Newbern and on to Wilmington.

At first all the territory in the colony of North Carolina was divided into two counties, Albemarle and Clarendon, the former being all the country around the Albemarle and Pamlico sounds and along the rivers flowing into them, and the latter the country on the Cape Fear river.

About 1670, Albemarle was divided into the precincts of Carteret, Berkley, and Shaftsbury, named in honor of three of the Lords Proprietors of Carolina. Fifteen years later, during the administration of Governor Seth Sothel, these three were abolished, and the territory divided into four precincts and given the names of Currituck, Chowan, Pasquotank, and Perquimans. When Bertie precinct was organized in 1722, the tide of immigration had flown westward across the Chowan river and was finding places of settlement along the banks of the Roanoke and on both the south and north sides of Fishing Creek.

HISTORY OF HALIFAX COUNTY

The first grants mentioned were in 1720, although one is referred to as early as 1714. These grants and deeds based thereon were located on the "south side of Morotuck river," which seemed to be the favorite localities for settlements, until some ten or fifteen years later when some grants were located on Fishing Creek, showing the gradual movement of population southward.

According to the records in the office of the Register of Deeds at Halifax, the first grants of land in the present limits of the county were on Roanoke river and near the mouths of Kehukee and Quanky creeks. The earliest that are on record were to William Jones on April 5, 1720, which lapsed and was regranted to William Pope, April 1, 1723. Quite close to that one in point of time was one to Philip Rayford, August 13, 1720, and to George Smith about the same time. The grant to William Pope is described as being "on the south side of Morotuck river and on Tuckahoe marsh;" those to Philip Rayford and George Smith on Conoconara Swamp.

There were many other grants located on Conoconara Swamp, Quanky Creek, Elk Marsh, Fishing Creek, Indian Creek, and Looking Glass Creek between 1720 and 1730 by Robert Long, Cornelius Pierce, Thomas Smith, John and Jacob Pope, Michael Aaron, and others. About ten years later grants by Edward Jones, Robert Hill, Joseph Hale, Henry Dawson, John Dawson, John Cotton, Joseph J. Alston, Marmaduke Norfleet, and others were located in the same section.

Other grants were about the same time, or a little later, made to the following, whose names are given because of the interest that may attach to some of them on account of the fact that their descendants are still living in the county: James Allen, Thomas Bradford, Thomas Bryant, James Bradley, Aaron Drake, William Drake, John Edwards, Charles Evans, John Green, Davie Hopper, James Hale, James Joyner, Thomas Jenkins, Nathan Joyner, Benjamin Johnson, James Moore, Thomas Matthews, Ephraim Owen, Edward Powers, John Rog-

EARLY SETTLEMENTS 11

ers, Edward Simmons, John Sojourner, James Saunders, Thomas Turner, James Thompson, Robert Wood, William Whitehead, Robert Warren, and others.

In 1722, a colony of Scotch Highlanders came across the Roanoke from Virginia and settled in a great bend in the river, and gave their settlement the name of Scotland Neck. The exact locality is not known, but it was somewhere in that large belt of fertile lands between the Caledonia farms and Palmyra. It is also unknown as to how many families were in this colony; but they were an industrious set of people, had built comfortable homes, and had raised several good crops of corn, tobacco, and wheat, when a tremendous freshet in the river swept away everything they had accumulated. Becoming discouraged, they abandoned the settlement and went to the Cape Fear country.

From 1732 to 1741, the period of contest over the validity of the establishment of Edgecombe precinct, there was probably no county seat, the county courts being held in private homes. There is a deed on record proved at a court held for Edgecombe precinct at the home of Robert Long on Elk Marsh, August 15, 1732.

It is reasonably clear that as early as 1732, people were living in all parts of what is now Halifax County. Immense grants of land had been located on Roanoke River north of Kehukee Creek as far north as the point where the old town of Gaston was situated. South and west of the Roanoke the tide of immigration had gone as far as the present town of Enfield and the neighborhood of Aurelian Springs. The early settlers were essentially an agricultural class and were looking for farming and grazing lands. They found them on the Roanoke near Looking Glass Run, Quanky Creek, Conoconara Swamp, Marsh Swamp, Chockayotte and Deep Creeks. Large farms were soon cleared in those sections and elegant country homes for those early times built.

Enfield, which at the time was known as Huckleberry Swamp, was selected about 1745 as the county seat of

Edgecombe County. By act of 1741, confirming the establishment of Edgecombe precinct in 1732, which had been changed from precinct to county in 1738, the Commissioners were empowered to levy a poll tax, not to exceed five shillings, for the purpose of erecting a court house. This was acted upon at an early date, and the building located at Huckleberry Swamp, which took the name of Enfield, probably in honor of old Enfield in England. This is the first mention of a town in the county. Enfield is, therefore, the oldest town in the present limits of Halifax County.

Soon after that event, by act of 1746, the judicial district of Edgecombe, Northampton, and Granville was formed, and Enfield was made the place of meeting of the new court. This distinction for Enfield of being the seat of the judicial district continued until about 1758. The writs and subpoenas were all issued from Newbern, at the time the capital of North Carolina, but the courts were held at Enfield.

In 1742, a settlement was made on Kehukee Creek which is of considerable note. This was a party of immigrants from Berkley, Va., led by William Sojourner. After establishing themselves in their new homes, they built Kehukee Baptist church, probably the oldest church of that denomination in eastern North Carolina. Some years later several Methodist churches were established on Fishing Creek. Episcopal churches had been built some years before in several sections of Edgecombe County. It is well authenticated that religion and sobriety characterized the early inhabitants of this section of North Carolina.

An attendant upon a yearly meeting of one of the churches on Fishing Creek in 1755 has the following to say about the inhabitants of Edgecombe County: "The inhabitants were principally from Virginia and some from Pennsylvania and Jersey. They are thrifty and intelligent." He further says that the prevalent population of the territory was English, the only settlement

EARLY SETTLEMENTS

of another nationality being the one at Scotland Neck, which failed.

The chief agricultural products of the times were rice, Indian corn, cotton in limited quantities, indigo, and tobacco. Naval stores, lumber, staves, pork, beef, hides, deerskins, furs, beeswax, and honey also formed a large part of the material wealth of the people. Tobacco, staves, and lumber were exported in considerable quantities as early as 1746.

CHAPTER FOUR.

FORMATION OF THE COUNTY.

As the population increased, it soon became apparent that the sections north and south of Fishing Creek in Edgecombe County were rivals of each other. It is probable that the northern part of the county, that is, what is now included in Halifax, was the more populous, because it was the first settled. From a report given to the British Board of Trade, the population of Edgecombe County in 1758 was: whites, over 16, 1674: blacks, over 12, 1091, making a total of 2765. Allowing for children below the ages given in the enumeration, the total population of Edgecombe County in 1758 was about 5000. As Edgecombe Parish, or the section north of Fishing Creek, was the more populous, it is probable that Halifax County as organized in that year had nearly 3000 people living in its borders.

In the latter part of the year 1757, Governor Arthur Dobbs and his council, sitting at Newbern, heard the petition of the residents of the parish of Edgecombe for the formation of a new county to be composed of all the territory of Edgecombe County north of Fishing Creek and Rainbow Banks on the Roanoke river. Early in the next year, the petition was granted and confirmed by the Colonial Assembly. A committee from the petitioners and the Assembly called upon Governor Dobbs and asked him to suggest a name for the new county and the place for the county seat. The governor immediately offered the name of Halifax, in honor of Charles Montague, Earl of Halifax, who was at that time President of the British Board of Trade, which had control of the commercial and economic affairs of the colonies, and Enfield was designated as the county seat. The name suggested was read-

FORMATION OF THE COUNTY

ily accepted, but the acceptance of Enfield as the capital was delayed because it was thought that the location of the county town should be more thoroughly considered. Later, Enfield was rejected because it was too far from the center of the new county, and the village of Halifax was chosen instead. Thus the county of Halifax came into existence without much formality, the parish of Edgecombe becoming Halifax and the parish of St. Mary's Edgecombe.

Halifax, which had thus drawn the prize of having been selected as the county seat, was an insignificant village. It is well authenticated that there were several families living on Quanky Creek near where it empties into the Roanoke as early as 1741. It was not until 1757, however, that this thrifty collection of homes on the Roanoke began to be thought of as a town. In that year, by act of the Colonial Assembly, one hundred acres of land were purchased from James Leslie at the price of one hundred and fifty pounds and vested in a board of trustees to sell to expected residents in town lots, the proceeds of the sale to go toward paying Leslie for the land, to build a bridge over Quanky Creek, and the surplus to go for town improvements. Four acres were to be reserved for municipal buildings. The town became of some importance in 1758, and when it was selected as the county seat, it immediately assumed a degree of thrift, that it maintained for a long number of years.

Enfield having lost out in the contest for the county seat of Halifax, and losing also, on account of geographical reasons, the court house of Edgecombe, was destined further to lose the distinction of being the seat of the district court of Edgecombe, Northampton, and Granville. As soon as the county of Halifax was organized, the following year the district court was abolished, and the court house was purchased from Edgecombe County and moved to Halifax, or such portions of the building as could be used in putting up the new structure.

The county, as established, embraced at first not only

16 HISTORY OF HALIFAX COUNTY

what is now included in its boundaries but also the larger part of what is now Martin County. The boundaries as defined at the time may be roughly stated as follows: Running from Rainbow Banks on the Roanoke river two miles below the town of Hamilton in a westerly direction to Fishing Creek about three miles above its junction with the Tar, thence up Fishing Creek to the Warren (then Bute) County line, and following that line to the Roanoke. It was a splendid domain for the making of a great county, about seventy-five miles long and averaging about twenty broad.

Thus established, Halifax entered the family of counties as the twenty-first on the list. Joseph Montford was elected first clerk of the County Court, and a full quota of officers was installed.

To the Colonial Assembly, which met in Newbern in 1760, the county sent as its first representatives Alexander McCulloch and Blake Baker. The town of Halifax, which had been made a borough, sent Stephen Dewey. These men at once took high rank in this legislative body of that early time. Being the first to represent the county in the legislative halls of the province, they have a distinction that others did not attain.

Alexander McCulloch came to this county from Scotland and located a few miles westward of the town of Halifax. He married the daughter of Benjamin Hill of Bertie County, and was a successful farmer. He represented the county several times in the Colonial Assembly and was afterwards for several years a member of the governor's council. Later he was deputy auditor of the province, having charge of the king's revenue, and still later he was clerk of the court of Halifax County. He was the ancestor of the family of McCullochs that have rendered the name honorable.

Blake Baker, the other represenative of the county in the Assembly of 1760, was the father of Blake Baker who was afterward attorney-general of the State and a judge. He himself was a lawyer and served on the judi-

WHITFIELD AVENUE, ENFIELD, N. C.

ciary committee of the Assembly. It is interesting to know that the family of Bakers that came to Halifax County from Virginia were distinguished for several generations, and the heads of the family for four successive generations were named Blake. The first Blake Baker came to the county from South Quay, Va. The second Blake, son of the first, was trained as a cabinet maker, but studied law and became prominent as a representative in the Colonial Assembly from Halifax County. Of Blake the third, the attorney-general and judge, it is said that he was bred for the law and by dint of hard labor, for he was not brilliant, he came to be considered one of the ablest lawyers of his day. He left a son also named Blake.

Joseph Montford, the first Clerk of the Court, was distinguished as a mason and citizen. A biography of him is given in Part II., "Builders of the County."

Stephen Dewey, the representative from the town of Halifax, was a lawyer and a man of considerable ability. He was a man of strong character. When he was elected, the town had just been made a borough and there was some delay in its official recognition. Governor Dobbs had failed to issue a writ for an election. The election, however, was held and Dewey elected. As soon as the question was raised as to the legality of the election, Dewey promptly declined the office. The governor was then appealed to for the necessary writ and another election held, and Dewey was again elected. He served two terms.

CHAPTER FIVE.

FORERUNNERS OF THE REGULATOR MOVEMENT.

In 1759, an incident occurred in Halifax County, which showed the resentment of the people of this section of North Carolina toward a system which was in operation at the time in the province. The spirit shown in that incident was the same as that which was exhibited some fifteen years later when North Carolina in convention at Halifax declared for the absolute independence of the colonies.

For many years previous to the formation of Halifax County, there had been much dissatisfaction in North Carolina on account of the exactions of the quit-rent collectors. The lands were not held in fee simple by the owners, but in addition to paying the regular price for the land they had to pay to the Lords Proprietors and later to the king an annual rental per acre. This was to be perpetual, for while a man might buy his land and get a deed for it, he was under obligation to the British Government to pay a yearly tax. There was no chance to escape this even though the settlers had paid the price asked for the land. The liberty loving North Carolinians did not like this system of feudalism, and often showed their resentment.

When the Proprietors sold their claims to the crown in 1729, Lord Granville reserved his right and refused to sell. His share, one-eighth of the whole, was allotted to him wholly in North Carolina. His line ran through the old town of Bath and the present town of Snow Hill and westward to the Mississippi river, taking in a large slice of the northern part of the province. Halifax County fell to the share of Lord Granville.

THE REGULATOR MOVEMENT 19

In the territory belonging to the king, the quit-rents were paid into the treasury of the province and helped to pay the expenses of the government. In Granville's district, however, the sums collected went into the coffers of his lordship, and hence were an additional cause for restiveness.

Francis Corbin and Thomas Bodley were the agents of Lord Granville for the collection of his rents, and had made themselves odious by extortions and other evil practices. Charges against them were being investigated by a committee of the Colonial Assembly, but the committee was slow in their deliberations and the Assembly adjourned without action. Irritated by this seeming indifference, the people in the district concerned became aroused and threatened to take action themselves upon the guilty agents. Matters hastened to a crisis in Halifax and Edgecombe counties.

In January, 1759, the feeling against Corbin and Bodley became violently demonstrative; and on January 24 a body of well mounted horsemen from Halifax and Edgecombe rode all the way to Edenton, the home of Corbin and Bodley, and seized the two agents in the night time and conveyed them to Enfield, where they were compelled to give bond for their appearance at the spring term of court. Having given bond and promising to disgorge all illegal fees and taxes collected, they were released.

Shortly afterward, Corbin and Bodley instituted suit against their abductors, and a number of them were put in jail at Enfield. Friends and sympathizers of the imprisoned men went to the jail one night and released them. Not content with emptying the jail, the rioters warned the agents that they had better drop the suits or worse results would follow. Accordingly the suits were dropped and Corbin and Bodley paid the cost.

Some months later, Corbin, who had been a member of the council, was dismissed by Governor Dobbs and removed from the agency by Lord Granville. This in a measure quieted the restlessness in the colony, and especially in Halifax.

A singular circumstance is that the Colonial Assembly was severe upon the rioters, while the governor was more favorable to them. Governor Dobbs intimated in some of his correspondence that his opponents in the Assembly found it to their interests to make up with Corbin, against whom the greatest charge was laid, and change sides, and there may have been some truth in what he said. Dobbs was a hot-headed Irishman who was in continual warfare with the Assembly throughout his administration, and the solution of the reason that the Assembly took sides against the rioters is that Dobbs was for them.

Colonel Saunders, in the Prefatory Notes to the Colonial Records, considers these rioters as the forerunners of the Regulators, who rose against the royal government of the province a few years later.

CHAPTER SIX.

MUTTERINGS OF THE COMING STORM.

For some years after the formation of the county, there is little to record except the mention of the rotation of the county officers and members of the Colonial Assembly. Joseph Montford continued to serve as clerk of the court until his death in 1776. He was also a representative in the Assembly for several terms, thus serving in a double capacity for a few years.

Until the adoption of the Constitution in 1776, the Colonial Assembly consisted of an upper house known as his Majesty's Council, composed of the Governor and a number of men appointed by the king, and the lower house made up of delegates elected by the people. The history of the different assemblies was one of continued strife between the governor and the lower house. To the lower house, Halifax County, as well as other counties of the State, sent its representatives. The following is a list of the representatives sent by the county and the town of Halifax for the sixteen years before the Declaration of Independence in 1776:

For the Borough of Halifax.

Stephen Dewey	1760-61
Alexander Elmsley	1762-63
Abner Nash	1764-65
Joseph Montford	1766-75

For the County.

Blake Baker and Alexander McCulloch	1760-61
Blake Baker and Joseph Montford	1762-65
John Bradford and William Branch	1766-68
Blake Baker and Alexander McCulloch	1760-61
Abner Nash and William Alston	1770-71
Benjamin McCulloch and John Alston	1772-74
Nicholas Long and Benjamin McCulloch	1775

Abner Nash, who represented the town and county at different times, afterwards became governor of the State. Halifax is not generally credited with having been the home of this Revolutionary governor, but it is quite clear that he lived in the town of Halifax for about twelve years before removing to Jones County. He owned a farm on Roanoke river and considerable real estate elsewhere in the county. While living in Halifax, he married the widow of the late Governor Dobbs, who was before her marriage with the governor, Miss Justina Davis. She died in 1771, before Governor Nash left the county, and is buried in the old churchyard at Halifax. Nash became Governor in 1780, but declined to serve longer than one year.

William Tryon was sent from England in October, 1764, to act as deputy governor with Governor Dobbs. Tryon was a dashing soldier and soon became popular with the people of the province. Governor Dobbs died in April, 1765, and Tryon succeeded to the governorship. Almost immediately upon his accession, Governor Tryon found himself in the midst of a nation-wide excitement about the passage of the Stamp Act. Wilmington, Edenton, and Newbern had their periods of excitement and clashes with the king's officers over the sale of the stamps. There were riots and disturbances in various parts of the province. Halifax County, being far removed from the ports where the stamps were to be landed for sale, was intensely interested, but made no particular demonstration. Governor Tryon found out the temper of North Carolina people when he asked John Ashe whether the people would continue their resistance to the Stamp Act duty and received as reply that "It will be resisted to blood and death." He, therefore, advised the repeal of the act, and it was done the next year.

In 1768, the movement of the Regulators in Orange County produced considerable excitement and some sympathy in Halifax. To show a kindred feeling with the

MUTTERINGS OF THE COMING STORM 23

Regulators, in their struggle against extortions and illegal taxes, the inhabitants of Halifax County petitioned the Governor and the Colonial Assembly that year to lighten the burdens under which they were living and to pass laws regulating the payment of fees for the issuance of all legal papers, the collection of quit-rents, and the payment of taxes. The petition was presented by William Branch, one of the representatives for that year, and shows some of the hardships that the people of that time endured. No action, however, was taken upon the petition.

When Governor Tryon called upon the counties of the Province, in 1771, to furnish troops to march against the Regulators, Halifax County refused to furnish any men to fight their comrades and friends in Orange and Alamance. It is to the credit of the county that it sent no soldiers to aid the royal governor in his merciless warfare upon the inhabitants of that section of North Carolina. With his sympathizers from other counties, he marched against the Regulators and defeated them at the Battle of Alamance.

At a meeting of freeholders in the town of Halifax, August 22, 1774, John Webb was chosen moderator, and the following set of resolutions was unanimously adopted:

1. We declare our loyalty to King George III.
2. That the proposed alteration in the administration of the criminal law in certain cases in Massachusetts would be unconstitutional and oppressive, and deprive the accused of the privilege of being tried by a jury of his peers, and their indigent circumstances would prevent them from having their witnesses transported to England.
3. That the Boston Port Bill was an illegal exercise of arbitrary power and an encroachment upon private property.
4. That the bill for changing the constitution of Massachusetts, now founded on charter, would be

5. That the Americans can only be legally taxed by those who represent them, and that it would be impracticable to send representatives across the sea.
6. That principles of honor, justice, and gratitude, as well as interest, should direct them on that occasion.
7. That all luxury and extravagance should be discouraged in order that debts in England might be discharged; and that sheep husbandry and manufacture of wool be encouraged, and that every person should apply himself with assiduity to his occupation in life.
8. That exports to England be continued until all debts were paid.
9. That the trade with the British West Indies be continued.
10. That after the twentieth day of September next we import no article, directly or indirectly, from Great Britain, nor purchase from those who do import, until the duty on tea be taken off, except certain articles absolutely necessary.
11. That the East India Company has insulted Americans in sending over tea contrary to the wishes of the Americans; and that we will use no more tea until the tax is taken off.
12. That unanimity and concord should be encouraged.
13. That, as Joseph Montford on account of indisposition cannot attend the meeting of the Assembly at Newbern, John Geddy be appointed in his place.
14. That the courts of law continue to exercise their jurisdiction.
15. That a copy of these resolves be inserted in the Newbern Gazette.

From the tone of these resolutions it will be seen that the spirit of opposition to Great Britain was becoming defiant. Notwithstanding the fact that they disclaim any intention of being disloyal to the British Government, they boldly assert that certain acts of the British ministry were arbitrary and tyrannical and that a peo-

GRAVE OF JOSEPH MONTFORD, 1776, HALIFAX, N. C.

MUTTERINGS OF THE COMING STORM 25

ple can be legally taxed only by a body in which they are represented. It is noteworthy that all extravagance and luxury was discouraged in order that debts in England might be paid. These sturdy yoemen of Halifax saw that a separation from England was coming, but they wanted, when it did come, to be free of debt to their enemy. Here was a tea party also when they declared solemnly that they would use no more tea nor import any article from Great Britain until the tea tax had been repealed.

This determined spirit of the people of Halifax was seen in all parts of the province, and when the first Provincial Congress met in Newbern on the 25th of August, 1774, there was strong evidence that North Carolina was taking a long stride toward independence. In that Congress, Halifax County was represented by Nicholas Long and Willie (Wiley) Jones, and the town of Halifax by John Geddy. The Congress took wise precaution to guard the safety of the province by the appointment of committees of safety for the various counties. The committee for Halifax was as follows: Willie Jones, Nicholas Long, John Bradford, James Hogan, Benjamin McCulloch, Joseph John Williams, William Alston, Egbert Haywood, David Sumner, Samuel Weldon, and Thomas Haynes.

CHAPTER SEVEN.

LEADING UP TO THE REVOLUTION.

December 21, 1774, the Committee of Safety met in Halifax and elected Willie Jones chairman, and transacted some business of special note. While in session, it was reported to the committee that Andrew Miller, a merchant in the town of Halifax, had refused to sign the resolutions that were passed by the freeholders, known as the Resolutions of the Association. A sub-committee was appointed to summon him before the full committee. Miller came and gave as his reason for not signing the resolutions that he had in his hands certain goods belonging to persons in England and that he could not ship these goods to England before the time given for the resolutions to go into effect. He stated that he did not think it just to sign as his creditors in England had no means to influence the repeal of the objectionable laws.

His explanation was not satisfactory to the Committee, and by vote it was decided that a general boycott be instituted against Miller and whatever partner or partners he might have. This was perhaps the first instance of the kind in the State. Governor Martin refers to these resolutions of boycott against Miller in a letter to Lord Dartmouth. It is evident that these Halifax patriots were determined that their resentment to the mother country for the unjust treatment of the American colonies should be forcible and unanimous.

A few words of explanation of the conduct of Andrew Miller in thus defying his fellow citizens may be necessary. He was a Scotchman by birth and a man of much ability and good standing in his community. Several of his letters are given in full in the Colonial Records, in one of which he speaks of expecting Governor Mar-

LEADING UP TO THE REVOLUTION 27

tin to spend ten days with him. The county records show that he was one of the executors of the will of James Milner, a prominent attorney of Halifax. As will be supposed, Miller became a Tory and soon afterwards fled from Halifax. His property was confiscated in 1779, and he was a refugee at Charleston at the close of the war. It is not known where he went from there when that city fell into the hands of the American army under General Greene at the close of the Revolution.

James Milner, mentioned in connection with the Tory, Andrew Miller, was a leading lawyer of the Halifax bar during the period just before the outbreak of the war. He practiced in the courts of the province even as far away as Hillsboro. He died before the beginning of the Revolution, and the records show that he left considerable property. Several of his letters appear in the Colonial Records.

When the second Provincial Congress met in Newbern, April 3, 1775, Halifax County was represented by Willie Jones, Benjamin McCulloch, and Nicholas Long, and the town of Halifax by Joseph Montford and John Webb. Little was done at this session and an adjournment was taken to Hillsboro in August the same year.

At this session, which met August 21, Halifax County was represented by Nicholas Long, James Hogan, David Sumner, John Webb, and John Geddy. The town of Halifax was represented by Willie Jones and Francis Nash, who was living at the time in Hillsboro. One of the important things done by this Congress was the division of the Province into five military districts and the appointment of a colonel for each district. The Revolution had actually begun; the Battle of Lexington had been fought; the Mecklenburg Declaration of Independence had been signed; Washington had begun the siege of Boston; excitement was rife throughout North Carolina.

The Congress also authorized the enrollment of five hundred minute men in each district. Nicholas Long was chosen colonel of the Halifax department, which was composed of the counties of Halifax, Edgecombe, Northampton, and Granville. Henry Irwin was chosen lieutenant-colonel and Jethro Sumner, major. For the county of Halifax, the following were chosen officers of the minute men that were to be raised: John Bradford. Colonel; William Alston, Lieutenant-Colonel; David Sumner, First Major; Egbert Haywood, Second Major. Congress allotted to the county the enrollment of three companies of the militia that had been authorized.

The Hillsboro Congress took a step toward State sovereignty by the organization of a provincial government called the Provincial Council, which was to exercise the executive functions that had been wielded by the royal governor, who was now a refugee on a British gunboat at the mouth of the Cape Fear river. Cornelius Harnett, of Wilmington, was the chairman of this council and was thus the chief executive officer of the province. Halifax County was honored in having as a member of this Provincial Council Willie Jones, who was among the first elected by the Congress. To act on the Committee of Safety of Halifax district, James Leslie, John Bradford, David Sumner, and John Webb were appointed from the county.

During these troublesome times, Halifax County was specially free from anything like dominating Tory influence. Only a few loyalists were found in the county, and these were kept under such surveillance that they exerted very little assistance to those who were trying to uphold the power of the king in North Carolina. Andrew Miller, as has been related, was a Tory, and John Hamilton, another merchant of Halifax, who, after his flight from Halifax in 1776, rose to high rank in the British army. Besides these two, there were a few others, who were obnoxious. All of them were watched by the patriots and arrested and brought before the Committee of Safety for punishment, if they made any move in behalf of the king.

LEADING UP TO THE REVOLUTION

At a session of the Provincial Council, held at Smithfield, December 18, 1775, John Branch, sheriff of Halifax County, brought before that body Walter Lamb and George Massenbird, charged with certain crimes, and prayed punishment upon them as Tories. Lamb was remanded for trial at the next meeting of the Committee of Safety of Halifax County; but Massenbird seems to have experienced a change of heart and became penitent, under pressure, took the oath of allegiance to the Provincial Council, and was released. It is not known why they were taken to Smithfield, but the presumption is that they had taken an appeal from the decision of the Halifax Committee.

CHAPTER EIGHT.

HALIFAX COUNTY AND NATIONAL INDEPENDENCE.

For Halifax County, North Carolina, and all America, the year 1776 was momentous. The preceding year had come to a close with the Revolution just commencing. In the beginning, the resistance to British authority was only rebellion. Except the Mecklenburg Declaration of May 20, 1775, there had been no intimation anywhere in America of a desire to separate from the mother country. All the colonies declared, in effect, that they were fighting for their rights as Englishmen and not to establish an independent nation. So firmly fixed in the minds of the people was the idea of loyalty to the British crown that, when the Mecklenburg Declaration was passed and Captain Jack despatched with a copy to the Congress at Philadelphia, he was coldly received even by the North Carolina delegation and the copy of the Declaration pigeon-holed indefinitely.

As time, however, passed and the struggle with Great Britain became more and more desperate, a change took place in the feelings of Americans toward England. Before even a year had passed, people all over the colonies began to think that the war, which had begun as a rebellion was fast becoming a revolution. In no colony was the growing spirit of independence more pronounced than in North Carolina, and in no county was it more alive than in Halifax.

Ominously did the year 1776 open in North Carolina. Everybody felt that the war now under way was to be long and fierce. Early in January, the British Commander-in-Chief, whose headquarters were in Boston, sent his agents to various points in North Carolina to arouse the Tories and organize them for service against

NATIONAL INDEPENDENCE

the patriots. In the central and western part of the province, there was a bitter struggle for several months between the two factions; but the Tories were finally defeated and forced to submit or flee the country.

In Cumberland County, where the Highland Scotch had settled, more than two thousand Tories assembled at Cross Creek and began their march upon Wilmington to meet a British army of invasion that was to make a landing on the Cape Fear. Before reaching Wilmington, however, they were totally defeated by the patriots, on February 27, and dispersed. The leaders of the Tories in this Battle of Moore's Creek Bridge, Colonels Donald and Allan McDonald, the latter being the husband of the famous Flora McDonald, were captured and brought to Halifax and confined in the jail there. Colonel Nicholas Long, in command of the militia of Halifax district, apprehended other Tories that were trying to escape capture after the battle and were passing through Halifax and confined them in jail. The names of forty-six of these refugee Tories are given in the reports of these captures besides others whose names are not given. They were detained in jail in Halifax until paroled some months afterward.

After the Battle of Moore's Creek Bridge, sentiment in North Carolina for independence rapidly crystallized. Although a British army of invasion and twenty-seven enemy gunboats were on the Cape Fear, the people of the province set their faces steadfastly toward a separation from England. In Halifax County, the spirit of revolution was unchecked.

So when the Provincial Congress met in Halifax April 4, 1776, it found a sympathetic people to give encouragement to its deliberations. Samuel Johnston, of Edenton, was elected president and James Green, Jr., secretary. Halifax County was represented by John Bradford, James Hogan, David Sumner, Joseph John Williams, and Willis Alston. Willie Jones was elected to represent the town of Halifax, but, having been appointed by the Continental Congress superintendent of Indian affairs for the southern department and being absent on account of the duties of that office, John Webb was chosen in his stead.

After matters of a minor nature were disposed of by the Congress, the discussion of national affairs was entered upon. The sentiment for independence was well nigh unanimous, and it was enthusiastically decided that the Congress should go on record in some expression regarding it. Accordingly, a committee was appointed to draft suitable resolutions. This committee, consisting of Cornelius Harnett, Thomas Burke, Allen Jones, Thomas Jones, Abner Nash, Thomas Person, and M. Kinchin, made their report on April 12. Cornelius Harnett was the chairman of the committee and made the report as follows:

"It appears to your committee that, pursuant to the plan concerted by the British ministry for subjugating America, the king and parliament of Great Britain have usurped a power over the persons and properties of the people, unlimited and uncontrolled, and, disregarding their humble petitions for peace, liberty, and safety, have made divers legislative acts denouncing war, famine, and every species of calamity against the continent in general. The British have been, and still are, daily employed in destroying people and committing the most horrid devastations on the country. The governors in different colonies have declared protection to slaves, who imbrue their hands in the blood of their masters. The ships belonging to America are declared prizes of war, and many of them have been violently seized and confiscated. In consequence of all which, multitudes of people have been destroyed, or from easy circumstances reduced to the most lamentable distress.

"And whereas, the moderation hitherto manifested by the United Colonies, and their sincere desire to be reconciled to the mother country on constitutional principles have procured no mitigation of the aforesaid wrongs and

usurpations, and no hope remains of obtaining redress by those means alone which have been hitherto tried, your committee are of the opinion that the House should enter into the following resolve, to wit:

"Resolved, that the delegates from this colony, in the Continental Congress, be empowered to concur with the delegates of the other colonies in declaring Independence and forming foreign alliances, reserving to this colony the sole and exclusive right of forming a constitution and laws for this colony, and of appointing delegates from time to time (under the direction of a general representation thereof) to meet the delegates of the other colonies for such purposes as shall be hereafter pointed out."

This resolution, the first of the kind in all America, was adopted unanimously on the twelfth of April, antedating the Virginia resolves of the same nature a little more than a month. As is well known, the Continental Congress acted upon this resolution of North Carolina, which was well seconded by Virginia by a like resolve on May 15, and a national Declaration of Independence was passed July 4, 1776.

April 14, the Congress appointed a committee, of which John Bradford was a member, to prepare a temporary civil constitution for the purpose of changing from a provincial to a State government. The word "temporary" was used in the naming of the committee probably for the reason that the decisive step for independence had not yet been made. It is not known how far the committee proceeded in their deliberations, but no constitution was adopted at this session.

Two men were appointed, by resolution, from each county, whose duty should be to receive, purchase, and procure firearms for the use of the troops. Egbert Haywood and David Crawley were appointed from Halifax County. The militia of the province was reorganized with brigadier-generals in command of the districts. Allen Jones, who lived at Mount Gallant in Northampton County, was appointed to command the troops of Halifax district. The following field officers for Halifax County were appointed: Willis Alston, Colonel; David Sumner, Lieutenant-Colonel; James Hogan, First Major; Samuel Weldon, Second Major.

Before adjournment, the Congress provided for the erection in the county of a powder mill, and appointed Willie Jones, Benjamin McCulloch, and Josiah Sumner to have control of it.

At this Congress, one of the most important ever held in the province, a great deal of business was transacted, that relating to Halifax County, owing to its peculiar interest, is given in full,—

It was resolved that a declaration be published that the Congress was compelled to remove the prisoners, captured in the late campaign, into other provinces on account of the public safety. This action relieved the pressure in the Halifax jail, where there had been incarcerated a large number of Scotch Tories.

A committee was appointed to look into the matter of the seizure at Newbern of a vessel belonging to John Hamilton, a Tory merchant of Halifax.

William Hooper, Joseph Hewes, and John Penn were appointed delegates to the general Congress to be held in Philadelphia.

John Webb was added to the committee for the county for procuring arms. Colonel Nicholas Long was directed to collect all the arms that may have been taken from Tories and hold them ready to supply recruits for the minute men.

Colonel Long was requested to proceed to the Virginia line, with a detachment of troops, and escort General Charles Lee, an officer of the Continental army, to Halifax. He was passing through to inspect the troops in this State and in South Carolina and Georgia.

It was ordered that 1500 minute men be enrolled in the districts of Edenton, Newbern, Halifax, and Wilmington, and proceed to Wilmington for the defense of the State. Halifax district was to furnish seven companies; from Halifax 100 men, Edgecomb 100, Bute 100, and Northampton 75.

All the militia of the colony was divided into six brigades, one brigade in each district, to be commanded by a brigadier-general. All males between the ages of 16 and 60 were declared subject to military duty. Each county was to be organized into a regiment, which was to be subdivided into companies of not less than fifty men.

Bills of credit were issued to the value of $1,000,000 for the purpose of defraying all expenses of armaments, bounties, and other contingencies that should occur during the recess of Congress. It was resolved that "Any person or persons, who should attempt to depreciate said bills of credit by refusing to take the same in payment of any debt or contract, or by speaking or writing with the intention to lessen their credit and currency, shall be considered as inimical to America."

The Provincial Council and the Committees of Safety were dissolved, and, in their stead, was substituted a Council of Safety to consist of one man to represent the Congress and two from each of the six districts, which should serve until the next meeting of the Congress. Willie Jones was chosen to represent the Congress and Thomas Eaton and Joseph John Williams to represent Halifax district.

After a session of a month and ten days, the Congress adjourned on May 14 to meet again in Halifax November 10, 1776, unless sooner called together by the Council of Safety.

CHAPTER NINE.

NATIONAL INDEPENDENCE PROCLAIMED IN HALIFAX.

During the incipient stages of the Revolution, the town of Halifax was the scene of many stirring events. After the adjournment of the Provincial Congress, the Provincial Council of Safety, of which Willie Jones was a distinguished member, was in session in Halifax for more than a month during the summer of 1776. While in session on July 22, news of the passage of the Declaration of Independence at Philadelphia was received. The Council immediately passed the following resolution:

"Resolved, that the committees of the respective counties and towns in this State, on receiving the Declaration of Independence, do cause the same to be proclaimed in the most public manner, in order that the good people of this colony may be fully informed thereof."

While in session, July 25, the Council proceeded to change the test oath so as to make it conform to the character of the State as free and independent. By resolution, the preamble to the oath was made to say that the "Colonies are now free and independent states, and all allegiance to the British Crown is now forever at an end." On the 27th of the same month, the Council set apart by resolution, in conjunction with the Committee of Safety of Halifax County, Thursday, August 1st, as a day for proclaiming the Declaration at the court house in Halifax.

Accordingly, on that eventful day, a great concourse of people from all parts of the county met to witness the interesting ceremonies. The Provincial troops, that were in Halifax at the time, and the militia companies were all drawn up in martial array to give interest

INDEPENDENCE PROCLAIMED IN HALIFAX 37

to the occasion. At midday, Cornelius Harnett ascended a rostrum which had been erected in front of the court house, and even as he opened the scroll, upon which were written the memorable words of the Declaration, the enthusiasm of the immense crowd broke forth in one loud swell of rejoicing. Harnett proceeded with his task in measured tones and read the immortal document to the mute and impassioned multitude with the solemnity of an appeal to Heaven.

When he reached the end and read the names of the signers, among whom were William Hooper, Joseph Hewes, and John Penn, North Carolina's members of the Continental Congress, a spontaneous shout went up from hundreds of mouths, and the cannon from the fort at Quanky and the Roanoke boomed the glorious tidings that the Thirteen Colonies were now free and independent States. Cornelius Harnett was lifted from the rostrum and carried through the streets upon the shoulders of the enthusiastic populace. It was a great day in Halifax.

Shortly before this great demonstration in Halifax, the following officers of the two companies of Halifax County militia had been appointed by the Council of Safety: James N. Parsons and Henry Dawson, Captains; P. Cox and William Noblin, Lieutenants; Caleb Munday and John Champion, Ensigns. The total strength of the two companies as reported at that time was 105.

At the same sitting of the Provincial Council of Safety at Halifax, the following singular order was made: John Webb, of Halifax County, was allowed to export 18,000 hogsheads of staves to any of the French or Dutch cities on giving bond that he would import the proceeds in salt, arms, ammunition, and other warlike stores.

Other matters relating to Halifax County came up during the session and were disposed of. An order of special note is one appointing a committee to examine certain lead mines said to have been discovered on Big Fishing Creek. It is not known what was the final report of this committee, but they made a partial report some time later in which they said that lead ore was not found in sufficient quantity to justify working.

It was ordered also that the treasurer of the State pay Colonel Willis Alston fifty pounds to employ guards for the town of Halifax. John Hamilton, the Tory merchant, came before the Council and asked an appeal from an order of condemnation of his vessel at Newbern shortly before that time. This was allowed. It is of interest to know that Hamilton soon found out that the atmosphere of Halifax was not wholesome for Tories, and he fled to the British. As he was the most influential of the Tories that joined the British army in North Carolina, the following sketch is given of him:

"Before the outbreak of the Revolutionary war, there lived in Halifax a prosperous and influential man by the name of John Hamilton, who came from Scotland, his native country, in early life. He engaged in merchandising in Halifax and acquired a considerable fortune. Being well educated, he was naturally a leader, affable in manner and popular.

"When the war of Revolution began, Halifax County, as a whole, was enthusiastically patriotic, and joined heartily in the movement for independence. It was a source of regret to the people of the county that so capable a man as Hamilton refused to join in this movement. His friends and neighbors urged and entreated him to enlist on the side of the colonies, but he steadfastly claimed allegiance to the king. He continued his business, however, in Halifax until toward the close of 1776, when Governor Caswell issued his proclamation, calling upon all residents of the State to take the oath of allegiance to North Carolina within sixty days or move to other scenes. This proclamation caused a great many Tories to leave the State, among whom was Hamilton. He seems to have been the leader of the Tories even at that time, for he did most of the correspondence with Governor Caswell in securing passports for them.

He, with others, went to Jamaica; but soon afterwards returned to the states, joined the British forces in Georgia in 1778, and assisted in the capture of Savannah that year. In the meantime, his property had been confiscated by the State government.

"Hamilton's career as a soldier in the British army was brilliant. He entered the army as a private, but rapidly won distinction, reaching the rank of colonel in little more than a year's time. In one of his many battles with the patriots, he was captured by Colonel William Washington in 1780, but shortly afterwards exchanged and rejoined the British army. He was placed in command of the Royal North Carolina regiment in 1781 and commissioned to enroll in his regiment Tories of North and South Carolina and Virginia. He was with Lord Cornwallis, in his campaigns in the South, and surrendered with him at Yorktown.

"After the treaty of peace, he went to England and lived there for several years. Later, he was British consul at Norfolk, Va., and often during his term of office there visited Halifax, and mingled freely with the friends he knew there before the outbreak of the war."

CHAPTER TEN.

THE BIRTHPLACE OF THE STATE CONSTITUTION.

While the Provincial Council of Safety was in session at Halifax, a resolution was adopted calling upon the people to elect, on the 15th of October, delegates to a Congress appointed to assemble at Halifax, November 12, 1776. This Congress was not only to make laws, but also to form a State constitution, and can, with propriety be called the First Constitutional Convention of North Carolina. The elections were held throughout the State in accordance with the call. The following were elected to represent Halifax County in the Congress and Convention: John Bradford, James Hogan, Willis Alston, Samuel Weldon, and Benjamin McCulloch. For the town of Halifax, Willie Jones was elected. During the session, James Hogan, having been elected Colonel of the seventh regiment of continental troops, tendered his resignation as delegate for the county, and Egbert Haywood was elected to the vacancy.

The Convention met, as called, November 12th, and proceeded to organize. Richard Caswell was elected President of the body; Cornelius Harnett, Vice-President; James Green, Jr., Secretary; and James Glasgow, Assistant Secretary. Willie Jones and Benjamin McCulloch were members of the committee of privileges and elections. John Bradford was a member of the committee to settle civil accounts of the State.

This convention was a notable body. Among its members were some of the most distinguished men of the State. In the list of members, there are such names as Maurice Moore, Cornelius Harnett, Archibald McLean, Phileman Hawkins, Thomas Jones, Richard Caswell, Thomas Person, David Caldwell, Waightstill Avery, Al-

From the painting by Gilbert Stewart

GEORGE WASHINGTON

BIRTHPLACE OF STATE CONSTITUTION

len Jones, William Hooper, Griffith Rutherford, Joseph Hewes, Willie Jones, Abner Nash, and many others, who have rendered the State illustrious service in peace and in war. With such a galaxy of heroes, the State could well make its beginning.

Soon after assembling, the committee on Bill of Rights and Constitution was appointed. Halifax County was honored with two members of this committee of twenty-eight, Willie Jones and James Hogan. The committee was composed of the ablest men in the convention.

One of the first matters of business was the admission of Watauga, in the district of Washington, Tenn., as a county. This was done by motion of Willie Jones and carried by a vote of 153 to 1. In waiting were the delegates from the new county, Charles Robertson, John Carter, and John Wade, and they were admitted and the oath administered to them. Some days later, John Sevier, afterwards renowned in the history of the State and nation, another delegate from Watauga, arrived, and was admitted. James Hogan was appointed to administer the oaths.

John Bradford and Willie Jones were appointed to examine the accounts of Colonel Nicholas Long, rendered at the last session of the Congress. The committee shortly afterwards reported that the accounts were correct and that the allegations against him were groundless. It is unknown just what these charges against Colonel Long were, but the inference was that he was charged with misappropriation of funds or extravagance. It is certain that the committee, of which Bradford and Jones were members, made a searching investigation and declared that Colonel Long was blameless.

By resolution, it was ordered that a battalion of volunteers be dispatched to the aid of South Carolina, which was, at the time, threatened by an invasion of British troops. Samuel Weldon was appointed major of this battalion and two of the lieutenants were Josiah Pearce and John Champion, of Halifax. Later, Josiah

Pearce resigned, and Albritton Jones, of Halifax was appointed to succeed him.

In the records of the meetings of this convention, several orders were entered relative to a magazine for the storage of ammunition for the State troops. It was probably located in the town of Halifax at or near the present spring of that name. From this magazine supplies were distributed to the troops operating anywhere in eastern North Carolina.

Additional regiments for the Continental line were ordered by the Congress, and James Hogan was appointed Colonel of one of these regiments, that was raised largely in Halifax County. The following men from the county were appointed officers in these regiments that were to be raised: Henry Dawson, Captain; William Noblin, First Lieutenant; Jacob Barrow, Second Lieutenant. James Hogan was shortly afterwards assigned to the command of the seventh regiment of Continental troops.

Henry Montford, of Halifax, asked permission to ship staves to the West India Islands, and his request was granted.

December 6th, Thomas Jones, of Chowan County, Chairman of the Committee on Bill of Rights and Constitution, reported that the committee was ready to make its report. He read the report to the Convention, which body, by motion, appointed December 18 for its consideration.

Automatically, therefore, the Constitution came up for discussion on the eighteenth. Thomas Jones, of Chowan, and Willie Jones, of Halifax, are generally credited with being the authors of the Constitution as reported to the Convention that day. They were, therefore, ardent champions of its adoption. Very little opposition was developed as the document as written seemed to meet the requirements. The paper was read paragraph by paragraph, discussed pro and con, and adopted after amendments and changes were made. An engrossed copy was sent to James Davis, the State printer, at Newbern with directions to print and distribute a number of copies in each county.

After the adoption of the Constitution, the Congress went into the election of State officers to serve until the next meeting of the General Assembly, which was, thereafter, to elect all officers of the State government. The following were elected: Richard Caswell, Governor; James Glasgow, Secretary of State; and the following Counsellors of State,—Cornelius Harnett, Thomas Person, William Day, William Haywood, Edward Starkey, Joseph Leech, Thomas Eaton.

By the same Congress, the militia of Halifax County was reorganized with the following officers: Willis Alston, Colonel; Samuel Weldon, Lieutenant-Colonel; John Geddy, First Major; John Wheaton, Second Major.

Having completed the task before it of drafting a Constitution for the new State and making laws and regulations, needed during that time that tried men's souls, the Congress and Constitutional Convention adjorned a few days before Christmas, thus giving to the world a gift, which has been a blessing to a large part of civilization.

CHAPTER ELEVEN.

EARLY DAYS OF THE REVOLUTION.

To give anything like a connected account of the services and activities of Halifax County soldiers during the Revolution is impossible for the reason that the rosters of the Continental line do not give the counties from which the companies were enlisted. The militia of the county was, also, embraced in the rosters of the district of Halifax, and it is not at all clear what counties of the district should be credited with certain troops.

Two companies from the county, those of Captains Parsons and Dawson, numbering 51 and 54 respectively, are mentioned in the reports as being with General Ashe at Wilmington in July, 1776. It is possible, therefore, to give in only a general way the part which Halifax took in winning on the battlefield the independence of the State. It is quite sure that these companies went with General Ashe the next year, and were with him in the campaign in Georgia when that State was conquered by the British.

In the early part of 1777, a recruiting camp, called Camp Quanky, was opened at Halifax, for the purpose of recruiting the older regiments and for forming the three battalions ordered by the Congress. Colonel John Williams was in command of the camp and, according to the reports sent in from time to time, he was successful in enlisting the required number of men in a comparatively brief time. The older regiments were brought up to the required number of men, who were quickly dispatched to the front.

During the summer of 1777, the cause of liberty and independence was hanging in the balance. Washington's army in the North had dwindled to a few thousand men,

EARLY DAYS OF THE REVOLUTION 45

and these were poorly equipped and supplied with arms. In great contrast to the condition of the American army was that of the British which had landed at New York, in July, numbering thirty thousand men, and was seeking to attack and destroy Washington's little command.

Washington had sent out urgent appeals for reinforcements to all the states. Governor Caswell issued orders for North Carolina's quota of Continental troops to hurry to Washington's assistance. Halifax was made the place of rendezvous for all these troops before setting out for the north. Here about four thousand men assembled. In July, under the command of General Francis Nash and with such able leaders as Colonels Hogan, Sumner, Buncombe, and Davidson, the troops set out, and, after marching about five hundred miles, joined Washington at Philadelphia just in time to assist in the disastrous battles of Brandywine and Germantown, in which General Nash and Colonel Buncombe were killed besides a considerable number of the rank and file.

It is interesting to note that Halifax jail appears to have been at this time the general prison for Tories captured at different places in the State. Shortly before the establishment of Camp Quanky, the celebrated Flora McDonald spent some time in Halifax in the interest of her husband, Allan McDonald, who was captured at the Battle of Moore's Creek Bridge and confined in the Halifax jail. It is said that, during his confinement, she exhausted her means in trying to effect his release, which she finally succeeded in accomplishing.

In the spring of 1777, the Tory hydra began to show itself in a limited way in Halifax County. The county records of that date show that the jail was filled with persons charged with disaffection to the patriot cause. Willie Jones, in a letter to Governor Caswell, speaks of these prisoners as being very obnoxious. It is worthy of note that these Halifax County patriots were vigilant enough to prevent anything like organized bands of marauders among the Tories, and, as soon as a Tory showed his hand, he was promptly arrested and put into a dry place in jail.

In Edgecombe County, there had been considerable trouble with the Tories. A marauding party of them had made an attack upon Tarboro, but Colonel Irwin, of that county had forestalled them and disarmed the whole crowd, forcing them to take the oath of allegiance. It is quite clear that some of these men who were giving trouble in Edgecombe had fled from Halifax.

John Hamilton and Andrew Miller had left the county and State some months before. Other Tories had gone with them, and it was thought that Toryism was at an end; but William Brimage, a man of considerable influence in Halifax, in 1777, became outspoken in his allegiance to the British crown and made himself especially obnoxious. Governor Caswell issued a special order for his arrest at all hazard. General Allen Jones, in command of the brigade of the Halifax district, in one of his reports, speaks of William Brimage as one of the leaders of the cut throats. He fled from Halifax and was arrested near Edenton and lodged in jail there. His wife is buried in the old churchyard at Halifax. With him ended Toryism in Halifax County. Thereafter, there were no Tories in Halifax.

With Toryism thus stamped out, Halifax County passed the remainder of the year 1777 with very little excitement. The only other thing of note was the session of the court of oyer and terminer, held by Judge Samuel Spencer in the summer of that year. In a letter to the governor, Judge Spencer complained that he had great difficulty in securing persons to act as clerk of the court and State's attorney. This was one of the few sessions of that court that was held in Halifax during the Revolution, owing to the disordered condition of the country.

In the fall of 1777, an incident occurred that is worthy of mention. Lieutenant John Allen, a gallant soldier in the battalion of Continental troops from Halifax, performed a heroic feat in bringing from Baltimore to New-

EARLY DAYS OF THE REVOLUTION 47

bern $2485.50, which was to be used to pay off soldiers. Allen was selected by John Penn, member of the Continental Congress from North Carolina, for this special duty. He secured a swift horse, and, with the money concealed about his person, made the perilous trip through British and Tory lines to Newbern and delivered the money into the hands of Governor Caswell. Lieutenant Allen was highly commended by his superior officers for this act of heroism. The report of this heroic act is found in the Colonial Records.

CHAPTER TWELVE.

HALIFAX COUNTY AND THE AMERICAN NAVY.

In the summer of 1775, during the excitement incident to the war then going on, John Paul Jones, who afterwards won the title of "father of the American navy", came to Halifax and sojourned there for more than a year. He had, prior to that time, varied experiences, and had met with many misfortunes. In early manhood, he had gone from his native country, Scotland, as a sailor, had been master of a trader, had killed a man in self-defense during a mutiny of the sailors, and had to flee from the avengers of blood on account of that act. Coming to America, he had made his way to Virginia, and finally he found himself in Halifax.

One morning, as the story is told, Willie Jones came down the street from his home, the Grove House, and saw sitting in front of the Eagle Hotel a stranger. As was the custom of Mr. Jones, he came up to the stranger and accosted him.

"Where is your home?" asked Mr. Jones.

"I have none," replied the other.

"What is your name?" inquired the questioner.

"I have none", replied the disconsolate stranger.

Mr. Jones became interested, and, after a few more questions, succeeded in getting the stranger to tell him something of himself. He was invited to the Groves, and later, on account of his ready wit and gentlemanly bearing, became an adopted member of the family. The stranger was no other than the afterwards celebrated John Paul Jones. His name was John Paul, but, in compliment to Willie Jones, he assumed the name of Jones.

Through the influence of Willie Jones, Joseph Hewes, a member of the Continental Congress from North Caro-

HALIFAX COUNTY AND AMERICAN NAVY

lina, became acquainted with John Paul, probably during the Constitutional Convention in Halifax, and later nominated him for the position of Captain of the gunboat, Ranger, which position was tendered him by vote of Congress. John Paul accepted the position tendered him, and never again was a visitor to Halifax, but he retained his admiration of Willie Jones even among the stirring scenes he later witnessed.

As commander of the Ranger, John Paul Jones performed some daring deeds of valor in British waters and even upon British soil. He was received in France as a hero, and the French government, in the spring of 1779, fitted out a squadron, with the Bonhomme Richard as the flag ship, and put Jones in command. On the 23rd of September, 1779, the British frigate, Serapis, was encountered, and the Bonhomme Richard, at once, prepared for action. The following account of the battle that followed is taken from that of James Fenimore Cooper, who pronounced it "The most bloody and obstinate battle in the annals of naval warfare." While not a quotation from Cooper, the account that follows is in accordance with the facts as brought out by him.

When Jones sighted the enemy, it was about noon, and he at once ordered every stitch of canvas to be set. He did not, however, come in fighting position with the enemy until about seven o'clock in the evening, at which time objects on the water could be only dimly discerned, but the bright moon assisted the Americans.

When within pistol shot, the Richard hurled a broadside at the British ship, and the fight was on. The Serapis was a new ship, built in the best manner, and with a much heavier armament than the Richard. She was commanded by Captain Richard Pearson, of the British navy, a naval officer of experience and courage.

In the early part of the action, the superior sailing qualities of the Serapis enabled her to take several advantageous positions, which Jones was unable to prevent. Not long after the fight began, many of the 18-pound shot of the Serapis had entered the hull of the Richard below the water line, and she began to leak in a threatening manner. Jones ran the Richard up alongside the Serapis and prepared to board, but the flag pole of his ship was shot away and the Stars and Stripes dropped into the sea.

Just before the boats closed, however, Captain Pearson, of the Serapis shouted above the roar of the battle to Jones: "Has your ship struck her colors?"

Jones thundered back his defiant and famous reply: "I haven't begun to fight yet".

From the beginning to the ending of the battle, there was not a man on board the Richard, who was ignorant of the superiority of the Serapis. The crew of the Serapis were picked men, whereas the Richard's crew consisted of a part of English, French and American sailors, and a part of Maltese, Portuguese, and Malays, the latter contributing by their want of naval skill and knowledge of the English language to depress rather than encourage any reasonable hope of success in a combat under such circumstances.

The terror of the scene was soon heightened by both vessels taking fire; but the fight continued with unabated fury. A rumor ran through the crew of the Richard that Jones had been killed. A frightened sailor ran up to haul down the flag. The flag had been shot away and Jones arrived upon the scene in time to knock the coward down and force him to continue the fight. At last the mainmast of the Serapis began to totter to its fall, her fire slackened, and about midnight the British flag was struck, and Captain Pearson surrendered his sword to Jones.

So terribly was the Richard cut to pieces that it was found impossible, after the fight, to get her into port, and she sank soon after. Jones took his prize to Holland, and it is no exaggeration to say that the whole world was astonished at his bravery and success. He was received in Paris with the greatest demonstrations of honor and respect. On one side of the English Channel it was "the pirate Jones," and on the other, "Jones, the hero." The King of France gave him a gold mounted sword and asked the consent of Congress to decorate him with the Order of Military Merit. Congress voted him its thanks and a gold medal. Later, he was made a Chevalier of France.

Jones, now a hero of renown, remained in France until the early part of 1781 when he returned to America and was placed in command of the frigate America. He set forth his ideas of a navy, which the government was slow in adopting. He went again to France in 1783, where he remained for four years, and returned to America in 1787. The next year Jones entered the service of Russia, but was later humiliated by the jealousy of the Russian officers and compelled to resign his command. Returning to France, he remained in retirement during the rest of his life. He died July 18, 1792, in the forty-fifth year of his age.

His remains were buried in Paris, and, by neglect, the burial place was lost. In 1905, however, the remains were discovered by General Horace Porter, the American Ambassador to France, and transported to America and consigned to rest at the United States Naval Academy at Annapolis. There is a monument to the "Father of the American Navy" in Potomac Park, Washington, D. C.

CHAPTER THIRTEEN.

PASSING EVENTS.

Very little of historical importance occurred in Halifax during the years 1779 and 1780. Stirring events, however, in which troops from the county played a conspicuous part, were transpiring elsewhere. "Mad" Anthony Wayne, in one of the most daring and extraordinary bayonet charges in all history, captured Stony Point on the Hudson river from the British, July 15, 1779. Major Hardy Murfree, of Hertford County, with a battalion of North Carolinians, some from Halifax, led a portion of the attacking columns and performed heroic service. Horatio Gates was disastrously defeated at Camden, S. C., by the British under Cornwallis, and Benjamin Lincoln surrendered Charleston. In both of these disasters, soldiers from Halifax participated with signal though unavailing bravery.

At Charleston, James Hogan, who had shortly before been promoted to the rank of brigadier-general by the Continental Congress, fell into the hands of the British, was imprisoned at Haddrell's Point, S. C., and there soon afterward died. With him was captured, also, the regiment of 600 men he had enlisted at Halifax the year before. It is said of General Hogan, whose home was near where Hobgood is now, that he refused the offer of a conditional parole because his men were not offered the same favor and preferred to remain and bear the hardships of prison life with them. His grave is somewhere in South Carolina, but the exact location is unknown.

At Camden, the American army was almost annihilated by the veteran troops under Earl Cornwallis.

General Gates fled from the field early in the fight and left the doomed men to destruction. Hal Dixon's regiment of North Carolinians, some of them from Halifax, and some Marylanders, were the only troops to hold their ground to the last, retreating in good order from the field only when it was seen that all was lost. General Isaac Gregory, of Camden County, led the Edenton brigade, among whom were some Halifax militia, but he was wounded and forced to retreat.

Two sessions of the General Assembly were held in Halifax during 1779, the first beginning January 19th and ending February 13th, and the second extending from October 18th to November 10th. In both of these sessions, the County was represented in the Senate by Orondates Davis and in the House of Commons, the first session, by Egbert Haywood and John Whitaker, and the second session by Willie Jones and Augustine Willis. The town of Halifax was represented in the House of Commons, both sessions, by Henry Montford.

Not much legislation affecting the county was enacted. About the only thing of note was the petition of the people of the lower end of the county to be detached from Halifax and united to Edgecombe. There appears to have been no objection to this on the part of the Halifax members. John Whitaker, in response to the petitioners, introduced the bill for this slice of Halifax to be transferred to Edgecombe, and the generous deed was done. By vote of the Assembly, the following officers of the Halifax regiment of State Militia were elected: John Whitaker, Colonel; James Allen, Lieutenant-Colonel; John Branch, First Major; William Weldon, Second Major.

Halifax, being at the time the real capital of North Carolina, was well guarded by the militia of the State. Several regiments were continuously held in camp in and around the town. The jail was also still crowded with military prisoners. In June, 1779, General Allen Jones, in command at Halifax, in a report to the governor, said that he was compelled to give the prisoners all the liberty possible because of the crowded condition of the jail and because he feared an epidemic might break out among them. At the session of the General Assembly of 1780, the following officers of the Halifax regiment were recommended to the governor for appointment and were accordingly commissioned: James Allen, Colonel; John Branch, Lieutenant-Colonel; William Weldon, First Major; Thomas Scurlock, Second Major.

The year 1781, was a stirring one for Halifax County and its people. Several events, occurring elsewhere, but participated in by Halifax County men, deserve more than a passing notice.

At the Battle of Cowpens, South Carolina, January 17, 1781, Colonel Tarleton, with a command of British regulars, was signally defeated by General Daniel Morgan, of Virginia, with a small body of Continental troops and a few battalions of North Carolina militia. In this conflict, Halifax County soldiers performed heroic service.

Nicholas Long, a kinsman of Colonel Nicholas Long and a gallant soldier in the Halifax battalion of Continental Cavalry, was with Colonel William Washington in his celebrated chase of Tarleton from the battlefield, in which Tarleton received a sabre cut in the hand administered by Colonel Washington. In the pursuit Long became separated from his comrades and found himself assailed by two British troopers. He wheeled and took the back track, hotly pursued by the dragoons, who fired upon him but missed their aim. In the chase, the troopers became separated, and Long observing it, suddenly turned upon his pursuers, and, with his sabre, unhorsed both men in detail and held them at his mercy until assistance arrived.

In Morgan's race with Cornwallis for the Catawba river and in Greene's retreat to the sheltering waters of the Dan, Halifax County troops performed their part. When Greene recrossed the Dan and fought Cornwallis to a standstill at Guilford Court House, men from Halifax were in the thickest of the attacks and counter attacks. When the British army retreated to Wilmington about the first of April, 1781, it was clearly demonstrated that North Carolina had beaten the hitherto invincible Cornwallis and was sending him to his doom.

CHAPTER FOURTEEN.

THE BRITISH OCCUPATION OF HALIFAX.

After the retreat of Cornwallis from Guilford Court House to Wilmington in March, 1781, it was a matter of keen speculation as to what that discreet and intrepid officer would next undertake. Patriot leaders all over the State had their attention focused upon him and were endeavoring to forecast his next move. Lingering only three weeks in the city by the sea to rest his troops from their arduous campaign, Cornwallis proceeded northward to Virginia in response to orders he had received from the British Commander-in-chief in New York.

General Greene, instead of pursuing the defeated British, turned aside and led his army into South Carolina in order to expel the British from that State. Cornwallis was, therefore, left to march unopposed, across the State. Only a few regiments of State Militia were in arms, and they were busy watching the movements of the Tory forces that had begun to mobilize.

At Halifax, as soon as it was known that Cornwallis was marching northward, there was great excitement among the people and hurried preparation among the soldiers stationed there. General Allen Jones, in command of the troops of the Halifax district, with Governor Nash, was holding his forces in readiness to attack the invading enemy if an opportunity should be presented. General Jones had his headquarters in Halifax and the regiments from Northampton, Edgecombe, Warren and Halifax were encamped along Quanky in daily expectation that the enemy would appear.

About the first of May, it was known that the British had left Wilmington and were several days on the march. Scouting parties were sent out from Halifax to ascertain

BATTLE BETWEEN THE SERAPIS AND BONHOMME RICHARD

THE BRITISH OCCUPATION OF HALIFAX 57

their whereabouts. It was learned on May 3rd that Tarleton's dragoons had crossed Fishing Creek and were advancing along the Huckleberry Swamp road. Governor Nash and General Jones held a hasty conference together with the commissioned officers of the different regiments, and the decision was reached that it would be a useless expenditure of life to undertake to oppose the advance of the British with untried militia against Tarleton's veteran cavalry.

Accordingly, on the afternoon of May 3rd, General Jones retired with his command in the direction of Warrenton, leaving Halifax to the mercy of the enemy. Governor Nash and the Council of State, together with other State officials, also left the town. Halifax, therefore, readily and quickly put aside its military appearance and assumed the air of an unpretentious village.

The next day, Tarleton at the head of two hundred dragoons, crossed Quanky and rode into the town. The redcoats passed down the street, observed indifferently and scornfully by the people, and came opposite the Eagle Hotel where they halted. Tarleton and his aids dismounted and went into the hotel and secured rooms for Cornwallis and his retinue and himself and his aids. Again mounting, they rode back to meet Cornwallis and the rest of the army. The town was completely occupied on the afternoon of May 4th, and the British troops to the number of about four thousand encamped on Quanky, on the Grove estate, on the plantation of Colonel Nicholas Long, and in the homes of the residents in and around Halifax.

From Wheeler's History of North America the following incident of the occupation is extracted. It was originally published in the **People's and Howitt's Journal** of New York:

"On the march of the British army from Wilmington to Virginia, in 1781, Colonel Tarleton, near 'Twanky Chapel' in Halifax County, either from a scarcity of provisions or from a malicious desire to destroy the property of the American citizens who were opposed to the British, caught all the horses, cattle, hogs, and even fowls that he could lay hands on, and destroyed or appropriated them to his own use. The male, and most of the female inhabitants of the country fled from the approach of the British troops, and hid themselves in the swamps and forests adjacent; and when they passed through the upper part of the county, while every one else left the premises on which she lived, Mrs. Powell (then Miss Bishop) stood her ground, and faced the foe fearlessly. But it would not do; they took their horses and cattle, and among the former, a favorite pony of her own and drove them off to the Camp, which was about a mile distant. Young as she was, she determined to have her pony again, and she must necessarily go to the British camp, and go alone, as no one would accompany her. And alone she went, on foot, at night, and without any weapon of defence, and in due time arrived at the British camp.

"By what means she managed to gain an audience with Tarleton is not known, but she appeared before him unannounced, and raising herself erect, said, 'I have come to you, sir, to demand restoration of my property, which your knavish fellows stole from my father's yard.' 'Let me understand you, Miss,' replied Tarleton, taken completely by surprise.

"'Well, sir,' said she, 'your roguish men in red coats came to my father's yard about sundown, and stole my pony, and I have walked here alone and unprotected to claim and demand him; and, sir, I must and will have him. I fear not your men; they are base and unprincipled enough to dare to offer insult to any unprotected female; but their cowardly hearts will prevent them from doing her bodily injury.'

"And just then, by the light of a camp fire, espying her own dear little pet pony at a distance, she continued, 'There, sir, is my horse. I shall mount him and ride peaceably home; and if you have any of the gentlemanly feeling within you of which your men are totally destitute, or if you have any regard for their safety, you will

THE BRITISH OCCUPATION OF HALIFAX

see, sir, that I am not interrupted. But before I go I wish to say to you, that he who can, and will not prevent this base and cowardly stealing from henroosts, stables, and barnyards, is no better, in my estimation, than the mean, good-for-nothing, guilty wretches who do the dirty work with their own hands! Good night, sir.' And, without waiting further, she took her pony, uninterrupted, and galloped safely home. Tarleton was so astounded that he ordered that she should be permitted to do as she chose."

This was Tarleton's first defeat at Halifax at the hands of a woman. He met with another more crushing a day or two later. Mrs. Ellet, in her "Women of the Revolution", has recorded the names of two Halifax women, Mrs. Willie Jones and Mrs. Nicholas Long, whose patriotic zeal is greatly commended. Wheeler speaks as follows about Mrs. Jones:

"Mrs. Willie Jones was a daughter of Colonel Mountford (Joseph), and combined with much personal beauty, great brilliancy of wit, and suavity of manner. One of her acquaintances says that she was the only person, with whom he was ever acquainted, that was loved devotedly, enthusiastically loved, by every human being who knew her."

There is a well known story regarding a passage of wit between Mrs. Jones and her sister, Mrs. John B. Ashe, on the one hand, and Colonel Tarleton on the other. The incident occurred at the home of Willie Jones, the Grove house. Colonel Tarleton, in the presence of the two ladies, referred to Colonel William Washington, who had wounded Tarleton in the hand at the Battle of Cowpens, in an uncomplimentary way as an illiterate, ignorant boor, hardly able to write his name. Mrs. Jones quickly resented the language used by the British officer.

"Colonel Tarleton," she said, "You know very well that Colonel Washington, if he can't write as well as some men, knows how to make his mark." As she said this she glanced at Tarleton's hand, which bore the scar of Washington's sabre stroke. The fiery Briton turned red, but continued the conversation.

"I would be happy to see Colonel Washington," said Tarleton, sarcastically, trying to recover his lost ground.

"If you had looked behind you at the Battle of Cowpens, Colonel Tarleton," rejoined Mrs. Ashe, in the same spirit, "You would have enjoyed that pleasure."

That thrust was too much for the already chagrined officer, and his hand involuntarily grasped the hilt of his sword. At that moment, however, General Leslie, Tarleton's superior, entered the room, and, seeing the situation, rebuked the discomfited Briton, and the incident closed.

Wheeler speaks as follows of Mrs. Nicholas Long: "Mrs. Long was a Miss McKinney. Her husband, Colonel Nicholas Long, was Commissary-General of the North Carolina forces. She was a woman of great energy of mind and body, and high mental endowments. She died at the advanced age of eighty, leaving a numerous offspring. Her virtues and patriotism were the themes of the praise and admiration of the officers of the army of both parties."

While encamped at Halifax, foraging parties were sent out by Cornwallis into nearly every section of the county to gather supplies for his army before setting out to Virginia. Stedman, the historian who was with the British during the occupation of Halifax, records the fact that these foraging parties, or marauders, were guilty of some crimes that were a disgrace to the name of man. Tarleton, in his "Campaign in the Southern Provinces of North America", states that a sergeant and a dragoon were executed at Halifax for rape and robbery.

The patriot forces, who had retired from the town upon the arrival of the British, kept watch upon the movements of the enemy, and were ready at any time to pounce upon them. The Edgecombe regiment under Colonel Hunter, Halifax under Colonel Allen, and Northampton under Colonel Gee were still in arms and ready to strike the foe at a minute's notice. There were unimportant clashes between the opposing commands at

THE BRITISH OCCUPATION OF HALIFAX 61

Swift Creek, Fishing Creek, and near Halifax. In one of the bold dashes of the patriots into Halifax, one of the American cavalry-men became separated from his comrades, and, as he dashed for safety across Quanky bridge, was confronted on the bridge by several of the enemy. Beset behind and before, he reared his horse and made him leap the railing, plunging to the water thirty feet below. The horse was killed, but the daring hero made his escape. Tradition does not record his name.

After a delay of about a week, Cornwallis crossed the river at Halifax and retired slowly through Northampton and Brunswick County, Va., to Petersburg, where he was joined by the British army operating in the Old Dominion under General Philips and the traitor, Benedict Arnold. Halifax was thus rid of the enemy and was at once reoccupied by General Allen Jones in command of the Halifax brigade. Cornwallis, after a short and decisive campaign in Virginia, surrendered his entire command to General Washington on October 19, 1781.

CHAPTER FIFTEEN.

YEARS SUCCEEDING THE REVOLUTION.

News of the surrender of Cornwallis was received in Halifax, late in October, 1781, with demonstrations of joy. The militia in arms paraded the streets and fired salutes in honor of the glorious tidings. Everyone felt that the long war had victoriously ended, that the independence of the colonies was established, and that British dominion was forever terminated in the United Colonies.

Each of the thirteen states was now independent, and, there were, therefore, thirteen sovereign republics, where a few years before there had been thirteen provinces. Each one was independent of all others and owed no allegiance to any power on earth. An important question now uppermost in the minds of all was to determine where this spirit of sovereignty would lead and how to regulate its course.

In the solution of this important and perplexing question, Willie Jones, the sage of Quanky Creek, performed an interesting part. He had served as a delegate in the Continental Congress during the closing years of the Revolution; but now that the war had closed he refused to act in that capacity longer, saying that the Congress had been created as a war expedient, and, having done its work, there was no longer any reason for its existence. He, therefore, retired from the Congress to his home in Halifax, and refused to take part in any further business of a national character. North Carolina was the only sovereignty he acknowledged.

For several years after the close of the Revolution, there is very little to record. When peace was declared the men, who had been on the firing line, in garrisons, and in camp, returned to their homes, and began again the building up of their communities. Apparently, so glad was every one that the terrible war had closed that no one was thoughtful enough to perpetuate in writing, or otherwise, the part that the county had taken in the momentous struggle.

It is said that, after the close of the Revolution, there was not even a pamphlet written on State history for a period of about forty-five years. In consequence of this neglect, North Carolina has never received credit for what her people did during those times. Along this line a letter written from Halifax to Archibald D. Murphy by Allen J. Davie in 1826 will be illuminating. Among other things he said:

"In writing a history of this State, it will be almost absolutely necessary, in order to do justice to the part we bore in the Revolution to have access to my father's papers, particularly of some books of correspondence written from '79 to '83, which show that North Carolina supported the troops of the whole Southern States, and, that without the aid of the specific tax laid by this State and placed under the management of my father, General Greene would have been forced to disband his army and the cavalry of Virginia, which they could not feed; that both man and horse grew fat on the flesh pots of the Roanoke; circumstances for which, as a State, we have never, either as a State or as individuals, had justice awarded us."

Mr. Davie, in this letter, is referring to the services which his father, General William R. Davie, rendered the State while he was Commissary-General. It is clear, therefore, as "both man and horse grew fat on the flesh pots of the Roanoke," that Halifax County, occupying the greatest extent along the Roanoke, was a large part of the granary which supplied the needs of the southern army during the times that tried men's souls.

During this period of comparative silence, it can only be inferred that the people of Halifax County were "pursuing the even tenor of their way" with very little to characterize them above the people of other counties. Dr. Kemp P. Battle, of the University of North Carolina, in an address at the Centennial of Salem Academy in 1902, gave a pen picture of the conditions prevailing in North Carolina during the generation following the Revolution, much of which applies directly to Halifax County. Among other things, he says:

"Our geographer of 1802 speaks kindly of our people. He described them as mostly planters, living three or four miles apart in a plentiful country, but with no ready market for produce. Many farmers turned their corn into whiskey and their wheat into flour, and sent them on lumbering wagons to distant regions, while others converted the grain into hogs, and the produce of the fields thus became at once a savory article of food and a grunting but convenient vehicle for the transportation of itself. Hogsheads of tobacco were placed on little wheels, with axletree and shafts and then rolled hundreds of miles to market.

"The farmers with no near neighbors were extremely hospitable to travelers, who brought them the news from the great world; but they had a plentiful lack of literature and science."

For Halifax County farmers, the only markets, of any degree of importance, during the period from 1780 to 1800, were Petersburg, Richmond, and Norfolk. To these towns of the Old Dominion, the farmers along the Roanoke sent their produce, sometimes in wagons, and often in boats, down the river and sound to the ocean, and up to Norfolk. Droves of hogs, sheep, and cattle were regularly driven overland to these cities. Hogsheads of tobacco, as mentioned by Dr. Battle, were regularly transported on wheels to Petersburg, where tobacco factories had been located, and where there was a ready market. Halifax County, thus isolated, but naturally rich, began its slow development.

William R. Davie

CHAPTER SIXTEEN.

HALIFAX COUNTY AND THE NATIONAL CONSTITUTION.

Early in 1786, the question of North Carolina's attitude toward a central government for the thirteen independent States was uppermost in politics. In no county was it more discussed than in Halifax, where two distinct views were held. Willie Jones was an ultra States Rights man and looked with disfavor upon the proposition. Opposed to him was General William R. Davie, who had located in Halifax for the practice of law in 1783, and who was an earnest advocate of the proposition to unite the States in a stronger bond of union than existed under the Articles of Confederation. Each of these distinguished and able men had their earnest supporters.

When the Constitutional Convention was called to meet in Philadelphia, in May 1787, the General Assembly selected the following delegates: Richard Caswell, Hugh Williamson, William R. Davie, Alexander Martin, Willie Jones, and Richard Dobbs Spaight. Halifax County had two in this eminent body, Willie Jones and William R. Davie. Richard Caswell was, at the time, governor of the State and decline to serve, William Blount, of Beaufort County, being appointed in his place. Willie Jones refused to have anything to do with the convention and did not go. Davie went to Philadelphia and was present throughout the long session from May to September and had considerable influence in making and shaping the immortal document.

After the Constitutional Convention adjourned, General Davie returned to Halifax an enthusiastic advocate of the immediate adoption of the Constitution by the State. Willie Jones, however, counselled caution and delay. The State Convention to ratify or reject it was called to meet in Hillsboro in August, 1788. Both Willie Jones and William R. Davie were delegates from Halifax County, and were the real leaders of their respective views in the discussions.

Soon after assembling, it was ascertained that the Anti-Federalists were in the majority. Willie Jones was the recognized leader of that division of the delegates and had the convention in his grasp from beginning to end. Notwithstanding the eloquence of Davie and the logic of James Iredell in advocacy of the constitution, when the vote was taken, the constitution was rejected by a vote of 84 to 184. North Carolina thus refused to enter the union and took no part in the election of George Washington as president in the fall of 1788. The next year, however, another convention at Fayetteville ratified the Constitution, and North Carolina became a member of the Federal union.

On April 16, 1791, George Washington, in his tour of the Southern States, while he was president, arrived in Halifax and spent a night in the ancient borough. There is nothing definitely known as to how he was entertained during his stay. Tradition has given out the information that he was royally banqueted at the Eagle Hotel, which stood near the river in the lot almost opposite the old Allen home, now standing. The president seems to have been somewhat impressed with the town; for in his diary, which he kept on his journey from place to place, he has a lengthy paragraph conveying his impressions. The following is the paragraph referred to somewhat modernized as to punctuation and capitalization:

"Halifax, N. C., Saturday, April 16, 1791.

"At this place, I arrived at about six o'clock after crossing the Roanoke, on the south bank of which it stands. This river is crossed in flat boats which take in a carriage and four horses at once. At this time, being low, the water was not rapid, but at times must be much so as it frequently overflows its banks which appear to be at least twenty-five feet perpendicularly in height. The lands upon the river appear to be rich and the low grounds of considerable width, but these which lay between the different rivers, namely, Appomattox, Nottaway, Meherrin, and Roanoke, are all flat and poor and covered principally with pine timber. It has already been observed that before the rain fell, I was travelling in a continued cloud of dust; but after it rained some time, the scene was reversed, and my passage was through water, so level are the roads. From Petersburg to Halifax, in sight of the road, are but few good houses with small appearance of wealth. The lands are cultivated in tobacco, corn, wheat, and oats; but tobacco and the raising of pork for market seems to be the principal dependence of the inhabitants, especially toward the Roanoke. Cotton and flax are also raised but not extensively. Halifax is the first town I came to after passing the line between the two states, and is about twenty miles from this place, vessels by the aid of oars and setting poles are brought for the produce which comes to this place and others along the river; and may be carried eight or ten miles higher to the falls, which are neither great nor much extent; above these (which are called great falls) there are others, but none but what with little improvement may be passed. The town stands upon high ground, and it is the reason given for not placing it at the head of navigation being none but low grounds between (it) and the falls. It seems to be in a decline, and does not, it is said, contain a thousand souls."

One singular thing about this record in the diary of the "Father of His Country" is that he makes no mention of anyone he met at Halifax, notwithstanding the fact that a galaxy of brilliant men lived there at the time. It is said that Willie Jones was asked to be chairman of the committee to entertain the president during his sojourn, but he declined with the remark that he would be glad to meet Washington as a gentleman and soldier, but that he could not greet him as President of the United States. This is understood to mean that the veteran States Rights advocate had never been reconciled to the adoption of the Federal Constitution and was still opposed to North Carolina's membership in the national union.

In the first election of members of Congress from North Carolina, in 1790, Halifax County furnished one of the five that represented the State in the House of Representatives. John B. Ashe, who had served with ability in the Revolution, received an almost unanimous vote in the Halifax district. He was re-elected in the fall of 1791 and served until 1793. Halifax County was signally honored during these early years of the State and Country's history. John Haywood, a lawyer of ability, was elected Attorney-General of the State in 1790 and served until 1794, when he was elected Judge of the Superior Court. General William R. Davie was appointed Major-General, in 1797, of a division of troops raised in anticipation of war with France. The next year, the project of war having passed, Davie was elected Governor of North Carolina, but resigned in 1799 to accept the position of Ambassador to France.

During the years 1787-1800, Halifax County exerted great influence in both State and National affairs. Perhaps, no county in the whole country had more men of ability and influence. Besides Willie Jones, William R. Davie, and John Haywood, already mentioned, there were Egbert Haywood, Nicholas Long, Willis Alston, Henry Montford, Orondates Davis, John Webb, Benjamin McCulloch, John Branch, Matthew C. Whitaker, and Peter Quarles, who had already made a state-wide reputation as men of real worth and ability.

CHAPTER SEVENTEEN.

FIRST TWO DECADES OF THE NINETEENTH CENTURY.

For twenty years following the beginning of the nineteenth century, Halifax County had practically no history. Nothing beyond the ordinary routine of daily matters disturbed the equilibrium of public affairs. Great problems of national government were being worked out, it is true, and Halifax had a part to perform in their solution, but no memorials have been left.

In the Federal House of Representatives, Halifax was again prominent from 1799 to 1815. John B. Ashe had retired from that position in 1793, and for six years the county lost the representative. In 1799, however, Willis Alston, Jr., was elected, and was successively reelected until 1815, when he retired from national politics. Alston had no opposition for his first two terms, but, in 1803, he had the race of his life when his opponent was General William R. Davie, who had shortly before returned from France almost a national figure.

The campaign that year was bitter and exciting. Alston had always been a strong supporter of President Jefferson, and therefore, a Democrat, although his enemies called him an aristocrat. Davie was a Federalist, but had recently been appointed by President Jefferson to the position of Indian Commissioner for the Southern States, and had, in more ways than one, shown decided inclination toward the dominant party. Alston won by a narrow margin. General Davie looked upon his defeat as the greatest humiliation of his life, and, shortly after the election, left Halifax and spent the remainder of his life on one of his farms in South Carolina.

Alston was in Congress during the period of the War of 1812; and, although the war was not popular in North

Carolina, he was an earnest supporter of the administration at Washington in the conduct of military affairs. Halifax County furnished two companies for the national army in that war, but they saw very little service. In 1814, they were ordered to Norfolk to resist a threatened attack by the British upon that place. While encamped there, an epidemic of "Camp Plague" broke out among them and many died. It was during the epidemic that Colonel Andrew Joyner, who was in command of the third regiment of North Carolina Volunteers, endeared himself to the soldiers by his daily attention to their welfare.

On account of the interest in the record of these soldiers of Halifax County, who volunteered to resist the invasion of the British, the complete roster is here given:

Jeremiah Slade, Lieutenant-Colonel; James Hill, First Major, Andrew Joyner, Second Major; James Overstreet, Captain; William C. Whitaker, Lieutenant; William Brickle, Second Lieutenant; Moses Grimmer, Fifer; privates, John Vaughan, William Crowell, John Ricks, James Whitaker, Thomas Applewhite, Wallis Nicholson, Timothy Connell, Samuel Simmons, John Parker, John Scot, James Gaskins, Henry Bradford, Thomas Bradford, William Willey, John Bradford, George Goodwin, Willie Watson, Thomas B. Parker, David Douglas, Wilson Brantley, John Glover, Hall Hudson, John W. Branch, John Knight, James Merrit, Washington Turner, Samuel Brickle, John Shields, James Young, John Bryant, James Brantly, James Lawrence, Benjamin Pearce, John Matthews, Hansel Horne, Cullen Grimmer, Jethro Parker, Miles Cross, Willis Shelton, Robert Saunders, Patrick McDaniel, Wilson W. Carter, John Scott, Edward King, Hiram King, Jesse A. Brooks, Blake Baker, Lewis Lewis, Joseph Pulley, Kinchen Harris, Jacob Bartholomew, James Abington, composing the first company.

Of the second company, the following is the roster: Isham Matthews, Captain; Thomas Nicholson, Lieutenant; John Alston, Ensign; Privates, Zachariah Sullivan,

FIRST DECADES OF NINETEENTH CENTURY 71

Francis Anderson, Halrin Ashe, William Brown, James Ashe, William H. Ballance, Robert Brinkley, Jesse Blackburn, Asa Blackburn, William J. Bradie, John Coolin, John Curtin, Jesse Christie, Samuel Carter, Gideon Dameron, William R. Daniel, Roderick Easley, Allen Easley, Eaton F. Allen, Allen Flood, Wilson Green, Thomas Green, William Gurley, Thomas G. Grimestead, Benjamin Green, Jesse Hamblet, Miley Harbin, David Harris, Jesse Harlow, Gabriel Hawkins, John Hawes, Hansel Hathcock, Edmund Jackson, Beverly Jackson, Robert Jones, John Jordan, John King, Solomon Lochlear, Exum Low, Samuel Lochlear, John Lee, Jr., John A. Losset, Jesse Moore, Alfred Moore, John Moore, Jr., William Montford, William Moore, John Mann, James Mason, Arthur Manley, Guilford Nicholson, Thomas H. Green, William Onions, Eaton Powell, Rica Pullin, John Pugh, Ransom Powell, Frederick Pully, John Porter, Allen Powell, Michael Rand, Joseph Studivant, Abner Spear, Thomas Simmons, Peter Ship, Whiles Studivant, Arthur Spear, John Weaver, Lemuel Wilkins, John Wright, Sr., Caleb Woodard, Thomas Ward.

This command of North Carolina veterans spent the fall and winter of 1814-15 in the trenches near Norfolk, Va. They were in expectation of active service when the British landed near Washington, D. C., defeated a small body of Americans at Bladenburg, Md., and captured the capital city. When the American forces at Fort McHenry, near Baltimore, resisted the attacks of the enemy and beat them off, it was expected that the next attempt would be upon Norfolk. The American forces, at that point, among whom were the Halifax companies, were in daily and almost hourly expectation that a landing of the enemy would be made.

Admiral Cockburn, however, in command of the British fleet operating in Chesapeake Bay, made a demonstration against Norfolk, entered the mouth of the Elizabeth river, measured the American forces in that vicinity, and sailed out to sea without striking a blow. The Halifax boys were a little disappointed in not getting a chance to grapple with the red coats, and, after peace was declared, marched back to Halifax and were mustered out of service.

During this period, Halifax County continued to have commanding influence in the affairs of the State. Hutchins G. Burton, who lived near Enfield, was elected Attorney-General in 1810, resigned in 1816, was elected to Congress in 1819, and served until he was elected Governor in 1824. William Drew was chosen Attorney-General in 1816 and resigned in November, 1825. He lived in the town of Halifax. John Branch, of Enfield, became Governor of the State in 1817 and served one term. Joseph J. Daniel was elected to the Superior Court bench in 1816 and was later elevated to the Supreme Court. All of these men possessed more than average ability and reflected honor upon themselves and the county, as well as the State.

CHAPTER EIGHTEEN.

THE VISIT OF LAFAYETTE.

In 1824, General Lafayette, the great Frenchman, who came to America during the darkest days of the Revolution, and assisted Washington in achieving American independence, made a visit to the land he had fought for nearly fifty years before. Lafayette was a veteran of two Revolutions. After American independence was assured, he returned to France; and when the great French Revolution came like a nightmare upon Europe, he espoused the cause of the people, but was a Conservative. Different from other great Frenchmen of that period, he escaped the guillotine, saw the rise and downfall of the first French Republic, witnessed the beginning and ending of the First Empire, and beheld the Restoration of the Bourbon line of kings.

Now, in his old age, he had come back to revisit the scenes of the battles of his young manhood. In the party, besides the General, were his son, whose name is unknown, and his secretary, Lerasseur, besides others, who have left no memorials. Everywhere throughout the country, north and south, the party was received with every mark of honor and esteem; and nowhere more than in Halifax County.

Lerasseur wrote very entertainingly of the receptions tendered the aged patriot in the large towns and cities of the United States. His account of the trip through Halifax County is very meager. He says:

"From Murfreesboro we went next day to Halifax, where we crossed the Roanoke in a ferry boat amidst the thunder of artillery, which awaited the arrival of General Lafayette on the opposite shore . . . We only slept at Halifax, and, in two days, after traveling over frightful roads, reached Raleigh. Nothing was neglected by Governor Burton in doing the honors of his dwelling to the national guest." The night spent in Halifax was Feb. 27, 1825.

It is well established tradition that, in honor of the distinguished guest, a banquet was given at the Eagle hotel, and after the banquet, a ball occupied the attention of the guests until the "wee sma" hours of the morning. General Lafayette was said to have been a graceful dancer, and many a Halifax dame, before and after the Civil War, took pride in saying she danced with the General on that occasion. There was one circumstance that was the cause of much comment among the ladies present, that General Lafayette's hair was black while that of his son was gray. The illusion was dispelled, however, when the General frankly stated that he was wearing a wig.

Next day, Lafayette and his party were escorted, on the way to Raleigh, as far as Enfield by a delegation appointed for that purpose by Governor Burton. At Enfield, he was entertained at the Branch residence, outside of Enfield, where a great crowd assembled to meet him. A school of boys taught by Alexander McClellan, one mile from town, carrying cornstalk muskets, attended in a body and attracted much attention. General Lafayette made a speech from the porch to the assembled throng, complimented the school boys for their soldierly bearing, and pleased the older people by referring to the gallant conduct of their fathers in the Revolution.

Leaving Enfield, the party continued the journey to Raleigh, escorted by Adjutant-General Daniel, Colonel William Polk, and Chief-Justice Taylor, who had been appointed to conduct the party to Raleigh.

This visit of General Lafayette is commented upon as one of the big social events of the times. It is pointed out that the Eagle hotel, where the party was entertained in Halifax, had been honored before in having Washington, on one occasion, as its guest, and in being the headquarters of the members of the Provincial Congresses

THE VISIT OF LAFAYETTE 75

and the General Assemblies, before and during the Revolution. It was located on a slight elevation, on the right hand side of the street coming up from the river, and nothing is left now but the remains of the chimneys that tumbled to the earth some twenty-five years ago.

The house in Enfield, in which Lafayette was entertained, was owned at the time by Governor Branch, who was then United States Senator from North Carolina, and was the birthplace of General L. O'B. Branch, who rendered distinguished service in the Civil War and who was four years old at the time of Lafayette's visit.

Halifax town was, at the time, an important centre, both of commercial and social influence. The visit of the distinguished Frenchmen called together the principal men and women of the county, and, no doubt, the intellectual and social worth of the inhabitants was fully demonstrated.

CHAPTER NINETEEN.

INTELLECTUAL DEVELOPMENT.

Before, during, and for twenty-five years after the Revolution, there is no mention of schools in the County. Planters, who did not send their children away to school, either to England or some of the northern Colonies, employed private tutors for them. It is probable that several families, in some localities, united in employing a teacher and conducting a school at some central point, to which the children of the neighborhood were sent. There was no effort made, looking to public education, for more than thirty years after the close of the war.

The first school, of which there is any mention, was taught by James B. Benson in the town of Halifax in 1806. Of this school there was an advertisement in the Halifax Journal, Oct. 6, 1806, in which the principal stated when the school would begin its first session, that the price of tuition was twelve dollars per year, and that the principal would board four orderly, well bred boys in most ample and genteel manner. This school seems not to have existed long, as a rival soon appeared on the scene.

In the Halifax Journal of January 12, 1807, there appeared the following notice: "A school will be opened on Monday the 12th inst. in the town of Halifax for the reception of students, where will be taught the Latin and English grammatically, together with writing, arithmetic, the mathematics, geography, and the use of the globe. All persons interested in promoting a good school in this neighborhood are requested to meet at Mr. Hopkins' tavern on the 24th inst., in order to appoint managers to superintend this institution and to settle on terms of tuition &c." This notice was signed by Robert Fenner. Richard H. Long, and W. W. Jones.

INTELLECTUAL DEVELOPMENT 77

About the year 1810, Vine Hill Academy was organized in Scotland Neck. In the same paper of date 1811, there is a notice setting forth the fact that the trustees have secured as principal Mr. Daniel Adams of Stratford, Conn., "who has for two years been principal of a very respectable school there, and will now teach the learned languages and the various branches preparatory for a college education." The notice that "it is hoped from the great respectability of his character, his experience and success, that this institution will receive the patronage and support its infant state so much requires." This school continued as an important factor in the intellectual life of Scotland Neck for nearly a hundred years.

From its establishment in 1815 to 1821, there are frequent notices, in the press of that day, of Union Academy, which was located in the town of Halifax. This institution was in charge of William E. Webb, with Jesse N. Falcon as president of the Board of Trustees. Webb appears to have been a man of some ability and influence, for he represented the County in the General Assembly three times before he became Principal of Union Academy.

Farmwell Grove Academy, somewhere in the Aurelian Springs section, was established in 1820, and flourished until 1837. In "The Star" of June 21st, 1837, appears a well written report of the examination exercises of this school. Special mention is made of the address of Rev. S. J. Harris, in which was enforced the all-important point, that of the moral necessity of uniting religion and literature in order to insure the grand result of usefulness and happiness. This writer signs his name, "Spectator," and claims to have no interest in Farmwell Academy, other than philanthropy and a love of education.

In the Raleigh Register of December 30, 1823, there is a notice of Enfield Academy in charge of Mr. Philip B. Wiley, of Newbern, and again in "The Star" of December 4, 1828, when Thomas L. Ragsdale was principal and Governor John Branch was president of the Board of Trustees. This school advertised that board at five dollars a month could be obtained in families convenient to the academy, "which occupies a high and healthful site remote from all scenes of dissipation."

In 1828, a Mrs. Philips announced in the newspapers of the day that the first session of her academy for young ladies at Hyde Park closed on December 2nd by an examination, which was attended by a numerous assemblage of the ladies and gentlemen of the vicinity. She claimed in the announcement, that all the branches taught in the best seminaries, with many ornamental accomplishments, would be given in her school, including needlework and embroidery, drawing, painting, and music on the piano, all for the price of $80 for ten months. She also stated that the school was fourteen miles west of Halifax on the direct road to Warrenton, that it was remote from all scenes of dissipation and extravagance, had pure air and water, and a neighborhood society, which for urbanity of manners is inferior to none in the country.

Also advertised in "The Star" and the Raleigh Register, there are three other female schools, namely, the Scotland Neck Female Academy, La Vallie Female Seminary, and Mrs. E. C. Grant's Female Boarding School. One of these was on the road from Halifax to Warrenton, and was originally, perhaps, the school at Hyde Park already mentioned. Mrs. Grant's School was located a few miles from Enfield at the place called Shell Castle, which continued as a boarding school for young ladies until after the Civil War. The La Vallie School included in its Board of Trustees David Outlaw, of Bertie, Samuel Arrington, of Nash, J. J. Daniel, formerly of Halifax, but at that time living in Raleigh as a member of the Supreme Court of North Carolina, Isaac Williams, Rev. S. Willis and Mason L. Wiggins, of Halifax. The president of this school was Tippo S. Brownlow.

A few years prior to the Civil War, Mr. Richard Parker conducted a select boarding school for young ladies at his home near Smith's Church about five miles from Weldon.

Mr. Parker was a member of the County, or "Old Field," Court, as it was called, held many public offices, and was guardian for quite a number of wealthy young ladies. This last fact was perhaps the explanation of the origin of this school, as, in this way, his wards were under his personal supervision and enjoyed the privileges of a hospitable Christian home.

In all these schools, the fact is emphasized that accomplished teachers from the North were employed and that much attention was given to "manners" and deportment, and that pupils from those schools went out to adorn many high places in this and other States.

About 1840, the system of "Free Schools" was introduced in the county, but they were conducted in a desultory manner and very little good resulted from them. A maximum salary of $30 a month was paid teachers, and very inferior instruction was given in a one-roomed house with more than fifty pupils of all ages and grades. Still the foundations laid with the "Blue Back" speller in those log schoolhouses with backless seats has caused many an ambitious youth and maiden to win excellence in other halls of learning. They have, therefore, done a work that will stand for all time.

It was not the purpose of this chapter to give a complete account of the educational activities of the county, but merely to give some facts that will give the reader an idea of educational conditions from the earliest times to the outbreak of the War between the States in 1861. Since the close of that struggle, the system of public schools has been greatly improved until there is now not a corner of the county that is without excellent school facilities.

CHAPTER TWENTY.

SOCIAL AND ECONOMIC DEVELOPMENT.

Halifax County, and particularly Halifax town, was for a number of years the political centre of North Carolina. The ancient borough was in reality the Capital of the State during and soon after the Revolution. There, many of the officers of the Commonwealth lived much of the time, and there, most of the records of state were kept. Of course, when the seat of government was removed to Raleigh, everything pertaining to State affairs was transferred to that place. Halifax, therefore, lost much of its influence. Even after that, however, the town was a centre from which radiated social, literary, and economic forces that were felt in remote portions of the State.

One of the most potent of these influences was that of the press. In those early days of newspaperdom, the weekly paper had more power among its readers than the metropolitan daily had at a much later date. Its columns were eagerly scanned by an interested constituency and its statements ordinarily went unchallenged. Without telegraphic dispatches, or quick mail facilities, the newspaper of the first half of the nineteenth century, especially in Halifax County, was an unpretentious institution, but comparatively of immense influence.

The first mention of a newspaper in the county was in 1784. James Iredell, who was afterwards United States Supreme Court judge, was on a visit that year to the home of Benjamin McCulloch, on Elk Marsh. In a letter to his wife on March 28th, 1784, he says: "They have begun to print a newspaper at Halifax, which is to be continued weekly." This was doubtless, a venture of Thomas Davis, who, at the time, enjoyed the distinction of being public printer. There is a letter in the State

LAFAYETTE'S RETURN

From a painting by Percy Moran

SOCIAL AND ECONOMIC DEVELOPMENT 81

Records from Davis at Newbern to Governor Caswell asking the assistance of the State in getting his press moved to Halifax. There is not a copy of this paper in existence, so far as is known, and it is not by any means certain as to how long it continued.

July 23, 1793, the initial number of the North Carolina Journal was issued at Halifax, by Hodge and Wells. There is a file of this newspaper in possession of the North Carolina Historical Society, beginning with the issue of January 7, 1805, and ending March 2, 1807, edited and printed by A. Hodge at $2.50 a year. The paper is eighteen inches long and eleven inches wide, four page, four columns to the page, without head rules, the paper and type being fairly good. It had the largest circulation in the State for many years, and probably discontinued its publication about 1810, at the time under the editorial management of Wright W. Batchelor.

There is no mention of further newspaper ventures in Halifax until 1829, when the first issue of the Halifax Minerva made its appearance on January 24th of that year, edited and published by John Campbell. Its first number is a folio, eighteen inches long and twelve inches wide, and six columns to the page. In about one year, Edmund B. Freeman purchased an interest in the plant and became the editor, Campbell continuing to do the mechanical work. The name was changed to the Roanoke Advocate. There are four volumes of the Minerva and Advocate in the possession of one of the sons of John Campbell.

A feature of every number of these interesting papers is the method of advertising. In every issue is seen an advertisement for a runaway slave, accompanied by a picture of the fugitive with a bundle of clothes in his hand, or hanging from a stick across his shoulder. Another striking advertisement was that of cock fighting, illustrating two of the feathered heroes in a death struggle, and announcing the mains at a certain time and place with the stakes, sometimes reaching the sum of one thousand dollars. Those were the days before cockfighting was forbidden by statute.

As the town of Halifax was the main distributing point for merchandise brought up the Roanoke by sailing vessels, and later by steamboats, from Norfolk and intermediate points, each issue of these papers gave the names of all vessels arriving and departing from the port of Halifax since the previous issue.

From these papers, the information is derived that Halifax County was, at that time, exporting flour and meat. Large cargoes of those articles were sent down the river to Norfolk at every sailing of a vessel. In addition to the trade by the Roanoke, a large contingent of wagons and carts carried wheat, tobacco, cotton, and other products overland to Petersburg and Richmond. Hogs and cattle were driven afoot and bartered for such merchandise as was needed by the people of the county.

All public traveling was by means of stage coaches before the coming of the railroad. From Halifax there was a tri-weekly line to Raleigh, passing Enfield, Hilliardston, and Nashville, in Nash County. The trip was made in a day by leaving Halifax at 3 A. M. and arriving at Raleigh at 10 P. M. From Enfield, another line of stage coaches extended to Tarboro. There was also another from Halifax to Warrenton in one direction and across the Roanoke in another direction to Murfreesboro and Winton, branching off to the left in Northampton County to Petersburg and Richmond.

Not many accidents, or incidents even, are recorded of travel in those primitive days. Only one has been handed down as being serious enough to be remembered, and it occurred on the Raleigh line. In 1831, while crossing Culpepper bridge, the lead horse became frightened and unmanageable, and precipitated the vehicle, with its occupants, into Fishing Creek. One man was fatally injured in this wreck.

Religiously, the people of the county were divided as now into the several denominations. The Baptists and Episcopalians were perhaps the first occupiers of the land. The former had established a church and built a house of worship, the oldest in the county, on Kehukee Creek, a few miles southeast of the town of Scotland Neck in 1742. That old church was the scene of the schism in 1827, when the Baptist denomination was disrupted over the question of missions and secret societies. After the meeting of the Kehukee Association of that year at Kehukee Church, there were two distinct Baptist denominations in the State, the Primitive Baptists, sometimes called "Hardshells," and the Missionary Baptists, who are now much the larger body. Other Baptist Churches were built a little later, in different parts of the County, among them Conocanara and Antioch being perhaps the best known.

Among the earliest people, who settled on the Roanoke river and Fishing Creek, there were quite a number of Episcopalians. Rev. Thomas Burgess was the first minister of that denomination to reside in the county. He was in charge of the Parish of Edgecombe, which became the County of Halifax, before the two counties were separated. At the session of the Colonial Assembly of 1760, the first after Halifax had become a county, a bill was introduced to confirm an agreement made between Burgess and the wardens and vestry of the Parish of Edgecombe. The bill set forth the fact that he had been employed under an act of the Assembly, which had since been repealed, to serve the parish during his natural life for 120 pounds a year, and prayed that the agreement be confirmed.

Governor Dobbs stated, in a report to the Board of Trade, that there were only six preachers of the established Church (the Episcopal) in the province at that time, of whom two were worthless, calling them by name, and the other four, among whom was Burgess, were good and competent men. This indirect testimony of the Governor as to the sterling qualities of the first Episcopal minister in the county is fully confirmed by tradition. His remains lie buried in the old Conocanara churchyard.

In Halifax, the church in which Burgess officiated is

still standing. Although there are no records in existence to show when it was built, there is strong presumption that it was erected a number of years before the outbreak of the Revolution, probably about 1760. In Scotland Neck, on the edge of old "Clarksville," is another ancient Church of the Episcopal faith.

Soon after the formation of the county, another denomination, the Methodists, began to make its influence felt. John Wesley and George Whitefield had visited North Carolina some years before and planted the seeds of Methodism, which now began to flourish. Churches of that faith were built in various sections of the county, among the oldest being Ebenezer in the Aurelian Springs neighborhood, Haywoods near Halifax, Bradfords near Enfield, and the church in the town of Halifax.

In these early days the Methodist Church took a high stand in the county. As was generally the case, the Methodist Circuit Rider followed closely in the track of civilization and in 1846 a church was organized in Weldon with seven members. These were Mrs. W. T. Whitfield, Mrs. Mary Allen, Capt. James Simmons, Mr. H. Wyatt and three others whose names are unknown. Capt. Simmons, the "Class Leader" for this little band, was Sheriff of the County and was a man of such sterling integrity he was elected without opposition as long as he would hold the office. A small wooden building was erected on the banks of the canal, in which to hold public services. This was roughly built and rudely furnished, but was the only church building in Weldon until 1874 when another and better one was built by the same congregation.

People, in the early years of the nineteenth century, especially in Halifax County, were particularly free from the almost nerve racking complexities of the present. Mail facilities were extremely limited, and until 1840, when the first railroads in the county were built, if a community received mail three times a week it was considered fortunate. Halifax was reached by a tri-weekly mail from Petersburg, and by one with the same frequency from

SOCIAL AND ECONOMIC DEVELOPMENT 85

Raleigh. The only postoffices that are known to have existed as early as 1830 are Halifax, Enfield, Scotland Neck, Weldon, which was called Weldon's Place, Littleton, which was called Little's Ordinary, Brinkleyville, Palmyra, and Crowell's Cross Roads.

In the General Assembly of 1826, an act was passed incorporating the Roanoke Steamboat Company and authorizing the incorporators, Andrew Joyner and Cadwallader Jones, to build a steamboat to navigate the Roanoke river, the Albermarle sound, and the James river. Their plan to open a regular line of steamers from Halifax to Norfolk did not rapidly mature; for it was not until April 15, 1829, that the first steamboat to navigate the Roanoke arrived at Halifax. This was the rude steamer, Petersburg, in command of Captain McRae. After discharging freight at Halifax, it proceeded to Weldon Place and returned the next day, proceeding later to Norfolk.

This was the first trip ever made on the Roanoke by a steamboat. Since that time, Weldon, Halifax, Scotland Neck, Palmyra, and other points on the river have been visited by steamers that connected the Roanoke farms with Norfolk. After the introduction of the railroads, however, the boat line on the river was gradually discontinued above Hamilton in Martin County until now it is a rare thing for a steamboat to visit Halifax.

CHAPTER TWENTY-ONE.

COMING OF THE RAILROADS.

The early settlers who came to what is now Halifax County were either the enlarging or spreading out of the settlement of the first colonies of Virginia or adventurous spirits exploring the Roanoke River from the sound to the falls, about one hundred miles, of a navigable though dangerous stream of water.

This river, deep and turbulent, was impassable farther on account of the many rocks embedded in the stream and the tremendous falls over which the water swept, and the only means of passage was the small canoe or dugout then in general use.

At the point where the town of Halifax was built, the river is broader and the banks not so steep, so the trail was opened into a highway of travel, a ferry across the river established and the nucleus of the town begun.

The river to which the Indian had given the name of "Roanoke" or "River of Death" has been found navigable from the lower settlements on the sound up to this point and was for many years the only means of commercial transportation of any kind.

At certain seasons of the year, this river yielded an enormous supply of fish of the very finest quality, especially the white shad and the striped bass, or rockfish, which annually leave the sound and larger waters to deposit their spawn amid the rocks in the falls of the Roanoke. So fishing hamlets were established on either side of the river to provide shelter for the fishermen when not engaged in their dangerous though profitable work.

One of these villages was called Blakely, and was at

COMING OF THE RAILROADS

a point about three miles below Weldon on the Northampton side and was the head of navigation for any boat except the canoe or dugout. In the year 1832, a railroad was built out from Petersburg, Va., into North Carolina terminating at Blakely landing. The day of the opening of this road was celebrated with great rejoicing. The people came together for miles away and entered into the exercises with interest and enthusiasm. A dinner and speech making were then, as they often are now, features of the occasion.

In 1834 another Railroad was built out from Norfolk, Va., into North Carolina with its terminus on the Northern side of the Roanoke just across from the landing at the point now called Weldon. The land on the South side of the river was the holding of a man of importance whose name was Daniel Weldon. At this time there were many prosperous and influential men in this community, owning and cultivating large farms of grain and fruit. These were the descendants of the pioneer settlers, James Bradley, William Gary, Joshua Jones, William Whitfield, Mark Petway, Samuel Weldon, and many others.

The cultivation of fruit was a popular industry and apple orchards were fine assets for these early settlers. Every man of importance cultivated orchards and made quantities of genuine apple brandy. The dangerous chemicals now used were then unknown and the pure apple brandy was the product of these distilleries which were owned and operated almost universally. And so what is now the town of Weldon was then known as Weldon's Orchard, or Weldon's Place and was the seat of one of these primitive industries which were considered respectable and entirely moral. To illustrate this, it is said that Henry Sledge, a prosperous man of the county at this period and also a pious and devoted Christian gentleman, when told by his pastor that it was sinful to manufacture and use brandy, at once destroyed his large and profitable orchard, by cutting every tree to its roots, saying he would in this way remove the temptation to evil.

In the year 1835, Col. Andrew Joyner, who was elected to the State Senate this year and was re-elected to the same position for sixteen years, was also elected President of the "Roanoke Navigation Co.," an organization which had for its purpose the opening of a canal from a place called Rock Landing on the river, nine miles above Weldon, through which boats could pass and so avoid the rocks and falls in the river and find anchorage at Weldon's Orchard. A charter was procured, the canal became a reality and the orchard became a junction of it and the two railroads, as well as the transportation facilities of the river below the falls.

This canal was an important improvement at the time, as, in addition to the railroads mentioned, one had been built from Raleigh to Gaston in 1833, with its terminus at a landing on the river. A large basin was formed here and the boats from as far as Danville, Va., would bring the produce of the farms down the river to Gaston and then through this canal to Weldon. The Company which undertook this work did it thoroughly and well. There are three locks in the canal, the masonry of which is very fine, as is that of the aqueduct over Chockoyette near Weldon, and has stood without repairs for three fourths of a century. A large basin was formed just above the falls, at Weldon where the canal empties into the river, for the purpose of moving the boats which operated on the canal line.

A large brick warehouse was built near this basin, in which an immense amount of tobacco and other produce were safely stored. This opening up of a new method of transportation was of great importance to the farmers along its line, as previous to this the only means of marketing the tobacco was to convey it for sixty miles or more in large hogsheads on wooden sleds drawn by horses to Petersburg, Va.

Quite a group of buildings were erected as the out-

THE ROANOKE RIVER, NEAR WELDON, N. C.

COMING OF THE RAILROADS 89

come of this new enterprise. A man named Thomas H. Wyatt built a large storehouse with a small tavern or inn annexed on the corner of First and Sycamore Streets and these were the first of their kind on the ground. These stood until only a few years ago and were mementoes of these early days. A larger hotel was soon built by Mr. Michael Ferral and this was operated for a number of years.

In the year 1833 a charter was granted to the Wilmington & Raleigh Railroad. This was changed to Wilmington & Weldon, and in May, 1840, the first train of cars ran through from Wilmington to Weldon with William Hall as Conductor and G. G. Lynch as helper. Of these young men, Captain Hall died very early, but Mr. Lynch lived to a ripe old age. He was employed when quite a young man as route agent or mail inspector for the United States Government and was appointed to the same office by Thomas H. Reagan, Postmaster-General in the Confederate Cabinet, which office he held until the close of the War. When the War between the States began, he held in his possession $250.00 in gold which belonged to the United States Government. Through all the terrible four years, he held this as a sacred trust and at the close of the war returned the money to the Postoffice Department of the Government.

In 1855, the Raleigh and Gaston Railroad was extended from South Gaston to Weldon, thus making that village the centre from which radiated four important lines of railways, one of them the W. & W. being for many years the longest in the world. The large shed, which has so often been associated with Weldon, was built that year from under which the passenger trains of the four roads left for their different destinations, upon the ringing of a signal bell.

On the completion of the Wilmington & Weldon Railroad to Weldon, a bridge was built across the river and a junction formed of this and the Seaboard and Roanoke Railroad. The terminus of the road from Petersburg was moved from Blakely to Weldon and a bridge built for that line also. This was a wooden bridge and was burnt in the year 1856, and not replaced until after the Civil War, when a new steel structure was erected on the old pillars about one mile below Weldon. This was in use until Nov. 26, 1877, when both bridges were washed away by the highest freshet ever known in the Roanoke River. The Petersburg bridge was never rebuilt, both roads using the Seaboard bridge.

In the political campaign of 1844, Henry Clay, one of the Presidential candidates, came to Weldon on his way to Raleigh to speak in the interests of his party and to encourage and strengthen his constituents in the State. He was met and entertained at dinner at the Ferral hotel by Col. Joyner, the leading Whig of the section, who took him to spend the night at his home at Poplar Grove and accompanied him to Raleigh next day. The important issue discussed at this time was the annexation of Texas to the United States. Mr. Clay was supposed to favor this bill pending in Congress and his chances for election were considered good. In this speech, however, he strongly antagonized the bill and in the following election his opponent, James K. Polk, was elected.

In the meantime Weldon's Orchard had become the town of Weldon. Another and a larger hotel was built and operated by W. T. Whitfield, who came to Weldon in 1834, stores and business houses were multiplied, and other enterprises engaged in. Among the prominent men of this period were Dr. William Lunsford Long, John K. Campbell, Hamlin and Elisha Allen, James Simmons, and E. N. Peterson.

A weekly newspaper of modest pretensions was launched and flourished for some time. This was called the Weldon Patriot and was founded by J. T. Gresham and afterwards edited by Thomas L. Suiter. Two large mills, one for wheat and the other for corn, were built near the falls of the canal and were supplied with grain

COMING OF THE RAILROADS

from the neighboring farms, especially Mush Island, the fertile and prolific lands of Col. Nicholas Long, which at that time was called the Egypt of Halifax County.

Col. Joyner, besides being President of the Roanoke Navigation Co., was President of the Seaboard & Roanoke Railroad. For many years he was a member of the Senate of North Carolina and was promoter under the influence of Dorothy Dix of the Bill to establish a home at Raleigh for the Deaf, Dumb and Blind of the State. His wife, a lady of culture and refinement and wealth, was a veritable "Lady Bountiful," ministering to both the souls and bodies of men, and their home at Poplar Grove near what is now the City of Roanoke Rapids was a general dispensary for the neighborhood. Rev. Robert O. Burton of the Virginia M. E. Conference married a daughter of Col. Joyner and was often in charge of Roanoke Circuit, to which the Methodist church at Weldon belonged.

CHAPTER TWENTY-TWO.

"ROYAL WHITE HART LODGE."

One of the oldest and most famous institutions in the county is the Masonic Lodge at Halifax. Because of its historic importance a somewhat extended account is given of the rise, progress, and spirit of this lodge.

The first meeting was held April 20, 1764, in the home of David London, Halifax town, Province of North Carolina. Halifax was then one of the most important and flourishing towns in the State. It was at the head of navigation and was the home of a great many prominent people and statesmen. Here was held the Provincial Congress and here was the first demonstration after the one in Philadelphia celebrating the Declaration of Independence. Among its citizens was Joseph Montford, an Englishman of noble lineage and a Mason who was closely connected with this Lodge from his arrival in Halifax until his death.

It seems that at that time there were two Masonic lodges, but it is evident from its size and the amount of its funds that this one had been in existence for some years. From 1764 to 1772 and again from 1783 to the present time there is an unbroken record of these meetings. But it is a matter of regret that all records are missing from 1772 to 1783. It is believed that these records were carried home (for safekeeping during the Revolutionary period) by one of the members and they were lost to history. Diligent search continues to be made for them in the old homes in Eastern North Carolina.

On May 20, 1768, an important meeting of this Lodge was held in which the Worshipful Master produced a Charter from the Grand Master of England, to wit: "Henry Somerset, Duke of Beaufort, Grand Master of Masons in England, appointing Joseph Montford, Master; Joseph Long, Senior Warden, and Nathen Brown, Jr., Warden—a regular constituted lodge of free and accepted Masons by the name of Royal Hart Lodge, town of Halifax, Province of N. C." This charter was dated London, March 21, A. L. 5767, the same being No. 403 in the list of English Lodges.

It was unanimously and gratefully received and the Secretary was ordered to write a letter to the Grand Lodge of England returning thanks for the honor which the Grand Master had been pleased to confer on them.

It is noticeable that the minutes of all their meetings were signed by the Worshipful Master, and the utmost care was taken in their preparation. That these earnest men took masonry very seriously is evinced by the By-laws in which we read "To laugh in Lodge, fine five shillings. To whisper in Lodge, fine five shillings." In April, 1769, a meeting was held at which it was resolved to build a Masonic Temple and the following is a part of the interesting minutes:—

"Whereas we, the subscribers esteem it publicly beneficial to promote society, to laudably increase the means of obtaining benefit and happiness to those whom we are most nearly connected, and Whereas it is proposed and agreed to improve a lot in the town of Halifax, to wit: No. 111 so that the accommodation thereon may serve for various purposes, particularly that of a Masonic Hall and Assembly room;—We therefore, obligate ourselves, our heirs, executors and Administrators respectively to pay or cause to be paid the sum annexed to our respective names and for the purpose of improving the said lot, etc."

Joseph Montford—one house and lot (deed executed).
Joseph O. Long, ... ten pounds
Frederick Schulzer, ... ten pounds

John Thompson .... ten pounds
Alexander Telfair, ... ten pounds
James Milner, ... ten pounds
Charles Preston, ... five pounds
William Martin, ... five pounds
F. Stewart, ... ten pounds
David Stokes, ... five pounds
James Auld, ... three pounds
Peter Thompson, ... five pounds
Joseph Campbell, ... five pounds

The house and lot donated by Joseph Montford at that date was worth $1,500.00, making the whole amount $2,000.00.

This was indeed an enormous amount for these poor colonists, but it showed their intense devotion to the cause of Masonry. It is a noticeable fact that "Paid" was written after each amount promised.

This temple was built and was a very imposing and rather elegant building for that day and time. It was situated in a large oak grove facing the public road. It was 30 x 30 feet, two stories. The lodge room was on the second floor, and the lower story was used for a public school—although the last day of school in this building was in 1829.

A description of the temple written in 1820 is interesting. "The roof was slate color, the building was white with green blinds, mahogany doors, red brick foundation and chimney. The ceiling which is arched, is blue and the interior woodwork is white."

The beautiful silver candlesticks still used by this Lodge were purchased Feb. 26, 1784, and cost 11 pounds. The unique and handsome chair (with its approaching steps) was bought May 20, 1765. It is supposed these came from England. Visiting Masons say that the ballot-box is the finest they have ever seen tho' it is not so old as the other pieces, having been bought April 1, 1820.

On March 10, 1772, Joseph Montford presented the

lodge with a beautiful Masonic chart, painted on heavy cloth and to this day it is in a fine state of preservation. A few days later—March 13, 1772, a meeting of special interest was held—The following quotation is from the records: "Bro. Joseph Montford produced a charter from the Grand Master of England—the Duke of Beaufort—appointing him Provincial Grand Master of and for America—which was recognized, and for which he was congratulated by the lodge and offered the chair, which he declined."

For the third time we see this notable figure in this grand old lodge. First, with the charter from the Grand Lodge of England; second, generously giving to the Royal White Hart Lodge a house and lot towards the erection of a Masonic Temple; and now presenting his appointment as Provincial Grand Master of America—and in his modesty declining even a seat in the East. Thus we see that a history however brief it may be cannot be written without the name of the most prominent Mason in America at that time, viz:—the Hon. Joseph Montford.

He was also the first Clerk of the Court for Halifax County, Treasurer of the Province of North Carolina, Colonel of Colonial Troops and delegate to the Provincial Congress, not mentioning the father of two brilliant and beautiful daughters who became the wives of two of North Carolina's most distinguished statesmen, viz:— The Hon. Willie Jones and the Hon. John Baptista Ashe.

It is true that that Grand Lodge of England, which was organized in 1717, had, before this time, appointed other Provincial Grand Masters in America—but their authority was limited to their Province or territory, and they in turn were subject to the Provincial Grand Master for Foreign Lodges at London, who was the appointee of the Grand Master of the Grand Lodge of England. But the authority vested in Joseph Montford was absolute and supreme in all parts of America, and he established lodges and chapters at his will and pleasure, thereby attaining the highest masonic position ever held by any man on this continent. There are several reasons why he was selected to this high honor: his social and political prominence, the exactness and faithfulness that characterized everything that he attempted, his prompt and regular remittances to the Grand Lodge of England, and his idea of building a Masonic Temple which (at that time) was absolutely new in both England and America. This especially made a deep impression upon the Grand Lodge of England, and it undoubtedly inspired them to build "Free Mason's Hall" in London, for they began immediately to raise funds for this purpose and four years later this magnificent structure was completed. The contribution of "10 pounds 10 shillings from Joseph Montford—R. W. H. Lodge Halifax—Province N. C.," was the largest amount subscribed.

Benjamin Franklin and his associates erected Free Masons' Lodge in Philadelphia about this time, which was the first Masonic Temple in this country and also in the world, and the temple in Halifax (now standing in its somber dignity) was the second.

Up to this time it was customary for Masons to meet in Taverns or homes. Even the Grand Lodge of England was holding its meetings at the "Crown and Anchor in the Strand" (London), and the Royal White Hart Lodge met at "Bro. Martin's Tavern at the sign of the Thistle."

After 1790 the Lodge became very prosperous. The members paid $5.00 per pair for gloves, $10.00 a plate for banquets and gave $25.00 a month as pensions to needy widows. Surely they never dreamed of the abandonment of the river traffic, the decline of the town and lodge and the decay of their beloved temple. It is the cherished hope of the Masons to restore the temple as it was in the heyday of its glory.

Joseph Montford died March, 1776, in the early stage of the Revolutionary War, and was buried in the old Colonial churchyard where he had so often marshaled his lodge in a body for worship. We notice that the word

ROYAL WHITE HART LODGE, HALIFAX, N. C.

"Hart" is spelled in the old Records Heart until the arrival of the charter from England. In this charter this word is spelled "Hart" and from that time, all records conform to this spelling.

There are many amusing instances recorded in the old records. At one of the early meetings a Committee of one was appointed to furnish "1 gal. of brandy, 1 gal. of rum, 1 gal. of gin, 1 cheese, 1 baked ham and some crackers the same to be charged to the candidate for the night." Surely these brothers were in a hilarious (or sad) state of mind before the night ended. Tho' it is recorded that the members of this lodge were deeply religious, "observing feast days regularly and attending church on Sundays in a body." Copies of the sermons preached to them were carefully preserved. Marshall Delancy Hayward in his splendid work, "The Beginning of Free Masonry in North Carolina and Tennessee," records the lives of the members of this Grand Lodge and the great service they rendered the American cause during the Revolutionary War. It was the custom of Joseph Montford on the feast days of St. John to assemble his lodge in the temple at five o'clock before sunrise. He would open the Lodge until he came to the "Master's Station" when the opening stopped and a brother who was stationed at the East window would signal the first appearance of the Orb of Day—and at that instant rose also the only Provincial Grand Master that America ever had—to open and govern the only Provincial Grand Lodge that ever existed in America. The oldest Lodge in this country is St. Johns No. 1 Boston. The second oldest is Solomon's No. 1 at Savannah, Ga.

The charters issued by the Provincial Grand Lodge of America are the most beautiful and expensive Masonic Documents on this Continent. One of the finest specimens of this work is the charter issued to St. John Lodge in Newbern. It is as perfect as when it was proudly received by the Lodge 136 years ago. The second charter of Royal White Hart Lodge under which it works today was issued by the Grand Lodge of North Carolina, Dec. 27, 1800. Royal White Hart Lodge retained its English allegiance thirteen years after its sister lodges were working under the Grand Lodge of North Carolina, because it paid ten pounds for a charter giving it No. 1. After the Grand Lodge received the money, they changed their mind and wrote out another charter giving it No. 2. For years there was much bitter feeling in regard to this matter, but the lodge is well launched on its second century of faithful allegiance to the Grand Lodge of North Carolina, but this is mentioned merely as historic truth. It was incorporated in 1800.

CHAPTER TWENTY-THREE.

EVENTS LEADING TO THE CIVIL WAR.

For thirty years preceding the outbreak of the Civil War, Halifax County had more influence in national affairs than any other county in North Carolina. The only time the county ever had a United States senator and a member of the President's cabinet was during that period. John Branch, of Enfield, was elected senator in 1823 and re-elected in 1829. He, however, resigned the latter year to accept the position of Secretary of the Navy in President Jackson's Cabinet. Two years later, he resigned that position, also, because of the disruption of the cabinet on account of some social disagreements of the wives of the members.

Branch returned to Enfield in 1831, and was the next year elected to Congress. He served only one term when he was succeeded by Jesse A. Bynum, of Halifax, who continued in office until 1841, when he in turn was succeeded by another Halifax County man, John R. J. Daniel. Halifax County was, at the time, in the Sixth Congressional District, the other counties being Wake, Franklin, Warren, Edgecombe, Nash and Johnston. Daniel had been Attorney-General of the State, but was now elevated to a seat in Congress, where questions of great national importance were being discussed.

Not only in national affairs did the county wield influence during this period, but the affairs of State felt its energizing effect also. Spier Whitaker, of Enfield, was elected Attorney-General in 1842, holding that responsible position until 1847. Bartholomew F. Moore was chosen to the same post in 1848, and removed from his home in Halifax to Raleigh the same year. Joseph J. Daniel, of Halifax, was elevated from the Superior

Court to the Supreme Bench in 1832 and held the position until his death in 1848. During this period, therefore, the county was well represented in the councils of both State and nation.

Between 1840 and 1860, the county, along with the State and nation, passed through a crucial period leading up to the great climax of 1861. The question of slavery was to the fore, and the people of Halifax County were watching the trend of sentiment in the north with no little degree of uneasiness. The National Congress had been drawn into the discussion, first by the proposition to abolish slavery in the District of Columbia, second by the annexation of territory, and also by the passage of the Fugitive Slave Act. Some of the most brilliant men in the United States were arrayed on one side or the other of this absorbing question.

In 1840, according to the Federal Census taken that year, the county had a population of 24,325, of whom 16,865 were negro slaves. It is strange to note that when the census of 1850 was taken, the population had decreased to 16,584, nearly the whole of the decrease being in the slave population, which dropped to 8954, nearly fifty per cent. No reason is assigned for this remarkable decrease. There is no record of any unusual sale of negroes to the States farther South, nor any plague to reduce the number by death. Probably the most plausible conclusion is that a mistake was made by the census enumerators either in 1840 or 1850. The census of 1860 showed an increase over that of 1850 of about 3000.

From 1846 to 1848, the United States was at war with Mexico. In North Carolina and Halifax County, the war was unpopular because it was considered an unworthy attempt on the part of our Government to bully a weak neighbor. The State raised and equipped two regiments for the war, one commanded by Colonel Robert Treat Paine, of Elizabeth City, and the other by Colonel L. B. Wilson, of Tarboro. Halifax County furnished no soldiers for either regiment. The result of the war brought

EVENTS LEADING TO CIVIL WAR

new problems in the way of new territory to increase the tension over the slavery question.

Some ten years before that time, the country was thrown into violent excitement over the Nat Turner insurrection in Southampton County, Va. Turner was a slave, who incited the negroes of his neighborhood to rise against their masters, and, with himself at their head, they slaughtered a number of men, women, and children before the rebellion could be checked. Turner was finally overpowered, captured with a number of his deluded followers, given a trial, and hanged.

During that period of excitement, the people of Halifax County were in a state of wild suspense. It was not known how far the conspiracy among the slaves extended, and many rumors of similar risings in the county were current. None of these rumors, however, had foundation; and when the Southampton insurrection collapsed, there was no further fear.

Another insurrection that produced intense distrust and alarm was the John Brown raid in 1859. Halifax County was a unit in condemnation of such efforts on the part of the abolitionists. There were, it is true, in the county many who believed in a gradual emancipation of the negro race from bondage; but such acts as the John Brown raid and the Nat Turner insurrection solidified sentiment against the agitators. After Brown and his followers were captured at Harpers Ferry, Va., given a trial, convicted, and hanged, sentiment in the county was well nigh unanimous that the abolitionists of the North, by their agitation and indiscreet utterances about the slavery question, had brought the country to the verge of war.

CHAPTER TWENTY-FOUR.

IN THE LEGISLATIVE HALLS OF THE STATE.

Before following in the wake of the part Halifax County took in the tremendous cataclysm of the War between the States, a retrospective view of the part taken by her sons in the State's legislative halls will be interesting. From the first, the county sent to the General Assembly some of her best men. Among them are many names that are familiar and honorable in the county. Some of them reached great prominence in State and Nation. The following list is of interest to every native of Halifax County. They were the representatives from the adoption of the Constitution in 1776 to the outbreak of the war in 1861.

Halifax Town.

Year	House of Commons	Year	House of Commons
1777	Willie Jones	1806	Allen J. Davie
1778	Willie Jones	1807	Joseph J. Daniel
1779	Henry Montford	1808	William P. Hall
1780	Henry Montford	1809	William Drew
1781	Henry Montford	1810	Holcott J. Pride
1782	Henry Montford	1811	Jeptha Dupree
1783	Henry Montford	1812	Peter Brown
1784	Henry Montford	1813	William Drew
1785	Charles Pasteur	1814	William Drew
1786	Wm. R. Davie	1815	Joseph J. Daniel
1787	Wm. R. Davie	1816	William Drew
1788	Goodrum Davis	1817	Hutchings G. Burton
1789	Wm. R. Davie	1819	Thomas Burgess
1790	Wm. R. Davie	1820	Robert A. Jones
1791	Wm. R. Davie	1821	Thomas Burgess
1792	Richard H. Long	1822	Thomas Burgess
1793	Wm. R. Davie	1823	Jesse A. Bynum
1794	Wm. R. Davie	1824	Jesse A. Bynum
1795	John B. Ashe	1826	Robert Potter
1796	Wm. R. Davie	1827	Jesse A. Bynum
1797	Thaddeus Barnes	1828	Jesse A. Bynum
1798	Wm. R. Davie	1829	Wm. L. Long
1799	Richard H. Long	1830	Wm. L. Long
1800	Richard H. Long	1831	Wm. L. Long
1801	Isaac Hilliard	1832	Wm. L. Long
1802	Basset Stith	1833	Wm. L. Long
1803	William Drew	1834	Thomas Ousby
1804	Thomas Hall	1835	Robert C. Bond
1805	Allen Gilchrist		

By the Constitution of 1835, borough towns were abolished. Halifax town was, therefore, no longer entitled to a representative in the General Assembly. It will be observed that a considerable number of these men, who represented the town in the legislative body of the State, had already achieved a State and national reputation. Willie Jones was a national figure, though he held few positions of trust under the Federal government. William R. Davie, John B. Ashe, and Jesse A. Bynum, at different times, held positions of trust at the National Capitol. Hutchings G. Burton was afterwards Governor of the State. William Drew was Attorney-General for nine years. Joseph J. Daniel was afterwards on the Supreme Court bench for sixteen years.

In the list of members in the General Assembly for Halifax town, from which the above is taken, there is a note at the year 1825, which gives the following information: "No member was elected this year in consequence of the election having been broken up by a brawl between the contending candidates, Potter and Bynum, and their friends." It is known that Jesse A. Bynum and Robert Potter were on unfriendly terms because Bynum refused to introduce Potter to a certain lady. In 1825, they were contending candidates, and so bitter were the passions aroused between the candidates and their friends that on election day a fight ensued, in which one man was killed and a number bruised and disfigured. As all the election judges and poll holders participated in the fight, on one side or the other, no election could be held, and the town, therefore, had no representative that year.

Halifax County.

Year	Senate	House of Commons
1777	John Bradford	Jos. John Williams, Egbert Haywood
1778	Orondates Davis	Egbert Haywood, John Whitaker
1779	Orondates Davis	Willie Jones, Augustine Willis
1780	Orondates Davis	Willie Jones, William Weldon
1781	Orondates Davis	John Branch, Benjamin McCulloch
1782	Willie Jones	John Branch, Benjamin McCulloch

HISTORY OF HALIFAX COUNTY

Year	Senate	House of Commons
1783	Benjamin McCulloch	John Whitaker, John Geddy
1784	Nicholas Long	Benjamin McCulloch, John B. Ashe
1785	Nicholas Long	John Whitaker, John B. Ashe
1786	Benjamin McCulloch	John B. Ashe, Augustine Willis
1787	Nicholas Long	John Dawson, John Branch
1788	Willie Jones	John Jones, John Branch
1789	John B. Ashe	Peter Quarles, Marmaduke Norfleet
1790	Peter Quarles	John Dawson, Willis Alston
1791	Peter Quarles	Willis Alston, Thomas Tabb
1792	Peter Quarles	Willis Alston, Eaton Pugh
1793	Peter Quarles	Stephen W. Carney, James A. Tabb
1794	Willis Alston	Eaton Pugh, John A. Tabb
1795	Willis Alston	Eaton Pugh, Stephen W. Carney
1796	Willis Alston	John A. Tabb, Eaton Pugh
1797	Stephen W. Carney	Wood J. Hamblin, James A. Tabb
1798	Stephen W. Carney	Sterling Harwell, M. C. Whitaker
1799	Stephen W. Carney	Sterling Harwell, Wood J. Hamblin
1800	Stephen W. Carney	Mat'w C. Whitaker, Sterling Harwell
1801	Stephen W. Carney	Mat'w C. Whitaker, Sterling Harwell
1802	Stephen W. Carney	Mat'w C. Whitaker, Sterling Harwell
1803	Joseph John Alston	Mat'w C. Whitaker, Sterling Harwell
1804	John Alston	William Williams, M. C. Whitaker
1805	Gideon Alston	William Williams, M. C. Whitaker
1806	Gideon Alston	William Williams, M. C. Whitaker
1807	Matthew C. Whitaker	William Williams, Daniel Mason
1808	Matthew C. Whitaker	William Williams, Lewis Daniel
1809	Matthew C. Whitaker	Wm. E. Webb, Joseph Bryant
1810	Matthew C. Whitaker	Wm. E. Webb, Benjamin Edmonds
1811	John Branch	Wm. E. Webb, J. J. Daniel
1812	Matthew C. Whitaker	Wm. E. Webb, J. J. Daniel
1813	John Branch	James Barnes, W. J. Hamblin
1814	John Branch	J. Grant, R. Jones
1815	John Branch	Richard Jones, Wilson W. Carter
1816	John Branch	Richard Jones, Jesse A. Dawson
1817	John Branch	Richard Jones, Jesse A. Dawson
1818	John Alston	Jesse A. Dawson, Neville Gee
1819	John Alston	Richard Jones, Willis Alston
1820	John Alston	Willis Alston, Jesse A. Dawson
1821	John Alston	Willis Alston, Jesse A. Dawson
1822	John Branch	Robert A. Jones, Isham Matthews
1823	Thomas Burgess	Willis Alston, Robert A. Jones
1824	Isham Matthews	Willis Alston, R. B. Daniel
1825	Isham Matthews	Geo. E. Spruill, R. B. Daniel
1826	Isham Matthews	Geo. E. Spruill, Anthony A. Wyche
1827	Isham Matthews	Geo. E. Spruill, Wm. E. Shine
1828	Isham Matthews	Geo. E. Spruill, Rice B. Pierce
1829	Isham Matthews	Jesse A. Bynum, Thomas Nicholson
1830	Isham Matthews	Jesse A. Bynum, Thomas Nicholson
1831	Isham Matthews	Thomas Nicholson, John R. J. Daniel
1832	Isham Matthews	Charles Gee, John R. J. Daniel

LEGISLATIVE HALLS OF THE STATE

Year	Senate	House of Commons
1833	Isham Matthews	Wm. M. West, John R. J. Daniel
1834	John Branch	Wm. L. Long, John R. J. Daniel
1835	Andrew Joyner	Sterling H. Gee, Wm. M. West
1836	Andrew Joyner	I. Matthews, S. H. Gee, B. F. Moore
1838	Andrew Joyner	W. W. Daniel, M. A. Wilcox, S. Wh't'kr
1840	Andrew Joyner	S. H. Gee, B. A. Pope, B. F. Moore
1842	Andrew Joyner	S. H. Gee, B. A. Pope, B. F. Moore
1844	Andrew Joyner	S. H. Gee, B. F. Moore
1846	Andrew Joyner	L. M. Long, M. C. Whitaker
1848	Andrew Joyner	Wm. L. Long, Richard H. Smith
1850	Andrew Joyner	W. B. Pope, Dudley C. Clanton
1852	Andrew Joyner	Richard H. Smith, James D. Perkins
1854	M. L. Wiggins	Richard H. Smith, James D. Perkins
1856	M. L. Wiggins	William Hill, John W. Johnson
1858	Matthew C. Whitaker	William Hill, William L. Long
1860	Matthew C. Whitaker	Archibald H. Davis, W. B. Pope

Many of these men took high rank in the affairs of the State and the United States. Orondates Davis, in 1780, was chosen to serve on the Board of War for North Carolina. The other members were Alexander Martin, who afterwards became governor, and John Penn, one of the signers of the Declaration of Independence. Willis Alston was a member of Congress from 1799 to 1815 and again from 1826 to 1831. John Branch was a member of Congress for a long time, both in the Senate and the lower house, Governor of North Carolina, Secretary of the Navy in President Jackson's cabinet, and later Governor of the Territory of Florida. John R. J. Daniel was Attorney-General of the State and later member of Congress for twelve years. Spier Whitaker, and B. F. Moore were, at different times, Attorney-General of North Carolina. Perhaps no county can show an abler list of representatives in the General Assembly of North Carolina.

CHAPTER TWENTY-FIVE.

THE CALL TO ARMS.

The year 1860 was ominous. Mutterings of the coming storm were clear and distinct. National politics had become a national problem. The Whigs had disbanded. The Democrats were divided into factions. The Abolitionists had united with the disorganized elements of Whigs, Know-Nothings, Free-Soilers, and other political fragments until there was now in the northern states a compact, well organized party, determined to destroy the institution of slavery at any cost.

Early in the year the political pot began to boil. John C. Breckinridge, of Kentucky, was nominated for President by one faction of the Democratic party, and Stephen A. Douglas, of Illinois, was nominated by the other. The Abolitionists, now called Republicans, nominated Abraham Lincoln, of Illinois. The campaign was bitter and personal. Lincoln was elected by a big majority in the electoral college, but by a distinct minority vote. He received not a single vote in Halifax County.

As soon as it was known that Lincoln had been elected, the Legislature of South Carolina called a convention to consider the proposition of seceding from the union. The convention met, and, on December 20th, unanimously passed the ordinance of secession. The example of South Carolina was rapidly followed by Alabama, Mississippi, Louisiana, Florida, Georgia, and Texas. Early in February, the seven States met in convention at Montgomery, Ala., and elected Jefferson Davis, of Mississippi, President of the Southern Confederacy, and Alexander H. Stephens of Georgia, Vice-President.

North Carolina had as yet taken no official step in these rapidly happening events. Near the beginning of Febru-

THE CALL TO ARMS 107

ary, however, the General Assembly passed an act submitting the question of calling a convention to the people. The election, for or against calling a convention and for electing delegates, was held February 28th, and, by a substantial majority, the call for the convention was defeated. The vote in Halifax County was significant. For the convention the county registered a vote of 1,049, and against the convention 39. The county, however, selected two union men as representatives. The State, as a whole, elected an overwhelming majority of union men, and if the convention had met before the capture of Fort Sumter, North Carolina would probably have remained in the union.

An evil time was just ahead. Lincoln was inaugurated on March 4th, 1861, and declared, in his inaugural address, his purpose to collect custom duties at all southern ports. That declaration, of course, meant war. He, at once, dispatched reinforcements to Fort Sumter in Charleston harbor. The Confederate forces there fired upon the Federal ships and demanded the surrender of Fort Sumter. Upon the demand being refused, the bombardment of Sumter began; and, on April 12th, the fort was surrendered.

Immediately a thrill shot through the nation. President Lincoln called for 75,000 volunteers to put down the "rebellion" in the South. Governor Ellis refused to send North Carolina's quota in response to this call, and thus placed the State in direct conflict with the United States Government. The General Assembly was, at once, called in extra session. Halifax County's representatives that year were Matthew C. Whitaker in the Senate and Archibald H. Davis and W. B. Pope in the house. With other representatives, they voted to call a convention to meet in Raleigh, May 20th, 1861. The call was submitted to the people and carried almost unanimously. Halifax County sent Richard H. Smith, of Scotland Neck, and Dr. Charles J. Gee, of Weldon, as her representatives.

When the convention met on May 20, there was no other

thought than secession. A majority of the delegates were union men, but in the crisis that had come there could be no other solution than secession and war. The vote was taken on May 20, almost in silence. The two representatives from Halifax, along with the others, recorded their votes in favor of severing the political bonds that bound the states together. The vote for secession was unanimous.

For more than a month before the convention met, the feeling in the State was general that war was inevitable. In fact, Governor Ellis, anticipating the action of the convention, had authorized the mobilizing of the militia. Thousands of men volunteered within three days after the fall of Fort Sumter, and even before the State authorities were ready for them.

Among the first companies in the State to volunteer was the "Enfield Blues," a company composed of 109 men rank and file. The officers of the company were D. B. Bell, Captain; M. T. Whitaker, First Lieutenant; F. M. Parker, Second Lieutenant; Carey W. Whitaker, Junior Second Lieutenant. At Raleigh on April 17, 1861, along with other companies from various points in the State, the "Enfield Blues" were enrolled in what was afterwards known as the Bethel Regiment under the command of Colonel D. H. Hill.

After remaining in camp at Raleigh for a few weeks, the regiment was ordered to Virginia, and, passing through Richmond, marched up Main Street, receiving an ovation from the populace. As this regiment was the first from the State and the Enfield Blues the first company from Halifax County, it will not be improper, before mentioning other companies and other Halifax County men, to follow briefly the military fortunes of this heroic body of men, who risked life, fortune, and honor in a cause they thought right.

From Richmond, the regiment was ordered to join General Magruder, who was stationed near Yorktown, Va., and who was directed to check the advance of the Feder-

THE CALL TO ARMS 109

als from Fort Monroe. Hill was ordered to take position at Bethel Church, where, on June 10, he was attacked by a superior force under the command of General Pierce. In the battle which followed, the Enfield Blues, under the command of Lieutenant Parker, was stationed on the right wing and did splendid service. They aided in repelling the attacks of the enemy and in driving him from the field. Not a man of the company received a scratch in this remarkable conflict, in which about one hundred of the Federals were killed or wounded and only one, on the side of the South, killed and a few slightly wounded.

After the Battle of Bethel, the regiment was disrupted and the elements distributed through other commands. Captain Bell resigned August 31, 1861, and Lieutenant F. M. Parker succeeded him, Carey W. Whitaker succeeding to the position of Second Lieutenant and Carr B. Corbett becoming Junior Lieutenant. On October 16, same year, Captain Parker was elected Colonel of the Thirtieth Regiment, and, therefore, severed his connection with the Enfield Blues. Lieutenant M. T. Whitaker became Captain upon the resignation of Colonel Parker. Another member of the company, Spier Whitaker, was later made adjutant of the Thirty-third Regiment.

Through the vicissitudes of war the company passed, losing in battle and by disease, recruiting and diminishing, until at the last sad drama, at Appomattox, only three of the original company, that fought at Bethel, were left, John Beavens, J. S. Whitaker and Spier Whitaker. During the years between Bethel and Appomattox, many a deed of heroism and many a noble sacrifice were made; but history cannot throw a bouquet nor record a tear.

CHAPTER TWENTY-SIX.

WAR'S ALARMS.

During the spring and summer of 1861, North Carolina equipped and sent to the battle front in Virginia and Tennessee more than fifty thousand men. Regiments were organized at various points in the State, and camps of instruction in the school of the soldier were busy centers of military life.

Halifax County was not behind in furnishing the flower of her soldiery in this crisis. Immediately following the organization of the Bethel regiment, the First Regiment of volunteers was mustered in at the Race Track near Warrenton. Montford F. Stokes was elected Colonel; Matt W. Ransom, Lieutenant-Colonel, and John A. McDowell, Major. Halifax County sent one company of 157 men; and during the service of the company through the period of the war, the following officers served in turn: Captains, S. H. Gee, W. H. Day; First Lieutenants, A. L. Pierce, C. Branch; Second Lieutenants W. B. Williams John Wynn, D. E. Stokes, R. J. Day.

Upon its organization, the regiment was ordered to Richmond, and became a real fighting force in the Army of Northern Virginia. It was assigned to Holmes' brigade and received its first baptism of fire in the Seven Days Battle, where about one-half of the entire regiment were either killed or wounded. All the regimental officers were shot down and the surviving men continued the pursuit of the enemy without officers or orders. Colonel W. R. Cox, at the time in command of the Second Regiment, was ordered to take command also of the First. The pursuit was continued to Malvern Hill, where the Federals made a desperate stand and checked the Confederate drive. In the last charge of Lee's lines upon the union works at

Malvern Hill, the First Regiment performed heroic and herculean tasks, and its dead were afterwards found nearest the enemy's defences.

Later that year, the regiment participated in the Battle of Antietam, where it lost, in killed and wounded, about one-half of its total number. The next year it underwent another baptism of fire at Chancellorsville, and again at Gettysburg and Winchester. Continuing its career of martial glory, the first regiment met the enemy at the Wilderness, Spottslyvania, Cold Harbor, and Petersburg; and furled its banners at Appomattox.

It is beyond the compass of this work to give a narrative of the exploits of all the volunteer companies from Halifax County in the War between the States. It would require a much more extended volume than the one now being prepared. Hardly more than a mere mention can be made of them, together with a few references to the services rendered.

The Twelfth Regiment was organized in the summer of 1861, and Company E, Halifax Light Infantry, became an integral part of it. James H. Whitaker was chosen Captain; J. H. Brickell, First Lieutenant; and John Formey, Second Lieutenant. Along with many another this regiment was sent to Virginia to assist in holding the Confederate lines around Richmond. The Fourteenth Regiment was organized soon afterwards with Junius Daniel, a gallant son of Halifax County, as Colonel. Daniel rose to the rank of brigadier-general, and was killed, at Spottsylvania, while brilliantly leading his brigade.

In July, 1861, the Twenty-fourth Regiment of volunteers was organized at Weldon. Company D, David C. Clarke, Captain, Halifax County troops, was enrolled in this splendid body of men. It participated in the battles around Richmond, at Fredericksburg, and Petersburg. It formed a part of General Ransom's Command, sent into Northampton County in June, 1863, to repel a Federal raid from the Chowan river toward Weldon, having for its object the burning of the railroad bridge across the Roanoke river. Ransom met the enemy at Boone's Mill and inflicted upon him such a defeat that he fled precipitately to the shelter of his gunboats below Winton. The next year, Company D was a part of Ransom's brigade that made the memorable charge in the capture of Plymouth.

Later, in the summer of 1861, the Forty-First Regiment was organized with the Scotland Neck Mounted Riflemen as one of its best fighting units. At the head of this well equipped and well disciplined company were Atherton B. Hill, Captain; Benjamin G. Smith, First Lieutenant; Norfleet Smith, Second Lieutenant. It became a part of the cavalry division of the Army of Northern Virginia.

In March, 1862, the Forty-Third Regiment was organized at Camp Mangum, near Raleigh. Junius Daniel, who was at the time Colonel of the Fourteenth Regiment, was elected to command this valiant body of troops. Daniel was much in demand at the time and had been chosen to head the Forty-Fifth Regiment, which was mobilized about the same time. He accepted the latter position, and was shortly afterwards promoted to the rank of brigadier-general.

Halifax County furnished two companies for this regiment, Companies D and F, the former commanded by Cary Whitaker, Captain; Thomas W. Baker, First Lieutenant; John S. Whitaker, Second Lieutenant. During the period of enlistment, William Beavans and George W. Willis also served in the position of Second Lieutenant. Company F was officered as follows: William R. Williams, Captain; William C. Ousby, First Lieutenant; Henry A. Mason, Second Lieutenant. The foregoing were promoted during the progress of the war to the position of captain, and William R. Bond, J. H. Morris, W. L. M. Perkins, and Jesse A. Macon served in turn in the position of Second Lieutenant.

The Forty-Third Regiment saw active service at Kinston, Newbern, and Plymouth in this State, and at Gettysburg, Drury's Bluff in Virginia, and in the famous Val-

CONFEDERATE MONUMENT, WELDON, N. C.

ley campaign under General Early. In all of these struggles, the Halifax County men acquitted themselves heroically. When General Pickett was given the command against Newbern in January, 1864, the Forty-Third was assigned to his division, and was in the attacking force that met defeat on that occasion. In April, the same year, it was with General Hoke in his successful assault upon Plymouth.

When the Junior Reserves were mustered into the Seventieth Regiment in the summer of 1864, Halifax County furnished one of the regimental officers, perhaps the youngest officer in the southern army, Walter Clark, who has since become distinguished in State and Nation. He was first elected Lieutenant-Colonel, but shortly afterwards, upon a reorganization of the regiment to meet the wishes of Lieutenant-General Holmes for more experienced senior officers, Clark was chosen Major. Halifax County had no company in this regiment but its history is interesting because of the close connection with it of one of the most distinguished sons of the county. In the biography of Judge Clark, given elsewhere, will be found a brief summary of the services of this body of troops.

In December, 1864, the Seventy-First Regiment of Junior Reserves was organized at Weldon with J. H. Anderson as Colonel. Halifax County furnished one company officered as follows: W. R. Williams, Captain; David C. Whitaker, First Lieutenant; W. K. Martin and W. T. Purnell, Second Lieutenants. The regiment was in service only about four months, but the Halifax Company had been organized in July of the preceding summer and had done provost duty at Weldon until attached to the Seventy-First Regiment.

Almost immediately after its organization, Colonel Anderson was ordered to Belfield (now Emporia), Va., to check the advance of the Federals upon that place. This was gallantly done, and, upon the retreat of the enemy, he was pursued several miles. The weather was intensely cold and the soldiers suffered very much from the lack of proper clothing and bedding. For their gallant service, on this occasion, the General Assembly passed a resolution of thanks. Later, the regiment was attached to Hoke's division, and was under fire at Kinston, South West Creek, and Bentonville, surrendering with Johnston at Durham.

Just previous to the organization of the Seventy-First Regiment of Junior Reserves, by act of the Confederate Congress the Seventh Cavalry was formed, which body of troops was afterwards designated as the Seventy-Fifth Regiment. Halifax County furnished one company with the following officers: W. K. Lane of Wayne County Captain; John A. Collins, First Lieutenant; W. F. Parker, Second Lieutenant. No explanation is given why a man from Wayne County was elected Captain more than the fact that this was a company of Junior Reserves, and it was desired to have an experienced officer to command. During its term of service, John H. Branch also served as first lieutenant. The regiment served in eastern North Carolina, at Petersburg, and surrendered at Appomattox.

CHAPTER TWENTY-SEVEN.

THE CONSTRUCTION AND SERVICE OF THE ALBEMARLE.

During the entire four years of warfare, from 1861 to the surrender of Lee at Appomattox, April 9, 1865, not a foot of Halifax County soil was occupied by Federal troops. In a very important sense, we were remote from the war zone and felt no shock of arms nor heard the din of battle. Nevertheless, the county and particularly Weldon held a strategic position throughout the war.

Weldon was selected, early in 1861, as a mobilization camp for troops intended for the Virginia campaigns. Just across the Roanoke, in Northampton County, was established a school of instruction where raw recruits were drilled and seasoned into grim warriors. Here, many of the regiments were organized and trained before being sent to the firing line.

The railroad lines through Weldon were the main arteries that transported reinforcements and supplies to Lee's army from the South. With these railroads in the hands of the Confederacy, the war might be brought to a successful conclusion or prolonged indefinitely; with them severed, Richmond would fall and the gray line around Petersburg would be irretrievably broken. Hence the effort of the Federals, early in the war, to burn the railroad bridge at Weldon and the determined purpose of the Confederates to hold it.

Weldon was, therefore, a place of much importance, far more than its size, at that time, warranted. For a long time, Lieutenant-General Holmes, in command of the department of Eastern North Carolina, made his headquarters there; and later, during the closing months of the war, Brigadier-General Baker, in command of the same department, issued most of his orders from that point.

116   HISTORY OF HALIFAX COUNTY

The concentration camps for troops from many portions of the State and the far South were located on the outskirts of the town, and troops were constantly marching and countermarching through the principal thoroughfares. Weldon, therefore, presented all the appearances of war without any of its accompanying horrors.

Elsewhere in the county, also, there was considerable military activity, although no fighting occurred. Near Scotland Neck, at Edwards' Ferry, the Ram *Albemarle*, that performed such remarkable service in the recapture of Plymouth, was built. As that extraordinary vessel contributed such an important chapter in the record of the war in North Carolina, a general statement about its construction, equipment, manning, and services will not be inappropriate. As to the construction and equipment, the best authority is the builder of the wonderful naval prodigy, Gilbert Elliott, of Elizabeth City, who was when he began its construction just nineteen years of age. His report, taken from Vol. V of the North Carolina Regimental Histories, is here given:

"During the spring of 1863, having been previously engaged in unsuccessful efforts to construct war vessels, of one sort or another, for the Confederate Government, at different points in Eastern North Carolina and Virginia, I undertook a contract with the Navy Department to build an iron-clad gunboat, intended, if ever completed, to operate on the waters of Albemarle and Pamlico Sounds. Edwards' Ferry on the Roanoke river, in Halifax County, North Carolina, about 30 miles below the town of Weldon, was fixed upon as the most suitable for the purpose. The river rises and falls, as is well known, and it was necessary to locate the yard on ground sufficiently free from overflow to admit of uninterrupted work for at least twelve months. No vessel was ever constructed under more adverse circumstances. The shipyard was established in a corn field, where the ground had already been marked out and planted for the coming crop, but the owner of the land, W. R. Smith, Esq., was in hearty sympathy with the en-

CONSTRUCTION AND SERVICE OF ALBEMARLE 117

terprise, and aided me then and afterwards, in a thousand ways, to accomplish the end I had in view. It was next to impossible to obtain machinery suitable for the work in hand. Here and there, scattered about the surrounding country, a portable saw mill, blacksmith's forge, or other apparatus was found, however, and the citizens of the neighborhoods on both sides of the river were not slow to render me assistance, but co-operated cordially in the completion of the iron-clad, and at the end of about one year from the laying of the keel, during which innumerable difficulties were overcome by constant application, determined effort, and incessant labor, day and night, success crowned the efforts of those engaged in the undertaking.

"Seizing an opportunity offered by comparatively high water, the boat was launched, though not without misgivings as to the result, for the yard being on a bluff she had to take a jump, and as a matter of fact was 'hogged' in the attempt, but to our great gratification did not thereby spring a leak.

"The plans and specifications were prepared by John L. Porter, Chief Constructor of the Confederate Navy, who availed himself of the advantage gained by his experience in converting the frigate *Merrimack* into the iron-clad *Virginia* at the Gosport navy yard."

Mr. Elliott gives a very minute detailed statement as to the size and armament of the vessel. Continuing he says:

"The *Albemarle* was 152 feet long between perpendiculars; her extreme width was 45 feet; her depth from the gun-deck to the keel was 9 feet, and when launched she drew 6 1-2 feet of water, but after being ironed and completed her draught was about 8 feet. The keel was laid, and construction was commenced by bolting down, across the center, a piece of frame timber, which was of yellow pine, eight by ten inches. Another frame of the same size was then dovetailed into this, extending outwardly at an angle of forty-five degrees, forming the side, and at the outer end of this the frame for the shield was also dovetailed, the angle being thirty-five degrees, and then the top deck was added, and so on around to the other end of the bottom beam. Other beams were then bolted down to the keel, and to the one first fastened, and so on, working fore and aft, the main deck beams being interposed from stem to stern. The shield was sixty feet in length and octagonal in form. When this part of the work was completed she was a solid boat, built of pine frames, and if caulked would have floated in that condition, but she was afterwards covered with four-inch planking, laid on longitudinally, as ships are usually planked, and this was properly caulked and pitched, cotton being used for caulking instead of oakum, the latter being very scarce and the former almost the only article to be had in abundance. Much of the timber was hauled long distances. Three portable saw mills were obtained, one of which was located at the yard, the others being moved about from time to time to such growing timber as could be procured.

"The iron plating consisted of two courses, seven inches wide and two inches thick, mostly rolled at the Tredeger Iron Works, Richmond. The first course was laid lengthwise, over a wooden backing, 16 inches in thickness, a 2-inch space, filled in with wood, being left between each two layers to afford space for bolting the outer course through the whole shield, and the outer course was laid flush, forming a smooth surface, similar to that of the *Virginia*. The inner part of the shield was covered with a thin course of planking, nicely dressed, mainly with a view to protection from splinters. Oak knees were bolted in, to act as braces and supports for the shield.

"The armament consisted of two rifled 'Brooke' guns mounted on pivot-carriages, each gun working through three port-holes, as occasion required, there being one port-hole at each end of the shield and two on each side. These were protected by iron covers lowered and raised by a contrivance worked on the gun deck. She had two

CONSTRUCTION AND SERVICE OF ALBEMARLE

propellers driven by two engines of 200 horse power each with 20-inch cylinders, steam being supplied by two flue boilers, and the shafting was geared together. The sides were covered from the knuckle, four feet below the deck, with iron plates two inches thick. The prow was built of oak, running 18 feet back, on center keelson and solidly bolted, and it was covered on the outside with iron plating two inches thick, and tapering off to a four-inch edge, formed the ram.

"The work of putting on the armor was prosecuted for some time under the most disheartening circumstances, on account of the difficulty of drilling holes in the iron intended for her armor. But one small engine and drill could be had, and it required, at the best, twenty minutes to drill an inch and a quarter hole through the plates, and it looked as if we would never accomplish the task. But 'necessity is the mother of invention', and one of my associates in the enterprise, Peter E. Smith, of Scotland Neck, North Carolina, invented and made a twist-drill with which the work of drilling a hole could be done in four minutes, the drill cutting out the iron in shavings instead of fine powder.

"For many reasons it was thought judicious to remove the boat to the town of Halifax, about twenty miles up the river, and the work of completion, putting in her armament, machinery, etc., was done at that point, although the actual finishing touches were not given until a few days before going into action at Plymouth."

Having been completed, the *Albemarle* was placed under the command of Captain James W. Cooke, of the Confederate Navy, and manned by a complement of daring sailors. Being ordered to co-operate with General Hoke in his attack upon Plymouth, Cooke drifted down the river stern foremost until he came within a few miles of Plymouth. He then attacked the two Federal gunboats, the *Southfield* and *Miami*, sank the former, and chased the latter to the Albemarle Sound, silencing also the batteries on the river shore. The next day General

Hoke carried the Federal works by storm, captured the tov ⸳, and took the entire garrison prisoners of war.

As for the *Albemarle*, a few more months of glory ended her career on the spot of her greatest achievement. Shortly after the recapture of Plymouth, Captain Cooke proceeded down the Roanoke to its mouth and engaged, in the Albemarle Sound, a Federal fleet of seven vessels. After a teriffic battle of four hours, in which her smoke stack was riddled and she was otherwise crippled, at the cost of enormous losses to the Federals, she steamed back to Plymouth, and lay almost a wreck until the night of October 27, 1864, when she was torpedoed and sunk by Lieutenant William B. Cushing of the United States Navy. Subsequently, the *Albemarle* was raised and towed to the Norfolk Navy Yard, and, being stripped of her armament, machinery, etc., was sold October 15, 1867.

Thus ended the career of one of the first iron-clad gunboats ever built and the only war vessel ever constructed in Halifax County. Its riddled smoke stack is now in the museum of the Historical Commission at Raleigh.

CHAPTER TWENTY-EIGHT.

CLOSING INCIDENTS OF THE WAR.

Halifax County soldiers played an important, and frequently a conspicuous, part in many of the great events of the war. They were ever among the foremost in nearly all of the great battles. There was no deed of daring, no perilous duty to perform, no sacrifice to make, no suffering to endure that Halifax veterans were not ready to undergo. The story of their patriotism, their endurance, and their fortitude under most trying circumstances would more than fill a volume. Only a few references to their deeds and dangers can be made. It is difficult to tell the story of the private soldier because of the lack of information, but the record of the officers, in many a duplicate, will give a fair estimate of the heroism of the men in the trenches.

Halifax furnished to the Confederate service five brigadier-generals; namely, L. O'B. Branch, Junius Daniel, W. R. Cox, L. S. Baker, and David C. Clark, the last mentioned holding a State commission, while the others were commissioned by the Confederate Government.

Branch was promoted to the rank of brigadier-general in January, 1862, and given command of about 5000 troops with headquarters at Newbern. In March, of that year, he was attacked by about 15,000 Federals, and, after a stubborn resistance, was compelled to retreat, surrendering Newbern and the Pamlico country to the enemy. Branch afterwards commanded a brigade in the Army of Northern Virginia, and, at the Battle of Antietam, was killed.

Daniel, whose commission as a brigadier dated from September 1, 1862, was a gallant officer. His courage, endurance, and skill, were exhibited on many hard fought battlefields; and in one of the most stubbornly contested conflicts of the whole war, Spottsylvania, he was slain while cheering on his men.

"Last at Appomattox" is a legend that has long been claimed for North Carolina, and, in its glory, Halifax County is entitled to a share. General W. R. Cox, a native of Scotland Neck, led the last charge of the last attacking column that fired the last shot, on the morning of Lee's surrender, a few minutes before the capitulation took place. Cox's brigade, among whom were some gallant sons of Halifax, thus did the last duty for the Confederacy, and, when ordered, stacked their arms with the deepest feeling of humiliation and regret.

Brigadier-General David C. Clark, commissioned by the State government, was, for a time, in command of the district of the Roanoke, and guarded the county against invasion from the southeast, again and again foiling the raiding parties of the enemy from Plymouth and the Albemarle country.

General Baker was a cavalry officer. During the last six months of the war, he was in command of the District of Eastern North Carolina with headquarters at Weldon. Judge J. M. Mullen, of Petersburg, Va., at one time a resident of the county, has given, in Volume V of the Regimental Histories, an interesting account of "The Last Fifteen Days of Baker's Command at Weldon". With his permission, a part of that article is inserted here:

"After the evacuation of Plymouth, Washington, Kinston, and Goldsboro, Brigadier-General L. S. Baker was sent to Weldon, charged with the duty of holding on to that place, not only for the purpose of preserving railroad communication between the other forces in North Carolina and the Army of Northern Virginia, and those along the line of the Wilmington & Weldon Railroad from Goldsboro to that point, but of collecting supplies for these armies from that portion of Eastern North Carolina not actually in possession of the enemy. The authorities recognizing the importance of this position in these

CLOSING INCIDENTS OF THE WAR 123

respects, it being one of the principal sources of supply for the armies in the field, instructed General Baker to hold it until the last moment, and, at the same time, to watch out for and repel any raids of the enemy coming from the Blackwater and Chowan, and from Plymouth, Washington, and Goldsboro. With the force under his command, this was no light duty, and he was necessarily absent from Weldon most of his time looking after the various points under his supervision. Weldon, however, was the headquarters of his department, which was styled 'The Second Military District of North Carolina'. In his absence, the captain of our battery (Captain L. H. Webb, Company A, Thirteenth Battalion, North Carolina Light Artillery), was in command.

* * * * * *

"The task imposed upon this small force, consisting of two or three hundred infantry and our battery numbering about one hundred and twenty-five men, was no light one. For weeks it had been in a state of constant activity and excitement, enhanced towards the last with continued suspense and anxiety. It had been constantly on the move to meet threatened advances from the directions of the Tar and lower Roanoke, and the Chowan and Blackwater rivers. If I remember aright, during the month of March, it had been sent upon two expeditions through Northampton, Hartford, and Bertie counties, to repel reported raids of the enemy's cavalry from the Chowan, one, to and below Tarboro to meet a threatened advance from the lower Tar and Roanoke, and one, down at the Seaboard & Roanoke Railroad towards Franklin, to check a cavalry raid from the Blackwater. This last expedition, however, was in April, the command returning to camp therefrom the night of April 6. It was under command of Colonel Whitford, who had with him not to exceed two hundred infantry, (about fifty of whom were members of our company, armed with inferior rifles), and two guns from our battery. I was with the expedition as a cannoneer of one of the guns of the battery. I forgot to say that we were conveyed down the Seaboard road upon two or three flat cars, and possibly a box car or two. Upon reaching Boykin's Depot, about twenty-five miles from Weldon, we discovered that, all below that point, the enemy had torn up and burned the track so that it was impossible for us to proceed further on the train. Disembarking, we reconnoitered the situation for several miles around and remained there until next morning, when hearing that the enemy was making his way in the direction of Weldon, we boarded the train and started back. After passing Seaboard, a small station about ten miles east of Weldon, Colonel Whitford, who was riding on the engine, saw one or two men run across the track some six or seven hundred yards ahead. He at once ordered the train stopped. This precaution was not taken any too soon; for as soon as some of the infantry were put off as skirmishers and the situation was taken in, it was discovered that the track for some distance just ahead of us was torn up and that the enemy had ambuscaded both sides. We had passed Seaboard about a mile. As soon as the train was stopped the enemy opened fire upon us. Colonel Whitford caused the train to be run back to Seaboard, where the remainder of the command was put in position to await the return of the skirmishers, who were ordered to fall back as soon as they could ascertain with some certainty the force and purpose of the enemy. They soon reported that the enemy, consisting of a regiment of cavalry, had retired in the direction of Jackson, which was distant some eight miles in a southeast direction from where we were and away from Weldon. Colonel Whitford concluded to follow on after them, but I suspect with no hearty desire to meet up with them, for he could but know that our force was not able to cope successfully with a full regiment. Upon reaching Jackson, we learned there that the regiment was the Third New York Cavalry, about six hundred strong, well mounted and thoroughly equipped with Spencer repeating carbines, and had passed through that town some hours before, and then must be near Murfreesboro, some twenty-five miles distant. After waiting several hours at Jackson, our guns were ordered back overland to Weldon, while the infantry under Colonel Whitford's command retired to Halifax. I shall always remember with pleasure one little incident connected with this affair. Several weeks before, as we had more men than were required or needed to man the guns, about sixty of our company had been armed with rifles and acted with the infantry. When the train was halted and skirmishers thrown off, I was anxious to join them and endeavored to get one of the riflemen to exchange places with me. I knew he was disaffected, and it occurred to me that he would not hesitate to shirk danger; but I reckoned without my host. He rejected the overture with some indignation, and remarked that if anybody had to use his rifle he proposed to do it himself; and I ascertained that he behaved as gallantly as any man. This but illustrates that it was not cowardice that caused a great many of our soldiers to waver in their allegiance towards the close of the war, but the terrible hardships to which they were subjected, the distressing accounts of suffering of their loved ones at home, and the intuitive knowledge that defeat was inevitable. I remember with sadness, without any feeling of censure, many instances of desertion of as brave men as ever marched to the tap of a drum.

"On April 7, about 5 o'clock p. m., a telegram was received by Captain Webb, who was in command, from General Johnston, ordering that all trains north of the Roanoke river be recalled at once, all the artillery that could be moved got on the south side, and such heavy guns in the defences north of the river as could not be moved be destroyed, and the railroad bridge burned. Steps were at once taken to execute the order, and by hard service all night, the next morning (Saturday, 8th) found everything in the shape of guns, ordnance, quartermaster and commissary stores, removed from the north side of the river and delivered in Weldon, and combustibles at once gathered and placed at each end of the railroad bridge to fire it as soon as all the trains were safely over. The bridge, however, was not fired that day, why, I will let Captain Webb speak. I quote from his diary: 'General Baker came up about 10 o'clock A. M. and ordered me with my battery and Williams' section of artillery across the river again. Upon getting my battery over the river, I put my guns in position along the old line as I thought best, and awaited ulterior orders from headquarters. My only support were the feeble remains of a company of so-called cavalry under Captain Strange. In all the twenty men of his command, there was not a single man or officer decently mounted. With my old fiery Bucephalus, Duncan, I could have charged and overturned every skeleton of a horse in his company. But the men were all true Tar Heels, and there was no braver man than Captain Strange. On the afternoon of the 10th, the artillery was ordered back to the south side, and preparations made to leave Weldon.' According to Captain Webb, there were then at that point about five hundred men, including at least seventy-five stragglers, furloughed men, convalescents from the hospitals, and detailed men."

Judge Mullen proceeds, in his story, to tell of the abandonment of Weldon and the retreat of the command toward Raleigh, in an effort to join General Johnston at that place. The little army left Weldon on April 12th and had not gone far on the way when news of the surrender of Lee reached them, and the realization that the cause was indeed a lost one came upon them. Nevertheless, they continued to push on, hoping to join Johnston and with him to strike one more blow in behalf of the expiring Confederacy. At Ridgeway, the command separated, the bulk of the men returning to their homes, while fifty under the immediate direction of General Baker continued their efforts to join Johnston. At Earpsboro, however, on April 18th, General Baker received information that Johnston had surrendered. He, therefore, sent a flag of truce to General Sherman surrendering his command on April 19th.

CLOSING INCIDENTS OF THE WAR

At Weldon, after Baker's Brigade had left, the greatest excitement prevailed. People from the Northampton side of the river came crowding into the town to escape the imagined evils that they supposed would follow in the wake of the Federal army of occupation. The railroad bridge was the scene of the greatest interest and alarm. All the trains and engines in Weldon and vicinity were run on the bridge, and, on the 13th of April, fire was applied, consuming the structure and letting fall the engines to the bottom of the river. This was supposed to cut Weldon off from the danger of immediate occupation by the union forces. Such, however, was not the case, for not many days passed before the blue coats came and assumed general direction of affairs, coming from the Northampton side of the river as patrol parties from Grant's army in Virginia and from Goldsboro, that was then in the hands of Sherman.

In a few weeks, all the soldiers, surrendered by Lee at Appomattox and by Johnston at Durham, found their way to their homes, and people generally began to realize that the long war had ended. Halifax County men, who had surrendered, returned, feeling that they had fought a good fight in support of the old regime and had failed, and were now ready to accept the result in good faith and make the most of it.

The Federal forces lost no time in completely occupying the county. Patrol posts were established at Halifax, Enfield, and Weldon, and Federal soldiers and officers were seen in every community. The war was over, but the bitterness of defeat was present.

CHAPTER TWENTY-NINE.

RECONSTRUCTION DAYS.

Recovery from the effects of the war was slow but steady. The men, who had followed Lee in Virginia or suffered in the trenches around Petersburg and Richmond, now entered heartily into the task of rebuilding the waste places. Some of the soldier boys, who had been wounded or held in prison, did not get back to their homes until late in the summer or early fall of 1865. When they did return, however, they, too, began the work of rebuilding. The war, it is true, was ended, but the battles of peace, no less stern and unrelenting, had to be fought; and the manhood of Halifax, that had heard without fear the whistle of bullets, or seen without dismay, the glimmer of bayonets, did not hesitate to do their part.

Halifax County was in the gloom of defeat and in danger of alien domination; but it needed development. The four years of war had arrested the march of progress in almost every line of industry. There was no enterprise in agriculture, no manufacturing, no lumbering, no banking, and none of the many other lines of business now being conducted so successfully in the county. The red hand of war had blasted every important industry, and stagnation was stalking abroad.

But the heroes of the trenches were no less brave in home development than they had been on the battlefield. With no less courage, in the piping times of peace, than they had displayed on a hundred fields of carnage, the boys that went out to battle with enthusiasm in 1861 and returned in 1865, unconquered but overwhelmed, entered with zeal into the task of development. With industry and enterprise characteristic of a people determined to

THE GENERAL DAVIS HOME, HALIFAX, N. C.

RECONSTRUCTION DAYS

succeed, the county soon began to emerge from its stupor and to put on new life.

Gloom and disaster, however, almost as bad as the storm of war was just ahead. With the advent of peace and the freedom of the negro, grave feelings of uneasiness became apparent as to the status of the freedman and his political affiliations, if he should be given the ballot.

During the war, the county had been represented in the State Senate by Mason L. Wiggins and in the House by Henry Joyner and Archibald H. Davis. For the year 1866, Mason L. Wiggins was re-elected to the Senate. D. C. Clark and W. A. Daniel were chosen to represent the county in the House. To represent Halifax in the Convention of 1865, called to rescind the ordinance of secession and to ratify the emancipation of the slaves, Edward Conigland and W. W. Brickell were chosen.

In this time of stress and uneasiness, all eyes were focused upon the Federal Congress, anxiously awaiting action by that body regarding the restoration of the State to its position as a member of the union. It was not until 1867, however, that Congress decided definitely upon a policy for the seceded states. In March, that year, the first of the reconstruction acts were passed, organizing North and South Carolina into a military district with General E. R. Canby as military governor with headquarters at Charleston, S. C. The same year, Congress passed the Fourteenth Amendment, which conferred the franchise upon the negro men of the South, and, by statute, withdrew it from thousands of white men, who had taken part in the late war.

By this reconstruction measure, more than 3000 negro men became legalized citizens in Halifax county, and cast their ballots for the first time in the election of 1868. In that year, the number of votes cast were as follows: Democratic, 1,593; Republican, 3,206. This vote compared with that of 1856 shows a startling increase. In that year, the vote was as follows: Democratic, 688; Whig, 509. There was, therefore, an increase in 1868 of 3,602, at least five-sixth of which was the negro vote. The white voters, as is apparent, found themselves overwhelmed by this avalanche of negro ballots. An evil day consequently dawned; and Halifax County, that had hitherto furnished men of learning and ability to the councils of State and nation, now found itself in the hands of ignorant ex-slaves, designing scalawags, and worse carpetbaggers. Henry Epps, a former slave, was elected in 1868, to the State Senate, and two other negroes, H. T. J. Hayes and Ivey Hutchings, and a carpetbagger, John H. Renfrow, were elected to the House. The government of the county fell entirely into the hands of the negroes and their confederates, the scalawags and carpetbaggers.

This domination continued until 1888, when the alien government was completely overthrown, and the native white people again assumed control. During that period, however, of political stagnation, from 1868 to 1888, the county made decided advances in material prosperity.

In 1868, the towns in the county were of little note. Halifax had lost its pristine significance and was of small commercial importance. Weldon was noted only as being the terminus of four railroads. Scotland Neck was merely two villages, Clarksville and Greenwood, a mile apart, Enfield, with about five hundred people, was perhaps the largest town in the county. Littleton had just emerged from the stigma of being called Little's Ordinary and was a mere hamlet. Palmyra was a small neighborhood on the Roanoke. Hobgood, Roanoke Rapids, Rosemary, and Hollister were not as yet in existence.

Since 1868, however, the forces of industry have brought about a wonderful change in the commercial importance of the country. Tremendous strides have been made in the development of agriculture. Land, which, in 1868, produced no more than a half bale of cotton to the acre, now produces a bale and a half. In manufacturing, the most wonderful progress has been made. At the close of the civil war, there was not a factory of any kind in the county, and that record continued until about 1890.

RECONSTRUCTION DAYS 131

In that year a knitting mill was built in Scotland Neck. In 1892, Major Thomas L. Emry began the development of the water power of the Roanoke river at a point about five miles above Weldon, and from his efforts has come the magic town of Roanoke Rapids with its large cotton factories, knitting mills, and paper mill and a population of over six thousand people. Weldon has also become a manufacturing center. At Hollister, the Fosburgh Lumber Company has one of the largest plants in the county. In 1868, there was not a bank in the county. Now there are ten.

In railroad building, the county has been among the first in the State. Besides the two trunk lines that were built before the outbreak of the Civil War, two other lines, the Kinston Branch and the Norfolk and Carolina, have been completed since 1880. In all about fifty miles of railroad have been constructed since the civil war.

CHAPTER THIRTY.

SINCE RECONSTRUCTION DAYS.

Until 1880, the government of the county was entirely in the hands of the ignorant element. They held all the remunerative offices and sent to the General Assembly regularly from 1868 to 1880 a negro to the Senate and a negro and a white man, a carpetbagger or a scalawag, to the House. In 1880, however, the conservatives asserted themselves and elected to the General Assembly Spier Whitaker, representative in the Senate and William H. Day and M. T. Savage in the House. The "radical" element again triumphed at the polls in 1882, but, in 1884, it was again overthrown by the election to the Senate of J. M. Mullen, and David Bell and A. J. Burton to the House. Again in 1886 the alien government became established to be finally overthrown in 1888 by the election of Thomas L. Emry to the Senate and W. H. Anthony and Thomas H. Taylor to the House.

Since that time the following representatives have served terms in the General Assembly:

Year	Senate	House of Representatives
1891	W. E. Bowers	W. W. Hall, A. B. Hill
1893	W. H. Day	W. H. Kitchin
1895	I. E. Green	J. M. Grizzard, J. A. House
1897	E. T. Clark	Scotland Harris, J. H. Arrington
1899	E. L. Travis	W. P. White, H. S. Harrison
1901	E. L. Travis	W. F. Parker, W. P. White
1903	E. L. Travis	W. F. Parker, W. P. White
1905	W. H. Thorne	T. C. Harrison, Sandys Gale
1907	W. E. Daniel	John B. Neal, A. Paul Kitchin
1909	E. L. Travis	A. Paul Kitchin, H. S. Harrison
1911	A. Paul Kitchin	W. T. Clement, P. N. Stainback, A. H. Green
1913	W. E. Daniel	W. T. Clement, W. P. White
1915	W. L. Long	J. H. Darden, T. H. Taylor
1917	W. L. Long	J. H. Darden, T. H. Taylor

SINCE RECONSTRUCTION DAYS

These men, most of them still living, performed a part in rescuing the county from the grip of reconstruction evils that is little short of marvellous. Some of them attained positions of honor outside of the county, and, therefore, deserve more than a passing mention. W. H. Day afterwards removed to Raleigh and became one of the most prominent attorneys in the State capital. Kitchin had, in 1878, been elected to Congress defeating two negroes, John A. Hyman, of Warren, and James E. O'Hara, of Halifax, both running on the Republican ticket. Travis is now, 1917, chairman of the State Corporation Commission, having been elected to a position in that body in 1910. Daniel was solicitor for this judicial district from 1894 to 1906, making a splendid record in that capacity.

Previous to 1871, for ten years, Halifax County had been in the First Congressional District; but in that year it became incorporated in the Second. In 1870, Charles R. Thomas, a Republican, was elected to represent the district in Congress, and re-elected in 1872. Thomas was a scalawag from Newbern. In 1874, the district did an unprecedented thing in electing a negro, John A. Hyman, of Warren County, to the national Congress. Two years later, Curtis H. Brogden, of Goldsboro, who had been governor of the State for two years, was chosen; but in 1878 Brogden failed of the nomination on the Republican ticket and two negroes, John A. Hyman, of Warren, and James E. O'Hara, of Halifax, were candidates, both claiming to have been nominated by the Republican Convention. Seeing a chance of success, the Democrats nominated W. H. Kitchin, of Scotland Neck. A spectacular three-cornered fight was the result, and Kitchin was elected by a plurality vote.

For twenty years following that time, the second district was represented in Congress by negroes, James E. O'Hara, of Halifax, H. P. Cheatham, of Vance, and George H. White, of Edgecombe. In 1900, however, Claude Kitchin, of Scotland Neck, was elected and has been continuously in Congress since. He has taken high rank and is now Chairman of the Ways and Means Committee of the House and the floor leader of the Democrats.

Halifax County took an active part in the World War. Claude Kitchin, Chairman of the Ways and Means Committee of the House of Representatives of the National Congress, voted against the Declaration of War with Germany, April 6, 1917, but, finding himself in the minority, he accepted the result as conclusive and allied himself with the President of the United States in the greatest war preparation ever undertaken by a nation. The war measures that startled the world in the enormous revenue raised for the prosecution of the war and the transportation of two millions of soldiers to Europe were largely the product of his efforts.

More than twelve hundred men were sent by the Halifax County Exemption Board to the training camps, and about one hundred, besides, volunteered for different lines of service. Many saw active service on the battlefields of France, and some made the extreme sacrifice for country and humanity.

In every drive for Liberty Loans or for war work, the county went "over the top" early in the campaigns. In the fight, therefore, for the liberation of mankind and in making the world safe for democracy and Christianity, the county did no small part. Both men and money answered the call and answered it gloriously.

At present, Halifax County ranks as one of the foremost in the State in political influence, in educational progress, in religious development, in material prosperity, and in general industrial activity. Perhaps, there is no county in North Carolina that stands higher in any of these activities. On the Supreme Court Bench, the chief-justice, Judge Walter Clark, is a native of Halifax. The Chairman of the North Carolina Corporation Commission, E. L. Travis, lives in Halifax. The Chairman of the Ways and Means Committee of the Federal House of Representatives, Claude Kitchin, lives in Scotland Neck. William

W. Kitchin, who was a member of Congress for twelve years and Governor of North Carolina for four years, is a Halifax County man, though he now lives in Raleigh.

In educational activity the county ranks high. Weldon, Roanoke Rapids, Rosemary, Scotland Neck, Enfield, and Littleton have splendid systems of public graded schools with valuable brick buildings in which the schools are conducted. Halifax, Hobgood, and Hollister have also good schools. Religiously, also, the county is wide awake. In other lines of progress, the county is by no means a laggard.

If we compare Halifax County of the present with one hundred and fifty years ago, we shall see a wonderful difference. Then, a few hundred people lived here; now fifty thousand. Then, only two villages in the county; now five thriving towns with large industrial and commercial activities. Then, no roads worthy the name; now splendid sand-clay turnpikes traversing almost every section. Then, no industry of any note; now, almost every line of business in the modern world represented. Then, no schools; now, six city school systems besides other High Schools and rural schools of splendid efficiency. Then, few churches; now beautiful and substantial houses of worship in every neighborhood. In short, Halifax County in a few generations, has leaped from the desolation of the wilderness, unknown and unhonored, into the calcium light of railroads, telegraph lines, telephones, electric lights, schools, newspapers, churches, paved boulevards, factories, paper mills, and all the conveniences and improvements of the modern community. Well might it be said "What wonderful changes time hath wrought!"

CHAPTER THIRTY-ONE.

SOME ODDS AND ENDS OF HISTORY.

There are numbers of interesting incidents connected with the history of Halifax County, not vitally concerned in the story as given in the preceding pages, but are so absorbing that mention may very well be made in a chapter of "Odds and Ends."

The Crowell Family.

From Wheeler's History of North Carolina:
"Two brothers, John Crowell and Edward, came to North Carolina and settled in Halifax. They emigrated from Woodbridge, New Jersey. They are originally from England; and they or their ancestors were originally called Cromwell.

"In the year 1674, says the Annalist of Philadelphia, two brothers of Oliver Cromwell left England for America and settled in New Jersey. They fled from England, from the political storms that impended over the name and house of the late Protector.

"While on the voyage, fearing that persecution would follow from the adherents of Charles II., then on the English throne, they resolved to change the name. This was done with solemn ceremony, and by writing their name each on paper, and each cutting from the paper the M and casting it in the sea.

"The family pedigree on vellum, recording these facts, was with the family in North Carolina, in an ornamental chest with other valuables, when by a party of Tarleton's Legion, in 1781, this chest was seized and taken off. These facts are undoubted. The record was again made up from the recollections of the family, and is still preserved

OLD TRINITY CHURCH, SCOTLAND NECK, N. C.

SOME ODDS AND ENDS OF HISTORY 137

among them. From one of them, these interesting and curious facts are derived.

"Here, in the quiet retreats of North Carolina, the aspiring blood of Cromwell found repose, and in the peaceful precincts of Halifax, the exquisite poetry of Gray was fully realized:

> 'Some village Hampden, who with dauntless breast,
>   The petty tyrant of his fields withstood,
> Some mute, inglorious Milton here may rest,
>   Some Cromwell guiltless of his Country's blood.'"

This story of the Crowell family has been robbed of some of its interest in the last few years by the statement that Oliver Cromwell, the Lord Protector, was the only son of his father surviving infancy. These brothers, who came to America from England, could not, therefore, have been his. Another story of this interesting incident was found among the papers of the late S. S. Alsop, a part of which is here quoted:

"After the death of Oliver Cromwell, which happened about the year 1658, his eldest son, Richard Cromwell, having been named as his successor, quietly assumed the reins of government. It was very soon discovered, however, that the talent and disposition of Richard were by no means of an order to enable him to hold with firmness that which his father had won by the exercise of much energy, skill, and political address. Being a man of peaceful disposition, amiable, and unambitious, Richard allowed himself to be deposed without the least effort to prevent it. Charles II. was now recalled from Normandy and offered the throne. Richard Cromwell, in the meantime, had retired to his country seat, where, in the pursuit of more congenial employment, he lived to a very old age in the practice of all social and domestic virtues, and in the enjoyment of those rich and pleasant rewards which ever follow a well-spent life. After the death of Richard, his sons emigrated to America, about the beginning of the eighteenth century, and settled in New Jersey. Before landing, however, a family council was held when, in the known unpopularity of the family on this side, especially in the middle and southern provinces, it was agreed to drop from the name the letter (m), thus leaving it Crowell, as it is at present written.

"Shortly after the settlement of the family in New Jersey, Edward and Joseph Crowell were born, and from thence, about 1730, immigrated into this State. Here Joseph married a Miss Barns, a woman, says Wheeler, remarkable for her personal beauty.

"Edward Crowell, who settled near what is now known as Crowell's X Roads, married a Miss Raburn, a sister of Matthew Raburn, afterwards Governor of Georgia."

ADVENTURES OF A PRIVATEER.

A story from the pen of James Moore, father of B. F. Moore, at one time Attorney-General of North Carolina, is interesting enough to find a place in this volume. The following is his own account:

"In 1775-6, enlistments were made in the neighborhoods where the musters were held, and I was very anxiously concerned because I was not of the age required for a soldier (i. e. 16). At this time I was only ten or eleven years old, and during a part of the period from thence till I reached the required age, I was at school; but as soon as I was sixteen, which was in 1781, the year in which Cornwallis was taken, I entered on board a privateer schooner called the Hannah, which sailed out of Edenton on an eight weeks' cruise.

"Our captain's name was Kit Gardiner, an Englishman by birth. William Gold, of Connecticut, was lieutenant, and Daniel Webb, of South Quay, Nausemond County, Virginia, was first prize master.

"We sailed in March from Edenton and crossed the Ocracoke bar and soon was in the Gulf Stream with heavy surges. We sprung our bowsprit and put into Beaufort harbor and put another in. From there we sailed and cruised off Charleston, took four prizes and condemned three. The fourth was a Bermudean, a neutral, and he had two sets of consignments, one for a British port and the other for an American, by which means she was cleared at Wilmington, N. C.

"The first prize was a schooner from Cork, Ireland, to New York. She was taken first by a privateer out of Philadelphia and retaken by the Charleston frigate. This frigate was built in Newburyport, fifty miles eastward of Boston (I was shown the spot where it was said she was built) and was called the *Boston*. She happened to be in Charleston when the British took that city, and they changed her name and called her *Charleston*. After her capture she was their regular packet from Charleston to New York.

"In our cruise, we took a schooner called the Lord Cornwallis, laden with Governor Martin's effects. He was Governor of South Carolina and became traitor; and when laying in provisions against the siege, he caused the barrels to be filled with sand instead of pork.

"The second prize was from New Hampshire laden with salt and garden seeds, such as peas, beans, etc. I was put aboard of her. Our place of rendezvous was Beaufort, N. C. Now as we took the vessel near Charleston, the port to which she was bound, it was reasonable to suppose that her provisions were nearly exhausted, which was the case.

"With these, we undertook to make Beaufort, but instead of that, the first port was Newburyport, fifty miles eastward of Boston, and, sixteen days after, we were tossed and carried by contrary winds, going all around the different capes till we were off the Banks of Newfoundland and in view of the Agamenticus Hills, whose appearance, when seen at sea, is like three burly-headed clouds. We sailed along thence and arrived at Newburyport, sold our cargo (salt) at one dollar a bushel, and I received what the prize master saw fit to allow me, which was four dollars only."

Governor Burton's Apparition.

There is a well authenticated story connected with the death of Governor Hutchings G. Burton in 1836. The following account is the language of S. S. Alsop, who left some valuable notes on the history of the county:

"Governor Burton had a summer home in the western part of the county near Ringwood named Rocky Hill, at which he was residing at the time of his death. He had bought a large tract of land in Texas and had started to see it, with a view of removing if he liked it. Reaching Salisbury, where he had some business in court, he met with his cousin, Robert Burton, of Lincoln County, and started to spend some time with him. They stopped at the Wayside Inn, with some other lawyers to spend the night, when he was taken with cramp and died within twenty-four hours. His last words were, 'Oh, my dear wife and children. Lord, receive my spirit.' He was buried in Unity Church yard, in Lincoln County, a Presbyterian church, of which he was a member.

"His wife had been on a visit and was returning to her home, Rocky Hill, which is on a high elevation—about dusk. She was driven in a carriage by her servant William and had with her a grandchild, an infant, and a nurse. At the same time, she and William saw Governor Burton riding down the hill on a white horse, which he usually rode. Just then the infant cried and Mrs. Burton turned her head to see what was the matter. When she turned her head again expecting her husband to speak, the apparition had disappeared. She at once asked William where was his master. He did not answer and she repeated the question. He then said, 'Hush, Missus,' and told her he had ridden on down the hill and disappeared. He could never speak of it afterwards.

"On account of the slow mails of that day, Mrs. Burton did not hear of her husband's death until three weeks had passed, and found that the apparition had appeared at the very hour of his death."

SOME ODDS AND ENDS OF HISTORY

Historic Homes.

In the southern end of the town of Halifax, near Quanky Creek, was built about the year 1765, the famous home of Willie Jones, known as "The Grove Place". The four front rooms were built of material brought from the wreck of the home of Robert Jones, father of Willie Jones, in Northampton County. This home of the elder Jones was known as "Jones' Castle" and had been built near the beginning of the eighteenth century of material said to have been brought from England.

Willie Jones, the owner, was a man of considerable means, and greatly beautified not only the house but also the grounds. There was a race-track near the residence, which was used extensively by the residents of Halifax and by those who came from afar for the sport there afforded. Willie Jones owned blooded horses and was the leader in that line of sports as well as in many other lines.

The house is noted for having been, at different times, the headquarters of a part of three armies. During the Revolutionary war, Lord Cornwallis was entertained there while the British army was encamped in the town on its way to its Waterloo at Yorktown. In this house, also, Colonel Tarleton met his defeat in repartee at the hands of Mrs. Jones and her sister, Mrs. Ashe.

During the war between the States, Colonel McRae, by invitation of the owner, had his regiment quartered there for some weeks. At the close of the war, the house was unoccupied and was taken possession of by a part of the Federal army of occupation. For some years after the Civil War, the house was unoccupied.

Willie Jones, at his death, willed the home to his son, Willie W. Jones, who lived and died an old bachelor; and at his death, his sisters, Mrs. Eppes and Mrs. Burton, acquired possession. It remained in the Eppes family for many years and came to be called "The Eppes Home". It is now in decay, but an effort is being made by the Halifax Chapter of the Daughters of the American Revolution to reclaim and rebuild it.

It is sometimes erroneously called the "Paul Jones House". John Paul Jones did reside there for some time, but only as a guest or protege of the owner, Willie Jones.

Another historic house is "Quanky", where Colonel Nicholas Long, of the Revolution, lived. It was located just across Quanky Creek from the "Grove Place". Not one stone is left upon another now, and not even the site can be definitely determined. Here, during the Revolution, Colonel Long, who was, at the beginning of the war, in command of the Halifax regiment, entertained the high officials of the State and nation.

"Rocky Hill", the summer home of Governor Hutchings G. Burton, near Ringwood, is still standing, owned now by Mr. S. Harrison. Governor Burton, during his life as a public man, lived in the town of Halifax at the Grove House; but spent the greater part of the summers at "Rocky Hill", and was making it his permanent home at the time of his death in 1836.

Besides these historic homes, there are other buildings of more or less note. The home of General William R. Davie is still standing in the town of Halifax. The "Constitution Building", where the first State Constitution of North Carolina was written, is in a dilapidated condition, as is the old Town Hall, where the Convention met in 1776, both being in the town of Halifax. Here, also, is the Masonic Temple, a building venerable and historic. Between it and the river, on Main Street, is the site of the old Eagle Hotel, so famous during the Revolution and for years afterward. Now, hardly the foundations can be discerned.

CHAPTER THIRTY-TWO.

SUMMARY.

Halifax County was formed from Edgecombe County in 1758 and named in honor of Charles Montague, Earl of Halifax, who was, at the time, Secretary of the British Board of Trade.

The first settlements were made on Roanoke river and Conoconara swamp about 1723, and on Quanky Creek near the same time.

The first resistance to British oppression took place in Halifax County when armed men seized Corbin and Bodly, agents of Lord Granville, near Edenton and brought them forcibly to Enfield, in 1759, and lodged them in jail.

Joseph Montford, the first and only Grand Master of Masons for the Continent of North America, lived in Halifax.

April 12, 1776, the Provincial Congress, in session in Halifax, passed the famous resolution instructing the delegates in the Continental Congress from North Carolina to vote for a National Declaration of Independence, antedating similar resolutions from other colonies.

November 12, 1776, the first Constitutional Convention of North Carolina met in Halifax and organized the State government.

From 1776 to 1782, nearly every session of the General Assembly met in Halifax.

Halifax County had one of the representatives in the Continental Congress for several years, Willie Jones.

In the National Convention of 1787, Halifax County had two of the six representatives from North Carolina, Willie Jones and William R. Davie. Jones, however, refused to serve and afterwards opposed the ratification of the Constitution.

HISTORY OF HALIFAX COUNTY

Halifax County has had one ambassador to France, William R. Davie, and one member of the President's cabinet, John Branch.

The County has had the following members of the National House of Representatives:

John B. Ashe	1787—1788
John B. Ashe	1789—1793
Willis Alston	1799—1815
Hutchings G. Burton	1819—1825
Willis Alston	1825—1831
John Branch	1831—1833
Jesse A. Bynum	1833—1841
John R. J. Daniel	1841—1853
L. O'B. Branch	1855—1861
W. H. Kitchin	1879—1881
James E. O'Hara (negro)	1883—1887
W. W. Kitchin*	1897—1909
Claude Kitchin	1901—

(*Elected from Person Co.)

One Senator in the United States Congress was from Halifax County, John Branch, who served from 1823 to 1831.

The following Councillors of State were from Halifax County. Usually there were seven from the State at Large:

Willie Jones	1781—1782
Willie Jones	1787—1788
John Branch	1793—1798
John Branch	1801—1804
Gideon Alston	1807—1830
Isham Matthews	1834—1835
Henry Joyner	1866

Halifax County has given the following Governors to the State:

THE GROVE HOUSE

SUMMARY

Abner Nash .... 1780—1781
William R. Davie .... 1798—1799
John Branch .... 1817—1820
Hutchings G. Burton .... 1825—1827
W. W. Kitchin* .... 1909—1913

(*Elected from Person Co.)

The following Comptrollers:

John Craven .... 1784—1808
James Grant .... 1827—1834

The following Attorney-Generals were elected from Halifax County:

John Haywood .... 1791—1794
Hutchings G. Burton .... 1810—1816
William Drew .... 1816—1825
John R. J. Daniel .... 1835—1840
Spier Whitaker .... 1842—1846
B. F. Moore .... 1848—1851

The county has furnished two judges of the Supreme Court of North Carolina:

Joseph J. Daniel .... 1832—1848
Walter Clark .... 1889—

Clark has been chief-justice since 1903.

Five judges of the Superior Court have been chosen from Halifax:

John Haywood .... 1794—1800
Joseph J. Daniel .... 1816—1832
Walter Clark .... 1885—1889
Spier Whitaker .... 1889—1894
W. R. Cox .... 1877—1879

Halifax County furnished four brigadier-generals to the Confederate service.

HISTORY OF HALIFAX COUNTY

	Date of Rank
L. O'B. Branch (killed at Antietam)	Nov. 16, 1861
Junius Daniel (killed at Spottsylvania)	Sept. 1, 1862
Lawrence S. Baker	July 23, 1863
William R. Cox	May 31, 1864

David C. Clark held the rank of brigadier-general in the State militia and received his commission from the State government.

In the Revolutionary war, the county furnished one brigadier-general in the Continental service, James Hogan. The "Father of the American Navy", John Paul Jones, was appointed Captain of the Ranger while residing at Halifax.

The last soil held by Cornwallis, in North Carolina, was in Halifax just before his retreat to Virginia where he was soon bottled up and captured.

At the Eagle Hotel both President Washington and General Lafayette were entertained with elaborate ceremony at different times.

The Confederate iron-clad, the Ram Albemarle, was built near Scotland Neck, the first and only one built in the State.

Halifax has furnished more Governors (five) than any other county in the State; more attorneys-general (six); more members of Congress (fifteen); more brigadier-generals (six) than any other county.

Soldiers from Halifax have always stood in the front line. They were among the first to march to Washington's aid in 1776, among the first at Bethel, among the foremost at Gettysburg, and the last at Appomattox.

There are twelve townships, as follows: Halifax, Weldon, Roanoke Rapids, Littleton, Conoconara, Scotland Neck, Roseneath, Butterwood, Brinkleyville, Faucette, Palmyra, and Enfield. There are ten towns, Weldon, Halifax, Enfield, Scotland Neck, Roanoke Rapids, Rosemary, Littleton, Hobgood, Palmyra, and Hollister.

PART TWO

PART TWO.

BUILDERS OF THE COUNTY.

Unknown are most of the real builders of the county. The men, who with axe and hoe, smote the forests and turned a wilderness into towns, farms, and gardens, lie mostly in unremembered graves. Few of the thousands, who wrought unselfishly in carving the county from the heritage of the woods, achieved distinction. Very few can be mentioned in a story of their deeds. Pity it is that the pages of the Recording Angel are not accessible to the historian; for many a hero and heroine, whose deeds are, doubtless, recorded in letters of gold, will have to be passed by with not even a word. Such is the fate of the great masses of humanity that come into existence, play for a brief time upon the world's stage, and pass off to an eternal oblivion. 'Tis but a few that catch the ear and attract the eye of men.

In this part of the work, brief sketches of those who have had to do with the making of the county are given. Some, perhaps, who belong in the number, are not given for the reason that their footprints have become so dim that they could not be traced. Only those who have made a distinct impression upon the records of the county have been selected. The "uncrowned kings," who toiled and delved and dropped into unmarked graves, must be necessarily omitted. Even many of those who held rank and won honor among their fellows must go unrecorded.

I

JOSEPH MONTFORD.

Among those who became prominent about the time of the formation of the county was Joseph Montford, who was born in England in 1724 and came to North Carolina in early life. He received a liberal education in his native land before coming to America, an asset which was worth much to him in shaping his career in the land of his adoption.

Coming to North Carolina about 1750, Montford located on the north bank of Quanky Creek in what afterwards came to be called Halifax. Before Halifax County was formed and while the territory north of Fishing Creek was called Edgecombe Parish, he was elected Clerk of the Court of Edgecombe County and served in that capacity at Enfield, the County seat of Edgecombe, until Halifax County was organized in 1758, when he was elected Clerk of the Court of Halifax and was re-elected each year until his death.

In addition to his duties as Clerk of the Court, he was called upon to serve in other capacities. When the Halifax Judicial District was formed in 1760, Montford was chosen Clerk of the District Court. He was, also, one of the commissioners of the town of Halifax in 1764, and member of the Colonial Assembly in 1762, 1764, 1766, 1767 and 1773. He was chosen Colonel of the Halifax militia before the outbreak of the Revolutionary war, and, in addition to other duties, he was made treasurer of the Northern Counties of the province in 1764.

While serving in this last capacity, he came in direct antagonism with Governor Tryon, who was at the time engaged in his war with the Regulators. Tryon was organizing and equipping his army ready for his campaign against the rebels of Orange County and needed money to pay his soldiers. He drew drafts upon Colonel Montford, without authority of the Assembly, which Montford refused to pay. Tryon blustered and threatened, but his drafts were not paid until the Assembly authorized their payment.

An unusual honor came to Colonel Montford in March, 1772, when he received a commission from the Duke of Beaufort, Grand Master of Masons of Great Britain, ap-

BUILDERS OF THE COUNTY 151

pointing him Provincial Grand Master of and for North America. So far as is known, this was the first and only time such a signal honor was bestowed. This commission was held until his death in 1776.

Colonel Montford was a staunch patriot and strenuously advocated separation from the mother country, but an incurable disease was preying upon him and he was unable to do anything to bring about the desired condition. He died March 25, 1776, about the time the Revolution was getting fully under way. His remains rest in the yard of the Masonic temple at Halifax.

In 1753, Colonel Montford married Priscilla Hill, daughter of Colonel Benjamin Hill, of Bertie County. There were three children. Henry married Sarah Edwards, but died without offspring. Mary married Willie Jones; Elizabeth married John Baptista Ashe. These two won fame in their tilt with Colonel Tarleton in 1781 when the British were encamped at Halifax.

II

JOHN BAPTISTA ASHE.

John Baptista Ashe was the eldest son of Governor Samuel Ashe, of Rocky Point, New Hanover County, and grandson of John Baptista Ashe, who was presiding officer of the Colonial Assembly in 1727. He was born in 1748. As a young man, he was an enthusiastic admirer of Governor Tryon and was with him at the Battle of Alamance in 1771. Later, when the war of Revolution began, he joined the patriot cause and was at the Battle of Moore's Creek Bridge in February, 1776. He was appointed captain in the Sixth Continental Regiment in April, 1776; major in January, 1777; and Lieutenant-Colonel in November, 1778. That regiment was, in that year, consolidated with the first; but when it was surrendered at Charleston in 1780, Colonel Ashe was not present and so escaped captivity.

Under the command of General Jethro Sumner, Colonel Ashe organized, at Salisbury, another regiment of Continentals, which did splendid service, under his command, at the Battle of Eutaw Springs and at other points in South Carolina. He held this command until the end of the war.

In 1776, he married Elizabeth Montford, daughter of Joseph Montford, of Halifax, and thereafter made that town his home. At the close of the Revolution, he resigned his commission in the army and entered heartily into the business life of the town and county.

Entering politics, he was elected to the House of Commons in 1784 and again in 1786, and became Speaker of that body. In 1787, he was a member of the Congress of the Confederation and State Senator in 1789. He had, like his brother-in-law, Willie Jones, opposed the adoption of the Federal Constitution in 1788; but, after the amendments were practically secured, he favored its adoption, differing from Jones in that respect.

At the Constitutional Convention of 1789, which met in Fayetteville, Colonel Ashe was a member from Halifax and chairman of the Committee of the Whole, which had under consideration the Federal Constitution, and presided over the deliberations of the convention whenever the constitution was being discussed. He was an enthusiastic advocate of its final adoption, and was influential in securing a favorable vote for it.

At the first election of members of the Federal Congress, Colonel Ashe was chosen to that body and reelected in 1791, serving with distinction until 1793. In 1795, he again represented Halifax in the General Assembly, but retired to private life after his term of office expired. In 1802, he was elected Governor of the State, but when the committee from the General Assembly came to notify him of his election, they found him desperately ill; and in a few days thereafter he died without taking the oath of office.

He left one son, Samuel Porter Ashe, whose descend-

RECEPTION TO WASHINGTON

BUILDERS OF THE COUNTY 153

ants live in Tennessee. Colonel Ashe was an anti-Federalist, but later became an advocate of the Constitution, and still later a Jeffersonian Democrat.

III

WILLIE JONES.

In many respects, one of the most remarkable men of the Revolutionary period in North Carolina was Willie Jones, of Halifax. At one time, and through a number of years, he exerted more influence than any other man in the State; and stands out conspicuously as one of the really noted characters of that day.

The Jones family originally came from Wales to Virginia about the middle of the seventeenth century. Robert, or Robin, Jones, third of the name, moved to North Carolina and became agent for Lord Granville. He was a lawyer of ability, educated in England where he attracted the attention of Granville, and was appointed Attorney-General for North Carolina in 1761. By his profession as attorney for the crown and agent of Granville's great domain, he rapidly acquired wealth and became probably the largest landed proprietor on the Roanoke. He married first Sarah Cobb in 1737 and was the founder of the Jones family of Halifax and Northampton Counties.

Allen Jones, who held the rank of brigadier-general of State militia during the Revolution, was born December 24, 1739. Strange that the exact date of the birth of his more distinguished brother, Willie Jones, the subject of this sketch, is not given; but it was probably in 1741. Nothing is known of the boyhood and youth of the two boys, except that they were educated in England at the celebrated Eton College, where they were under the charge of Lord Granville. After completing their education, the brothers returned to North Carolina and became planters, Allen making his home at "Mt. Gallant,"

Northampton County, and Willie coming to Halifax about 1763 and building "The Grove" house in Halifax town.

The first appearance of Willie Jones on the political stage was as a member of the Provincial Congress that met in Newbern in 1774. He was also a member the next year when the Congress again met at Newbern, April 3, 1775, and at Hillsboro, August 20. The two meetings of the Congress in Halifax, April, 1776, and November, 1776, were the two most important sessions of that body. Jones was influential at both sessions. His election to all of these conventions, which could not but be regarded as preliminary to a separation from the mother country, shows him to have been the leader of the patriot cause in Halifax County; and his home is said to have been the meeting place for consultation between the prominent patriots from every section of the province.

At the Congress of November, 1776, he took a prominent part. He was a member of the committee on privileges and elections and, also, of the committee for drawing up a Bill of Rights and the Constitution. It is said that these documents were written by Thomas Jones, of Chowan County, but with the assistance of Willie Jones. It was said of him that he could draw a bill in better language than any other man of his day.

The Congress at Halifax organized what was known as the Council of Safety, consisting of representatives from each of the five military districts of the State. Willie Jones was elected president of the Council, and, therefore, was acting Governor of North Carolina until Richard Caswell was elected in December, 1776.

At the sessions of the General Assembly of 1776—1782 and 1788, he was a member either from the borough of Halifax or from the county. In 1787, he was elected a delegate to the convention which met in Philadelphia to adopt the Constitution of the United States; but he declined to serve because he was not in sympathy with the purposes of the Convention. He was a member of the Continental Congress in 1780.

BUILDERS OF THE COUNTY 155

One of the most spectacular events in his notable career was his opposition to the ratification of the national constitution by the Convention at Hillsboro. Jones was the leader of the opposition, and the manner in which he conducted the consideration of the measure was masterly. When the vote was taken it was found that the ratification was lost by a vote of 184 to 84. This was his last appearance as a public man.

He died in 1822 at his summer home near Raleigh and was buried in his garden, and the location of his grave has been lost. He has been honored by having a county, Jones, and a town, Jonesboro, named for him.

Willie Jones married, in 1776, Mary Montford, a daughter of Joseph Montford, who was a lady of many attractions and superior qualities. Their children were Anne Ward, who married Joseph B. Littlejohn; Sally, who married Hutchings G. Burton and, afterwards, Andrew Joyner; Patsy, who married John W. Eppes, and two sons, Robert Allen and Willie, who died unmarried.

Willie Jones was no orator in the ordinary acceptation of that term. Though he held the Hillsboro Convention in the hollow of his hand, he made no speech of more than a few sentences. He swayed the convention by his personal magnetism and his individual influence over the members. Feeling sure of his hold upon the convention, he made motion that the question of ratification be put without discussion, saying that he had made up his mind and that he supposed others had also, emphasizing the point that discussion would be a waste of time and an expense to the State. James Iredell, the leader of the Federalists, in reply, pointed out that discussion was involved in the very idea of the convention, and, if it had not been, the Assembly should have instructed the delegates to vote at their homes without coming together. Jones had the good sense to withdraw his motion, and the debate went on, participated in by Iredell, Davie, Johnston, and Maclain; but when the vote was taken it was found that Jones' position was sustained.

He left a lengthy will which is on record at Halifax, from which a few extracts are taken:

"Now, as it is possible and indeed probable that my wife will not be satisfied with the provisions which I have hereinbefore made for her, and consequently could refuse to be bound by this very will and claim dower in and a distribution share in my estate (he then revokes all provisions made in her favor and continues), and I leave to my wife to do better for herself, if she can, than I had hereinbefore done for her. I give to my wife the liberty of getting firewood for her own use on any of my lands, except my groves, and they are to be held sacred from the axe."

Another provision of his will directs that, if he should die in Raleigh, he be buried by the side of his little girl who is buried there; and, if he should die at Halifax, he be buried near his little girl in the orchard. About forty yards north of the site of the "Grove House" is a little thicket in which is the grave of the little child that is mentioned.

One other peculiarity of the will gives a trait of his character: "My family and friends are not to mourn my death even by a black rag; on the contrary I give to my wife and three daughters each a Quaker colored silk to make them hoods on the occasion."

With all of his peculiarities, Willie Jones was a remarkable man, and the county has not seen his like again.

IV

WILLIAM R. DAVIE.

Though acting such a prominent part in the history of the State and Nation, William Richardson Davie was not born on Carolina soil. He was born at Egremont, Cumberland County, England, June 24, 1756. He was brought to America by his father Archibald Davie in 1763 and left in charge of his maternal uncle, Rev. William Rich-

BUILDERS OF THE COUNTY 157

ardson, a Presbyterian minister residing in the Waxhans settlement, in South Carolina. Having no children, Mr. Richardson adopted the boy and made him heir to his estate. He was sent to school at the Queen's Museum, Charlotte, N. C., and afterwards to Princeton College, then in charge of Dr. Witherspoon.

In the summer of 1776, he served with a party of students in the American army, and in the fall returned to college and took the degree of Bachelor of Arts with the first honors. His uncle died before Davie's return to the State. Having selected the law as his profession, he began its study in Salisbury. In 1777, he joined a detachment of 1200 troops under the command of Allen Jones, ordered to the defense of Charlotte; but the attack on that city being abandoned by the enemy, the detachment returned after reaching Camden. In 1779, he joined a troop of cavalry raised in the Salisbury district, of which William Barnett was elected captain and Davie, lieutenant. The troop soon after joined the Southern army and was attached to Pulaski's Legion.

For distinguished service in the field, Davie was successfully promoted to the rank of captain and later to that of major. He took part in the Battle of Stono, in which he was severely wounded, which disabled him from any further service that year. While recuperating from his wound he secured his license to practice law; but in 1780, he answered again the call to arms, and, having obtained leave of the General Assembly, he raised a troop of cavalry and two companies of infantry, equipping them out of his own funds derived from his uncle's estate.

While in command of this troop, Major Davie took a brilliant part in several encounters. He arrived with his command after the defeat of the Tories at Ramseur's Mill, and was dispatched by General Rutherford in pursuit of the fugitives. He took an active part in the Battle of Hanging Rock, of which there is a good narrative in Davie's own words in Wheeler's History of North Carolina. After the Battle of Hanging Rock, Major Davie carried his wounded to Charlotte for surgical attention and set out to join the army of General Gates at Rugeley's Mill. When he came within a few miles of Camden, S. C., he met General Gates himself in full retreat. Gates ordered Davie to fall back to Charlotte, saying that Tarleton's dragoons were in pursuit and would soon be upon them. Davie's reply was characteristic. He said, "My men are accustomed to Tarleton and do not fear him." He then hurried on toward Camden. Meeting General Huger soon after, Davie asked him how far Gates' orders should be obeyed. Huger answered,"Just as far as you choose, for you will never see him again." Finding the rout complete, Major Davie retraced his steps and took post at Charlotte.

On September 20, 1780, Davie having been promoted to the rank of Colonel with instructions to raise a regiment of cavalry, with 150 dragoons fell upon about 400 of the enemy at Wahab's Plantation and routed them, killing and wounding about 60 and capturing ninety-six horses and 120 stands of arms. This remarkable feat of arms was accomplished after a ride of sixty miles, and all done within twenty-four hours. Shortly after this he was joined by Sumner and Davidson with about 1000 poorly equipped militia.

When Cornwallis advanced on Charlotte, September 26, 1780, Colonel Davie had only 150 mounted men with him and a few volunteers under Major Graham. Posting one company near the Court House, where the men would be sheltered by a stone wall, and two others where they were sheltered by dwellings, he repulsed three attacks of the British and held his ground until he was outflanked and was forced to retreat. The coolness and skill of Colonel Davie, in this affair, in which with a handful of men, he kept the whole British army at bay for hours, have been highly praised. After the disastrous defeat at King's Mountain, Cornwallis retired into South Carolina followed by Davie's command, that harassed his rear guards no little.

BUILDERS OF THE COUNTY 159

In December, 1780, General Nathanael Greene took command of the Southern army at Charlotte. Greene at once appointed Davie Commissary-General, which he accepted with reluctance because he regretted leaving active military service, and began his new duties in January, 1781. He was with the army of the South for five months, being present at the Battles of Guilford Court House, Hobkirk's Hill, the evacuation of Camden, and the Siege of Ninety-Six. In the summer of 1781, Colonel Davie was sent by General Greene as a confidential messenger to the General Assembly of North Carolina for the purpose of representing the wants of his army, a mission, which he, by reason of his tact and knowledge of the members, successfully accomplished, securing a liberal contribution of men and supplies.

In July, 1781, he became Commissary-General of North Carolina with headquarters at Halifax, which position he held until the close of the war. During this period, the credit of the State had fallen so low that Davie was obliged to pledge his individual credit in order to obtain supplies. It was during this period also that the Roanoke lands furnished supplies for nearly the whole of Greene's army.

After the close of the war, Colonel Davie, in February, 1783, resumed the practice of law and located in the town of Halifax, and about the same time married Sarah Jones, the daughter of General Allen Jones, of Mount Gallant, Northampton County.

There were seven judicial districts in the State at that time and Colonel Davie practiced law in all of them except the Morganton district. He was a brilliant advocate and soon built up a large and lucrative practice. It was said of him that, in the fifteen years he was at the bar, there was not a capital case in the State in which he was not retained by the defense. One of the most famous of the capital cases, in which he appeared, was the trial of the celebrated Tory, Colonel Samuel Bryan, for treason, at Salisbury. Davie and Bryan had been enemies on the battlefield. They had met in mortal conflict at Hanging Rock. Davie had done all that he could to destroy Bryan and his command; but now, peace had come and Davie was employed by Bryan to defend him. True to his client, Davie left no stone unturned to clear him; but the prejudice against the Tory was too great and Bryan was convicted. Later, however, he was pardoned by the Governor.

In 1787, Davie was a delegate from North Carolina to the Constitutional Convention, which met in Philadelphia, in May, to prepare a Federal instrument of government. He was then thirty-one years old, but, by his eloquence and knowledge, made a decided impression upon the convention. A critical question before the convention was the equal representation of the large and small states in the Senate, the large states contending for representation according to population and the small states for equal representation. North Carolina was then one of the large states. In order to avoid a disruption of the Convention, a committee of one from each state was appointed to decide the question, and Davie was appointed as the member of that committee from North Carolina. In this matter, Colonel Davie voted with the small states, and, by a majority of one, secured for the small states equal representation in the senate. He left the Convention a few days before adjournment in obedience to the call of a client, and for that reason his name does not appear among the signers of that document.

He was active in the State Convention of 1788, at Hillsboro, in advocacy of the ratification of the Federal Constitution, but it was defeated then under the leadership of Willie Jones. After the Constitution was ratified at Fayetteville the next year, President Washington tendered Colonel Davie the appointment of District Judge, but it was declined.

He represented the borough of Halifax in the House of Commons in 1786, 1787, 1789, 1791, 1793, 1794, 1796, and 1798. While a member of the General Assembly, he la-

THE ROANOKE MILLS, ROANOKE RAPIDS, N. C.

BUILDERS OF THE COUNTY 161

bored unceasingly for the establishment of the State University, and finally secured the act of incorporation in 1789. He was the real founder of that great institution, and as Grand Master of Masons of North Carolina laid the corner stone of the first building in 1793.

In view of the probability of war with France, Colonel Davie was appointed by Governor Spaight, in 1794, Major-General of the third State division of militia; and, in 1798, Congress having provided a provisional army of 10,000 men, he was appointed by President Adams Brigadier-General and confirmed by the Senate on July 1, 1798. In the same year, he was elected Governor and inaugurated, December 27.

On June 1, 1799, he was appointed by President Adams Ambassador to France, and, on September 10, resigned the governorship to accept this foreign post of duty. He was one of the three men to draw up a treaty with the French government, which was ratified by Congress, September 10, 1800. General Davie was the most distinguished looking man in that trio of eminent men. An eyewitness of the meeting of the American embassy with the French Emperor said, "I could but remark that Bonaparte, in addressing the American Legation at his Levees, seemed to forget that Governor Davie was second in the mission, his attention being more particularly to him."

General Davie returned from France in 1801, and, in 1802, he was appointed by President Jefferson Commissioner on the part of the United States government for the settlement of the affairs between the State of North Carolina and the Tuscarora Indians. He met the agents of the State and the Indian Chiefs at Raleigh, and the treaty was signed December 4, 1802, by virtue of which the remnant of the Tuscaroras, who had continued to hold their lands in the "Indian Woods," removed to New York in June, 1803.

In the spring of 1803, General Davie was prevailed upon to become a candidate for Congress against Willis Alston, who had recently abandoned the Federalist party and had become a disciple of Thomas Jefferson. Davie made no canvass, but party spirit ran high. He was charged with being an aristocrat and being opposed to Jefferson, and on election day he was defeated. This was his last appearance in a public capacity.

Having lost his wife, soon after his return from France and having met defeat at the polls, he retired altogether from public life. In November, 1805, he removed from Halifax to Tivoli, an estate he had in South Carolina just across the line, where he spent the remainder of his life in ease and dignity.

In his retirement, however, he was not forgotten by his countrymen. He was appointed by President Madison Major-General in the United States army during the War of 1812 and confirmed by the senate, March 2, 1813; but he declined the appointment.

General Davie died November 18, 1820, and was buried at Waxhaw Churchyard just across the river from his plantation. Governor Gaston, of South Carolina, who is said to have written his epitaph, called him "a great man in an age of great men."

His memory is perpetuated by the name of one of the counties in the State and by the name of a poplar on the campus of the State University.

V

JAMES HOGAN.

James Hogan was prominent in North Carolina history during the Revolution; but there is very little known about his early life. He was born in Ireland, but the date and place are unknown. Nor is it known when he came to the New World. He was a scion of that sturdy Irish stock that was restive under British domination, and had come to America to escape its tyranny. It is not known when he came to North Carolina, but he found his way to Halifax County, in early life, and made his home about two miles from the present town of Hobgood. In October 3, 1751, he was married to Ruth Norfleet, a young woman of that section of Halifax County.

When the Provincial Congress met in Halifax, April 4, 1776, James Hogan appeared as one of the delegates from the county. He was enthusiastically in favor of the resolution for independence passed by that body on April 12. He was again a delegate to the Provincial Congress and Constitutional Convention that met in Halifax, November 12, 1776. But early in that session, he was elected Colonel of the Seventh North Carolina Continental Regiment; and at once resigned membership in the Congress.

After the organization of the regiment, and after being disciplined in the school of the soldier at Halifax, Colonel Hogan led his troops northward, along with other regiments that had been mobilized at Halifax, and joined General Washington in time to take part in the battles of Brandywine and Germantown. After these two disastrous battles, Washington dispatched Colonel Hogan to North Carolina to raise reinforcements. Having established a recruiting station at Halifax, Hogan soon had another regiment of 600 men under arms. He led them North and joined Washington at Valley Forge. He was with the Army of the North during 1778 and 1779.

When General Robert Howe was promoted to the rank of Major-General, the General Assembly of North Carolina recommended Colonel Thomas Clark, of Newbern, for the vacancy; but General Washington said that Hogan, on account of his conspicuous gallantry at Germantown, was entitled to the honor. He was, therefore, elected and commissioned brigadier-general, January 9, 1779, and continued to serve with the Army of the North, his brigade consisting of the four North Carolina regiments then with General Washington.

In February, 1780, the tide of war having rolled southward, Hogan's brigade was sent to the relief of General

Lincoln at Charleston, S. C. The brigade passed through Halifax on its long march from Philadelphia to Charleston, and reached its destination in April, finding that General Lincoln was shut up in Charleston with less than twelve hundred men, Hogan joined him with about fifteen hundred regulars, but he was unable to restore confidence. Lincoln surrendered, May 12; and with one stroke of bad fortune, General Hogan and nearly the whole of the North Carolina Continentals became prisoners of war. Of the 1800 regulars, surrendered at this time, the North Carolina line numbered over 1200. With the exception of some officers, who were at home on furlough and several troops of militia, the entire fighting force of North Carolina was put out of the conflict. Halifax County was struck hard by this blow.

General Hogan and his brigade were imprisoned at Haddrell's Point, S. C., near the present location of the town of Mount Pleasant. There, Hogan and his brigade endured extreme suffering on account of the lack of food and the ravages of disease. Even permission to fish was denied the men thus imprisoned, and they were more than once threatened with deportation to the West Indies. Once was General Hogan offered a parole to return home; but seeing the misery of his men, he indignantly refused the parole unless the rank and file were to have the same privilege.

At that point, General Hogan disappears from history. It is certain that he died in this prison camp at Haddrell's Point, and now lies buried, probably, where the busy feet of the people of Mount Pleasant go tramping over his remains. Chief Justice Clark says, "History affords no more striking incident of devotion to duty, and North Carolina should erect a tablet to his memory and of those who perished there with him."

VI

SAMUEL WELDON.

Another man, who has left an impress upon the county and yet is comparatively unknown, is Samuel Weldon, in honor of whom the town of Weldon is named. The place and date of his birth are unknown; but he became prominent in the affairs of Halifax soon after the formation of the county in 1758.

In 1776, the Provincial Congress, in session in Halifax, elected Weldon Major of the county militia. On Dec. 23, 1776, he was promoted to the rank of Lieutenant-Colonel, and, on April 24, 1778, he became Colonel. His rapid promotion would indicate ability and popularity. This last rank, he was, soon afterward, forced to resign on account of ill health. He retired to his farm on the Roanoke river near where the present town of Weldon is.

He was a member of the Provincial Congress of 1776, that met in Halifax, and it is known that he exercised influence of note in that body. For some years he held the position of Justice of the Court of Pleas and Quarter Sessions. Not much else is known of his public services. His will was probated in 1782.

VII

JOHN HAYWOOD.

John Haywood was born in Halifax County, March 16, 1762. He was a son of Egbert Haywood, an officer of the Revolution and a representative from the County in the Provincial Congress of November, 1776, being elected to fill the vacancy caused by the appointment of James Hogan Colonel of the Seventh Regiment of Continentals. He also represented the county in the House of Commons in 1778.

But little is known of the early life of John Haywood.

He was but thirteen years old when the war of independence began, and, on account of his youth, took no active part in the struggle that followed. Near the close of the war, however, young Haywood became attached to the staff of a North Carolina officer, though the name of the officer is unknown. Wheeler, in his "Reminiscences," has the following to say of him:

"From the distracted condition of the country, at this time, the opportunities to acquire an education were few; but young Haywood entered the profession of the law, in which he was destined to become distinguished, under many disadvantages. To the lack of a systematic education was added an ungainly person and an unpleasantly harsh voice. Possessing, however, great determination, an ardent love of study, and a lofty ambition, he overcame those disadvantages, and soon rose to the head of the profession."

In many of his legal battles, he was often pitted against William R. Davie. Chief-Justice Walter Clark has this to say in an address delivered some years ago: "It is stated of him (Davie), in comparison with his great legal rival, John Haywood, that while the latter carefully prepared every point, Davie would size the strong points of the case and throw his whole strength upon them."

His success as a lawyer was shown by his election, in 1791, as Attorney-General of the State, when he was not yet thirty years old. He held this position until 1794 when he was elected Judge of the Superior Court to succeed Samuel Spencer, deceased. In both of these positions of trust and responsibility, Haywood displayed unusual ability and efficiency.

In 1800, however, his career on the bench was terminated in a remarkable way. James Glasgow, Secretary of State, was indicted for issuing fraudulent land warrants. The indictment was drawn by Attorney-General Blake Baker, a native of Halifax but at that time living in Edgecombe County. In drawing the bill of indictment, Baker sought the counsel of Haywood. Before the trial came off, Glasgow approached Haywood with a retainer's fee of one thousand dollars. Judge Haywood at once resigned his position on the bench and accepted Glasgow's offer. In the trial, however, Glasgow was convicted; but Haywood moved an arrest of judgment alleging thirteen errors in the bill of indictment, which he had assisted the attorney-general to formulate.

On account of his conduct in this case, Haywood became the victim of a torrent of criticism. While there was no moral turpitude in what he did, the public never forgave him for what seemed so. Shortly afterward, he removed to Tennessee and settled on a farm near Nashville, where he lived and died.

During his residence in Halifax County, he lived near Crowell's, where he taught a law school. His memory is perpetuated by Haywood's Chapel because he gave the land on which the church was built. After leaving Halifax, Haywood resided for some years in Franklin County about six miles north of Louisburg. Just before moving to Tennessee, he lived in Raleigh.

In Tennessee, Haywood began almost a new career. He soon became one of the leading lawyers of that new State. Often he was matched with Felix Grundy, one of the most noted orators of the west, and he always appeared to good advantage. He continued at the bar in Tennessee, building up a lucrative practice until 1812, when he was elevated to the Superior Court bench. Six years later he became Judge of the Supreme Court of Tennessee, and held that position until his death in 1826.

Judge Haywood's memory is perpetuated in Tennessee by the name of one of the Counties in that State. Haywood County, North Carolina, is named in honor of John Haywood, of Edgecombe County, for forty years State Treasurer.

VIII

WILLIS ALSTON.

Joseph John Alston, father of the subject of this sketch, came to Halifax County about the year 1730. He came from what is now Gates County, where his father, John Alston lived. Later he married a daughter of Willis Wilson, of Norfolk, Va., and from that union was born, in 1750, Willis Alston, usually referred to as Willis Alston, Sr., to distinguish him from his more celebrated son of the same name.

Willis Alston was a strong and sturdy character. He early became a leader among his neighbors and friends and even in his teens, he was a champion of the rights of Americans against the growing tyranny of England. During the Stamp Act troubles and the discontent over the tea tax, Alston was an undaunted patriot for one so young.

When the Provincial Congress met in Halifax, April 4, 1776, he was a member from the county, and took an active part in the passage of the famous independence resolution, which has been read around the world. He was also a member of the Constitutional Convention of November 12, 1776, and was an important factor in the framing of the first State Constitution.

Upon the organization of the State militia at the session of the Provincial Congress that met in Halifax at the same time with the Constitutional Convention, Willis Alston was elected Colonel; Samuel Weldon, Lieutenant-Colonel; John Whitaker, First Major; James Allen, Second Major. Alston, however, resigned in 1778 and was succeeded by Weldon.

There is no record of the war service of Willis Alston more than the bare mention of his election as Colonel of the Halifax regiment. It is more than probable that this regiment was used throughout the war as a garrison for the town of Halifax and saw no active service in battle.

A TYPICAL SOUTHERN SCENE

BUILDERS OF THE COUNTY

IX

WILLIS ALSTON, JR.

Willis Alston, son of the first of the name, was born on his father's farm, in the upper part of the county, in 1770. He was given as liberal an education as the exigencies of the times would permit. In spite of disadvantages along that line, by close application and diligent study, he became one of the best informed men of his day.

He early turned his attention to politics, and, in 1790, when he was just twenty-one years of age, he was elected to the House of Commons, and served in that body during the sessions of 1790, 1791, and 1792. In 1794, he was elected to the Senate and served in that branch of the General Assembly two years. Again, having served many years in Congress, he returned to the House of Commons in 1819 and again in 1820, 1821, 1823, and 1824.

Alston early became an earnest admirer of Thomas Jefferson and an ardent disciple. As a Republican (Democrat), he was elected to the Federal Congress in 1799, and was biennially reelected until 1815, when he retired from Congress for ten years and was again elected in 1825, serving until 1831.

In 1803, he was opposed for re-election to Congress by William R. Davie, who had recently returned from France. It was thought that the great popularity of Davie would win the election; but the result showed a majority for Alston. This was, perhaps, his greatest political triumph. During the agitation preceding the war of 1812, Alston was distinctly a war advocate, because he thought England had violated every right of nations.

Willis Alston was married twice, first to Pattie Moore, of Halifax County, and second to Sallie Madeline Potts, of Wilmington. There were no children of the first marriage, but of the second the following were born: Charles J. P., who married Mary Janet Clark, whose oldest son is Dr. Willis Alston, of Littleton; Ariellah, who married

Colonel James B. Hawkins; Leonidas; Missouri, who married Archibald Davis Alston; and Edgar. Willis Alston died in Halifax, April 10, 1837. He served in the Federal Congress longer than any other man from Halifax County, and, while not brilliant, he was a safe and wise representative.

X

NICHOLAS LONG.

Nicholas Long, the founder of the Long family of Halifax County, came to North Carolina when a young man and settled near what is now the town of Halifax. The exact date of his coming to the county is unknown, and the date and place of his birth are likewise obscure. Shortly after coming to Halifax, Long built his country home, "Quanky," which was just across Quanky Creek from the "Grove House."

He is mentioned in Wheeler's "Reminiscences" as being a wealthy planter and his home as being the headquarters for prominent men who from time to time visited Halifax. It is said that, when President Washington visited Halifax on his tour of the South, he stopped with Colonel Long for several days. In similar ways the reputation of "Quanky" came to be more than State wide.

Before John Harvy issued his call for the first Provincial Congress to meet in Newbern, August 24, 1774, he came to Halifax to consult with Willie Jones and Nicholas Long. Both Jones and Long were at the time members of the Provincial Assembly; and when the Congress was called, they were elected members and served in the double capacity at Newbern. Long was also a member of the Second Provincial Congress at Newbern the next year and also at Hillsboro. At the latter Congress, the State was divided into military districts, each district to raise and equip five hundred men. Nicholas Long was appointed Colonel of the Halifax district.

A grant of land was made to Robert Long in Halifax

BUILDERS OF THE COUNTY 171

County, but it is not known whether he was an ancestor of Nicholas Long. The grant is dated 1725.

Later, in the progress of the struggle for independence, each county was empowered to raise and arm a regiment of minute men, and the position of Commissary-General of the State forces was created. Colonel Long was chosen to this latter position. He personally superintended, together with his wife, the work shops on his own farm for the purpose of manufacturing implements of war, ammunition, clothing, and other supplies for the soldiers.

Mrs. Long possessed great energy and firmness with mental power of no common order. Her praises were the theme of conversation among the officers, who knew her. She died at the advanced age of eighty leaving a numerous offspring.

Colonel Long held the position of Commissary-General of the State troops until 1781, when he resigned and was succeeded by William R. Davie. The last public service he rendered, of which we have any record, was in the senate the sessions of 1785 and 1786. As a legislator, or soldier, or planter, Colonel Long proved his worth and has left a worthy name to his numerous descendants.

XI

ORONDATES DAVIS.

Very little is known of the early life of the subject of this sketch. He lived in that portion of the county near the old Conocanara Church. Receiving a limited education, he became a lawyer and practiced in the courts of the Halifax Judicial District, just before and during the Revolutionary War.

He was a member of the State Senate four consecutive terms, 1778, 1779, 1780, 1781. He was a man of considerable influence and strength of character as is shown by the commanding position he took in the General Assembly. When the Board of War was created in 1781 to direct the war in North Carolina, Davis was elected as a member of the Board. The other two members were Alexander Martin, who afterwards became Governor, and John Penn, one of the signers of the Declaration of Independence.

On account of the fact that the Board of War did not have its duties clearly defined, it was in frequent collision with the Governor on questions of jurisdiction, and was soon discontinued. General Davie, who had business before the Board several times without its being settled to his satisfaction, severely criticised the personnel of it. He said, in speaking of it:

"Nothing could be more ridiculous than the manner in which it (the Board) was filled. Martin, being a *warrior* (?) of great fame, was placed at its head. Penn, who was only fit to amuse children, and Davis, who knows nothing but a game of whist, were placed on the Board."

General Davie was no doubt prejudiced, but the Board was soon afterwards discontinued and Davis retired to private life.

XII

JOHN BRADFORD.

Only fragments of information regarding John Bradford have come down to us. He was one of the early settlers in the Enfield section, and built a home about two miles southwest of that town. He was living there at the time the county was organized in 1758, and had commanding influence in shaping its policies. He was a man of natural ability and high character.

In 1766, he was elected to represent the county in the Colonial Assembly and re-elected in 1767, and 1768. He was, therefore, a member of the law-making body of the Province during a very critical period of its existence. The third Provincial Congress at Hillsboro, in August, 1775, appointed John Bradford a member of the Committee of Safety for the District of Halifax. He served in that capacity as long as there was need for the services of such a committee. In 1776, he was a member of both sessions

BUILDERS OF THE COUNTY 173

of the Provincial Congress that met at Halifax. The next year he was elected to represent Halifax County in the State Senate, as the first from the County.

After the close of the Revolution, he was the Presiding Justice of the County Court, and held this position many years. He died about 1786 and left a number of children, one of them, Henry, became a minister and gave his name to Bradford's Church. Most of his descendants left the County and went South.

XIII

JOHN PAUL JONES.

The most famous man connected with the history of Halifax County is John Paul Jones, the Revolutionary hero, who won the title of "Father of the American Navy." He was born in Kirkbean, Scotland, July 6, 1747, and died in Paris, France, July 18, 1792. He was the youngest son of John Paul, a gardener, and was christened John Paul, the same name as his father; but after coming to America, for reasons that are apparent, he added the surname Jones. His mother was Jean Macduff, the daughter of a Highlander.

Having lived near the sea during his boyhood days, it was natural that he should follow life on the sea. He began early, being apprenticed at the age of twelve to a ship owner, and by the time he was a little beyond man's estate he had sailed all over the North Atlantic in trading, smuggling, and slaving vessels, and had climbed to the top of his calling, the Captain's berth.

In the meantime, his brother William had settled in Virginia, on the banks of the Rappahannock river as manager of the estate of William Jones, from whom William Paul, it is said, had inherited some land. William Paul died in 1773, and John Paul came to Virginia that year to take charge of his brother's property.

Previous to that time, John Paul had met with varied experiences on the sea. He had, in the spring of 1770, flogged a mutinous carpenter on board the merchant ship, John, of which he was master. Shortly after the flogging, which was light, the man died and John Paul had to face the charge of having caused his death. He was, however, acquitted. Soon after this occurrence, a mutiny broke out among the crew of the *John*, and John Paul, in defending himself from them, was forced to kill their leader. On account of this unfortunate circumstance, he was obliged to resign his position as master of the trader. Then it was he came to Virginia.

In the Mentor Magazine of October 16, 1916, the following paragraphs, in connection with John Paul Jones occur:

"One day in the early part of the year 1775, Willie Jones, a planter of North Carolina, came into the little town of Halifax from his estate, and found a young man sitting on a bench in front of the tavern, who seemed to be in the deepest throes of melancholy.

> 'What is your name?' he asked him.
> 'I have none', was the answer.
> 'Where is your home?' he asked.
> 'I have none', was the reply.

"He then talked with him a little further, and invited him to share his home. The dejected stranger was none other than John Paul, who later took the name of Jones with the permission of Willie Jones; and from that time on he used the name of John Paul Jones. Later he dropped his first name and used simply Paul Jones on his visiting cards."

At the "Grove," it is supposed, John Paul Jones sojourned for a year or more, and was treated with the greatest courtesy. It was here that he became acquainted with Joseph Hewes, who was a delegate from North Carolina to the Continental Congress, and served on what is now called the Naval Committee. The two immediately became intimate friends, and Hewes used his influence in having John Paul Jones commissioned in the Continental

BUILDERS OF THE COUNTY 175

Navy as an officer. Later, by the same influence, he became Captain of the United States Gunboat Ranger.

Although John Paul Jones was identified with Halifax but a short time, his sudden rise to eminence is traceable directly to his association with Willie Jones and through him with Joseph Hewes. All he needed was, at the psychological moment, to be brought to the attention of Congress and to be given an opportunity to display his wonderful talent. To Willie Jones and Joseph Hewes belong the credit of having been chiefly instrumental in doing this. To those two eminent North Carolinians is given the honor of having "discovered" John Paul Jones.

Reference has already been made, in this work, to the splendid achievements of John Paul Jones. His brilliant victories on the ocean together with his illuminating views as to the building and equipping of a defensive and an aggressive fleet have justly won for him the title of "Father of the American Navy." He was worthy of all the honor that came to him and more. Of natural brightness of intellect, of pleasing manners, and of tireless application, he had made himself an accomplished man of the world. With little advantage of an education in the schools, he taught himself until he could speak French as his mother tongue, and was equally at ease in Spanish.

His daring, his defiance of great odds, his harassing of the British commerce, his capture of numerous prizes, his influence in securing France as an ally, all make a thrilling story that leads us to see what a capable man he was and what a wonderful genius Halifax County gave to the world.

After the Revolution, he was at different times in the service of the Prussian government and of Russia. His last days were spent in France, where he died and was buried. After lying in French soil for more than one hundred years, his body was disinterred in 1905 and brought to America. It now rests in a crypt in the Chapel of the Naval Academy at Annapolis.

Albert Bushnell Hart, the eminent American historian, has the following to say in praise of John Paul Jones:

"Jones was still a young man, barely forty-five years old, at the time of his death; and his meteoric career was compressed into the fourteen years between 1775 and 1789. For the paling of his glory in later years, he was in part to blame. His killing of the mutineer threw a cloud upon his early life. He was gay, extravagant, over fond of the ladies, and often in money difficulties. Beginning so young, shooting up so rapidly, he made enemies that followed him to the end. A man as eager, as adventurous, as impetuous as John Paul Jones was bound to outrun cooler and more sagacious men like Franklin and John Adams.

"Against these faults is to be set the amazing brilliancy of Jones's character and deeds. His successes were not those of a dashing adventurer who took all the chances and was usually lucky in winning. Jones's splendid results came from his careful preparation, his personal interest in his men, his ability to execute naval manoeuvers at the precise moment. He was a naval genius also in his constructive plans. Throughout his life, Jones showed a wonderful spirit of organization. He was one of the first men to suggest a plan for the systematic building and use of the American Navy, which would have been much to the advantage of the nation had it been followed."

XIV

ABRAHAM HODGE.

Abraham Hodge was born in the State of New York in 1755 and died in Halifax, August 3, 1805. During the Revolution he conducted the Whig press of Samuel London of New York. For a time, he was in charge of Washington's traveling press while the army was stationed at Valley Forge. He was thus employed, during those dark days, in disseminating Republican principles and cheering the drooping spirits of his countrymen.

Soon after the close of hostilities, he came to Halifax

WASHINGTON AVENUE, WELDON, N. C.

County and established a printing office; and in 1784 or 1785, he was elected public printer by the General Assembly. He held that position until 1798 and discharged the duties of the office with ability and satisfaction. During that time, Hodge conducted his printing plant at Halifax, and at the same time had presses in Fayetteville, Newbern, and Edenton. July 23, 1793, he began, at Halifax, the publication of the North Carolina Journal, a newspaper that reflected the Federalist views of government. The State was Jeffersonian, and Halifax County particularly so at the time. Hodge was, therefore, displaced as public printer in 1798 and Joseph Gales elected to succeed him.

Undaunted, however, by this political rebuke, Hodge continued to edit his newspaper, the North Carolina Journal, as his conscience dictated, and the interests of the State, in his opinion, required. He was conspicuous as a man of natural ability and of acquired learning. He was one of the first men in the State to contribute to the library of the University of North Carolina, and thereafter until his death he was regular in his gifts to it.

Some months before his demise in 1805, he made a will in which he made his partner, William Boylan, his executor, and bequeathed to him his printing plants and other property. Hodge had been public printer for fifteen years previous to 1798, and had otherwise done a great work. He had three printing plants in the State, and was editor of one of the most influential newspapers in the South, the North Carolina Journal, published at Halifax.

XV

JOHN BRANCH.

John Branch was born November 4, 1782, about two and a half miles northwest of Enfield, on what is still known as the Branch plantation. His father, also named John, took an active part in the Revolution, and was specially vigilant in running down the few Tories in the county. While sheriff of the county, in 1776, he took two Tories to Smithfield before the Council of Safety for trial. He also represented the county in the House of Commons in 1781, 1782, 1787, and 1788.

But little is known of the boyhood of John Branch. After being prepared for college, he entered the University of North Carolina, from which he graduated in 1801. During his college career, he became well acquainted with Thomas H. Benton, the great North Carolinian who rose to eminence in Missouri, and who was an alumnus of the University of North Carolina. Benton, in his "Thirty Years in Congress," says: "I was particularly grieved at this breach between Mr. Branch and the President, having known him from boyhood, been school-fellows together, and being well acquainted with his inviolable honor, and long and faithful attachment to General Jackson."

Branch's first appearance in public life was in the State Senate in 1811. He was again chosen to that body in 1813, where he served continuously until 1817, and again in 1822. In 1817, he was elected Governor of the State and served the constitutional term of three years.

He carried the simplicity of his early life into the Executive Mansion. Once, during his term as Governor, a stranger rang the bell. Governor Branch, dressed in a suit of homespun jeans, answered the call. Upon inquiring for the Governor, the stranger was greatly astonished when informed that he was speaking to him. He was an educational governor of the early days. He was alive to the importance of a public school system, and, in his message to the General Assembly in 1819, he urged the appropriation of means to that end. He was, however, disappointed, for it was several years later before the public schools became an actuality. Upon his retirement from the office of Governor, President Monroe tendered him the office of Judge of the district of the Territory of Florida, which he declined.

In 1822, while a member of the State Senate, he was

BUILDERS OF THE COUNTY

elected United States Senator, the only time the county has ever had that honor, and was re-elected in 1828. While in the Senate, Branch differed with his colleague, Nathaniel Macon, on the question of internal improvements, and voted for an appropriation to build the Dismal Swamp Canal while Macon voted against it. Branch, however, was on the winning side.

Soon after his entrance upon his second term as senator, he was tendered by President Jackson the portfolio of Secretary of the Navy, which he accepted. John H. Eaton, at that time living in Tennessee but a native of Halifax County, was made Secretary of War. Thus, there was the singular coincidence of two natives of Halifax County being in the President's cabinet at the same time.

President Jackson's cabinet was disrupted in a singular way, and, as two Halifax County men were closely identified with the incident, it is here related. Secretary Eaton had married a widow Timberlake, about whom there were some uncomplimentary rumors. As a consequence of these rumors, she was not received in the best circles of Washington. President Jackson was an intimate personal friend of Secretary Eaton and noticed the snubs that Mrs. Eaton was receiving. He, therefore, undertook to have the social ostracism removed. He sent R. M. Johnston, of Kentucky, to Secretary Branch to express to him that the President thought the rumors regarding Mrs. Eaton were untrue, and intimated a wish that Branch might use his influence in Mrs. Eaton's favor.

Branch resented the effort of the President to influence his social relations, and at once tendered his resignation. His example was immediately followed by the other members of the Cabinet. President Jackson thus found that his diplomacy in social matters was not equal to his skill on the battlefield. Even Martin Van Buren, the Secretary of State, who was only remotely connected with the affair, left the cabinet.

After his return home from Washington, Branch wrote several articles for the Roanoke Advocate, published at

Halifax, explaining his connection with the affair, and thereby strengthened himself with the people. At the time of his retirement from the cabinet, the campaign was on for the nomination of a member of Congress. Jesse A. Bynum, of Halifax, was a candidate for the nomination, but there was a feeling that Branch ought to be nominated. Bynum, therefore, retired from the contest and Branch was nominated and elected to the Congress of 1831-32.

In 1834, Branch was again elected to the State Senate. In 1835, he and Joseph J. Daniel represented the county in the Constitutional Convention, held that year in Raleigh. On motion of Branch, Nathaniel Macon, of Warren County, was chosen President of the Convention. Both he and Daniel voted against the amendment to elect the Governor by the people instead of by the General Assembly. When the amendment to abolish the borough system came up, Branch voted in favor of it, but Daniel opposed it. Both were in favor of abolishing the religious restrictions in the constitution.

Later, when the new instrument of government was submitted to the people for ratification, the vote of Halifax County was 239 for and 441 against ratification. The vote of the State was 26,771 to 21,606 in favor of the new constitution. This was the first change in the Constitution since its adoption in 1776, which shows the conservatism of the people of North Carolina.

In 1838 Branch was the Democratic candidate against Edward B. Dudley, the Whig candidate, for Governor. Dudley was elected. Branch's defeat may have been brought about by his course in the Constitutional Convention of 1835. It was his last appearance before the people as a candidate for office. In 1843, he was appointed by President Tyler to the position of Governor of the Territory of Florida, and, after the expiration of his term of office, he retired to private life.

He died at Enfield, January 4, 1863, and is buried at the family cemetery near that town. He was married twice, first to Miss Fort and second to Mrs. Bond. He left a large family of children, whose descendants are numerous in the county.

No man connected with the county ever had so many honors bestowed upon him. He was, at different times, a member of the General Assembly, Governor of the State, Senator and Representative in Congress, Secretary of the Navy, and Governor of Florida. To have held so many offices shows that he was no ordinary man. The most striking traits in his character, to which his success is due, were his incorruptible integrity, indomitable will power, and urbanity. He was a gentleman of the old school, who went to his grave full of years and honors.

XVI

HUTCHINGS G. BURTON.

Hutchings G. Burton was born in Mecklenburg County, Va., in 1782. His father, John Burton, was an officer in the Revolutionary war; and, dying when his son was three years old, made his brother, Colonel Robert Burton, of Granville County, N. C., guardian of the child, requesting his brother to adopt him into his own family and rear him as his own son. The uncle took the boy to his home in Williamsboro where he grew up and remained until he entered upon his business career. His mother also accompanied him to Granville County.

He was given a liberal education for that day. After attending the academy at Williamsboro, he entered the University at Chapel Hill, but did not complete his college course. Leaving the University, he read law under Judge Henderson, one of the ablest jurists of his day. Upon receiving his license to practice law, he located in Charlotte. In 1809 and again in 1810, he represented Mecklenburg County in the House of Commons. His advance at the bar must have been rapid, as, in 1810, he was elected Attorney-General of the State, which position he held until 1816, when he resigned.

In 1812, he went to Halifax on a visit to a former schoolmate, Willie Jones, Jr. There he met Sarah, the youngest daughter of the late Willie Jones, and they were married in the following December. He immediately located in Halifax and made his home at the "Grove House." In 1817, he represented the borough of Halifax in the House of Commons. In 1819, he was elected to Congress and served two terms.

He was elected Governor of North Carolina in 1825 and brilliantly occupied that position for two years. One of the first things Governor Burton did was to urge, in his message to the General Assembly, the prime importance of the Public Schools; and, the same year, an act drawn by Bartlett Yancy was passed, entitled "An act to create a fund for the establishment of Common Schools." This was the beginning of our public school system, and makes memorable the administration of Governor Burton. It was during Governor Burton's first term that Lafayette made his visit to the State, and was magnificently entertained at the Governor's home in Raleigh.

In 1826, he was nominated by President John Quincy Adams as Governor of the Territory of Arkansas, but his nomination was never confirmed by the Senate. He retired from the executive mansion in 1827 to private life, and lived the remainder of his days quietly at his home.

Governor Burton was an orator of rare ability and a stump speaker of unusual power; but while in Congress, he rarely ever spoke upon the questions before the house. He explained that, himself, by saying that in the Congress, at the time, were such lights as Clay, Calhoun, Webster, and Randolph, and they overawed him. Burton felt under restraint in their company, but had he felt inclined he could have displayed ability of no ordinary kind.

He had a summer home in the western part of the county near Ringwood, named "Rocky Hill," where he was residing at the time of his death, the circumstances of which were rather singular. Some time previous to 1836, he had bought a tract of land in Texas with a view of going to the "Lone Star Republic" to live. He left his family at "Rocky Hill" and set out by stage coach to see his farm in Texas. Reaching Salisbury, where he had some business in court he met with his cousin, Robert Burton, of Lincoln County. After completing his business in Salisbury, he intended spending a few days with his cousin before going to Texas. On the trip to Lincoln County, the party stopped at the Wayside Inn to pass the night. Here, Governor Burton was taken, during the night, with cramp and died within a few hours. His last words were, "Oh, my dear wife and children! Lord, receive my spirit." His death occurred April 21, 1836. His remains were buried in Unity Churchyard, in Lincoln County.

Mrs. Burton, at her home at "Rocky Hill," did not hear of his death until three weeks after the funeral, and, even then the first intimation of it was a newspaper account of his death and burial.

XVII
JOSEPH J. DANIEL.

Joseph J. Daniel was born in Halifax County, November 13, 1784. Very little is known of his boyhood. It is said that his early education was defective; but, later he became a close student of the law under the tutelage of William R. Davie. By diligent application, he overcame his early deficiencies and became in early manhood one of the most brilliant lawyers in North Carolina.

His first appearance in public life was in 1807, when he was elected to the House of Commons from the borough of Halifax. He was but twenty-three years of age at the time, but showed wisdom and discretion far beyond his years. He was elected to the House of Commons from the county in 1811 and 1812, and to the same body from the town in 1815. In 1816, he was appointed Judge of the Superior Court, and, in 1832, was elevated to the Supreme Bench, which position he held until his death in 1848.

There are but scanty details regarding the career of Judge Daniel. It is said that he was never out of the State but one time and that was when he attended the trial of Aaron Burr in 1807 in Richmond, Va. He was devoted to the State and County, and was always grateful to both for the honors he received. He was not a good speaker at the bar, but a fine conversationalist. His ready wit and strong personality were the chief means by which he advanced so rapidly in his profession. He was judge of the Superior Court for sixteen years, and served the same length of time on the Supreme Bench. This long tenure of office, in itself, shows that he was a man of no ordinary ability. His reports of cases decided in the Supreme Court and his written decisions are models of conciseness and terseness, not a superfluous word being used.

Judge Daniel is said to have had an artless simplicity of character, and not to have been practical in the every day affairs of life. One, who knew him well, said that the simplest details of the farm were Dutch to him. He could not even plant a row of corn. Another who also knew him said that he was kind and charitable, and that he had known him to send around a servant with meal and meat to his indigent neighbors. In Judge Daniel's day, it was no reflection upon a man to "take a drink" with a friend; and whenever he did, Judge Daniel insisted on the English custom of paying for his own drink.

He owned a residence in the town of Halifax and a country home at his farm, "Burnt Coat," near Heathsville. He married Maria Stith, whom he survived. Several children survived him, and his descendants are numerous in this State and others.

Chief-Justice Ruffin had the following to say of Judge Daniel on the occasion of the adoption of resolutions by the bar on the occasion of his death:

"Judge Daniel served his country through a period of nearly thirty-two years acceptably, ably, and faithfully. He had a love of learning, an inquiring mind, and a memory uncommonly tenacious; and he had acquired and re-

COLONIAL CEMETERY, HALIFAX, N. C.

BUILDERS OF THE COUNTY 185

tained a stock of varied and extensive knowledge, and especially became well versed in the History and the Principles of the Law. He was without arrogance or ostentation, even of his learning; had the most unaffected and charming simplicity and mildness of manners, and no other purpose in office than to 'execute justice and maintain truth'; and, therefore, he was patient in hearing argument, laborious and calm in investigation, candid and instructive in consultation, and impartial and firm in decision."

XVIII

JOHN R. J. DANIEL.

The subject of this sketch was born in Halifax County in 1802 and graduated from the State University in 1821. After his graduation, he located at Halifax for the practice of law, which he pursued with great success. No man, in the early part of the nineteenth century, was more brilliant at the Halifax bar than John R. J. Daniel.

In 1831, he was elected to the House of Commons and re-elected in 1832, 1833, and 1834. In the last mentioned year, he was chosen Attorney- General of the State, which position he held until 1841, when he was elected to Congress as the representative in the House of Representatives from the Second District. He was re-elected continuously until 1851 when he retired from active participation in public affairs. While in congress, he was for several years chairman of the Committee on Claims, a post of duty for which his unquestioned integrity, clear and discriminating mind, and patient industry especially fitted him.

He was a good speaker and debater. Thomas H. Benton, in his book, makes several extracts from his speeches while in Congress and pays him a deserved tribute. He is said to have been a man of iron will, sometimes overbearing and tyrannical, tenacious of his rights and fond of having his own way. Once he became involved in a law suit with a neighbor over two acres of farm land, which both claimed; and, after considerable litigation and the expenditure of much ill nature and display of temper, he was beaten in the final adjudication and had to pay the bill of cost amounting to $2700.00. It may be supposed that this was done with no very amiable disposition by a man, who believed in his own case and saw no show of reason in the contentions of his opponent.

After serving his last term in Congress in 1851, he bought a farm near Shreveport, La., where he resided much of the time until his death in 1868. He was a cousin of Judge Joseph J. Daniel, father of General Junius Daniel, and immediately or remotely connected with the large family of that name in this and adjoining counties.

XIX

BYNUM AND POTTER.

During the early years of the nineteenth century, two men, Jesse A. Bynum and Robert Potter, lived a number of years in the town of Halifax and had considerable weight in the administration of public affairs. They possessed brilliant intellects, but because of violent tempers, they became involved in many difficulties that have brought reproach and almost ignominy upon their names. Because of their bitter rivalry, mention is made of them in the same connection.

Bynum was born in Northampton County and educated at Union College, New York, but came to Halifax quite early in life and began the practice of law. He represented the borough of Halifax in the General Assembly in 1823 and 1824 and again in 1827 and 1828. In 1825, he and Robert Potter were opposing candidates, and so warm did the campaign become that on election day the voting was broken up by a street fight between the adherents of the two candidates. Consequently, there was no election and no representative from the town that year. Robert Potter was elected the next year.

BUILDERS OF THE COUNTY

In 1833, Bynum became a candidate for Congress; and conducted such a brilliant campaign, he was elected by a big majority over his Whig opponent. He was re-elected continuously until 1841, when he retired to private life and removed to Louisiana. While in Congress he had two personal difficulties, one with Congressman Jenifer, of Maryland, resulting in a duel, which terminated, after several ineffectual shots, in a reconciliation; and another, on the floor of the House, with Congressman Garland of Louisiana. His career after his retirement from Congress is unknown.

Robert Potter was born in Granville County but lived for several years in Halifax. He was a man of ability, but of such violent temper and perverse nature that his career was a reproach upon his name. He and Bynum were on bad terms, it was said, because Bynum refused to introduce him to a certain young lady. Their bitter personal rivalries were carried into the political campaigns and fisticuffs were frequent. As already related, the election of 1825 was broken up by a street row; but, in 1826, Potter was elected as the representative in the House of Commons from the town of Halifax.

In 1827, Potter removed from Halifax to Granville County, and so lost connection with this immediate section; but because of his remarkable subsequent career, the story of his life is followed, though its recital reveals the ignominy of his character.

In 1828, he was chosen to represent Granville County in the House of Commons, and made himself very popular by championing a bill to inquire into the condition of the banks, some of which at the time were very corrupt. In 1830 he was elected to Congress and re-elected in 1832; but on account of the commission of a nameless crime, for which he was arrested, tried, convicted, and sentenced to jail, he did not serve his term out. Strange to say, however, that after serving his term in jail, he was again elected to the House of Commons from Granville County; but was expelled for cheating at cards.

After this second disgrace, Potter became an object of detestation; and, to escape public censure, he fled to Texas. There he took part in political matters and rose to prominence. Later, he moved to Louisiana and located near Caddo Lake. There he led a life of gross immorality, and, after forbearance had ceased to be a virtue, he was warned by his indignant neighbors to leave the community. He did not, however, obey the warning. Shortly afterwards a number of men came to his house by night, took him outside, and told him he richly deserved death; but they would give him a chance for his life. They then gave him a start of one hundred yards and told him that his life would be the forfeit if any of his pursuers should get in shooting distance of him. Potter immediately ran for the lake and plunged in to escape death by diving. His pursuers came to the edge of the lake, and, as he came to the surface for breath, fired upon him and he sank to a watery grave.

Thus died in disgrace and ignominy one of the most brilliant and corrupt men ever connected with Halifax County.

XX

BARTHOLOMEW F. MOORE.

Bartholomew Figures Moore was born at Sycamore Alley, Halifax County, January 29, 1801. His father, James Moore, came to the county from Northampton, Va. He was a sailor in the Revolutionary War, and saw service of a very exciting nature in that eventful struggle. Some of his adventures have already been narrated in a former chapter.

"Bat" Moore, as the distinguished son is familiarly known, entered the University of North Carolina in 1818 and graduated therefrom in 1820. He then read law under Thomas N. Mann, a prominent lawyer of Nash County, securing license to practice and locating at Nashville, N. C., in 1823. At first he had but little success, and, it is said, practiced several years without making expenses. He persevered, however, overcoming all difficulties by his indomitable will power until he reached the very summit of the profession in the State.

In December, 1828, he was married to Louisa, daughter of George Boddie, of Nash County. She died the next year, and, in 1835, he married Lucy, another daughter of George Boddie. In that year, he removed to his native County and began the practice of his profession in the town of Halifax, where he met with great success. He entered politics in 1836 and was elected to the House of Commons that year. He was a candidate in 1838, but was defeated at the polls by a majority of one vote, said to have been cast against him because he voted for an appropriation for the building of the Wilmington and Weldon Railroad. He was again elected in 1840 and re-elected in 1842 and 1844.

In 1847, he was appointed by Governor Graham to the position of Attorney-General of the State, and elected by the General Assembly in 1850. The next year he was appointed by Governor Reid on the commission to revise the statute laws of the State, in accordance with an act of the General Assembly of that year. The Revised Code was reported to the Legislature of 1854, and, with some modifications, passed into law. He was a member of the Commission appointed to edit and publish the code, which was done in 1855.

During the whole period of his residence at Halifax he was laboriously and successfully engaged in the practice of the law in all the courts in his circuit except the county courts, all of which, except Halifax, he discontinued upon his appointment to the office of Attorney-General. He removed to Raleigh in 1848, where he resided at the time of his death in 1878.

In Oakwood Cemetery, Raleigh, stands one of the most beautiful and costly monuments in North Carolina. It occupies a prominent position, and its symmetrical proportion and artistic beauty make it a notable object. Its total height is twenty-three feet. The design is Gothic and the spire is surrounded by a crown and cross. On the west side is the following inscription:

"Bartholomew Figures Moore, LL. D.
Born January 29, 1801,
Died November 27, 1878
Citizen, Lawyer, Statesman
To himself, his family, and his country
He was true.

To evade a duty was to him impossible. In the discharge of duty he was diligent; difficulty intensified his effort. A devoted son of North Carolina. A never failing friend and liberal benefactor to her interests, an uncompromising foe to oppression, a profound jurist, and a fearless patriot."

XXI

ANDREW JOYNER.

One of the most universally popular men that ever lived in Halifax County was Colonel Andrew Joyner, who was born, November 5, 1786, near the town of Halifax. His father, Henry Joyner, was a prominent planter and business man. Not much is known of the early life of Andrew Joyner. He was probably as well educated as the limited means of acquiring an education in that day would allow.

His first service of a public nature was during the War of 1812. He was enrolled in the Third Regiment of North Carolina Volunteers, and before the regiment was ready for service he was given the rank of Major. Shortly afterwards he was promoted to the rank of Lieutenant-Colonel in the First Regiment of North Carolina Volunteers. He served in that capacity during the period of the war.

In 1814, his regiment was ordered to Norfolk, Va., to assist in repelling a threatened British attack upon that town. Admiral Cockburn, the ranking British Naval officer in the Chesapeake, had been threatening a descent

BUILDERS OF THE COUNTY

upon the place. Finding it, however, well fortified and garrisoned, he did not attack; but sailed away to the South. During the stay of the First Regiment at Norfolk, an epidemic of "Camp Plague" broke out, and almost every man in the command suffered from it. During the prevalence of the epidemic, Joyner was so indefatigable in his efforts to relieve the sufferings of the men that he endeared himself to the survivors to such an extent that, in his political campaigns in later life, not one of them ever voted against him.

In 1835, he was elected Senator from the county to the General Assembly, and re-elected continuously until 1852. He was the presiding officer of the Senate in 1838, 1840, and 1846. In his campaigns for election, he usually won easily. He was a Whig, but sometimes he was elected unanimously. Not an old soldier of any political faith ever voted against him.

Colonel Joyner turned his attention to "big" business enterprises. He was an earnest advocate of internal improvements, voted regularly for railroads every time he had an opportunity, and was a promoter of steamboat lines on the Roanoke river. He was President of the Roanoke Navigation Company, that put on the first steamboat that ever made a trip on the Roanoke. He was also President of the Weldon and Portsmouth railroad, which afterwards became the Seaboard, and directed the affairs of that company from his headquarters in Weldon for many years.

While Colonel Joyner was so closely indentified with the railroads, he would never allow one of his children to ride on a pass. He had a highly developed judicial mind and was particularly active in settling disputes between neighbors. So well known was he in this respect that his home near Weldon was generally spoken of as "Colonel Joyner's Court of Equity."

He was twice married, first to Temperance Williams and second to Sarah Jones Burton, widow of Governor Hutchings G. Burton. Numerous children survived.

Colonel Joyner died Sept. 20, 1856, and is buried at Poplar Grove near Weldon.

XXII

LAWRENCE O'BRYAN BRANCH.

One of the Brigadier-Generals, furnished by Halifax County to the Confederate army during the War between the States, is the subject of this sketch. He was born, in Enfield, November 28, 1820, was a grandson of John Branch, sheriff of Halifax County during the Revolution, and a nephew of John Branch, member of Congress, governor, senator, and cabinet member. His ancestry and immediate family relationship were brilliant.

His father, Major Joseph Branch, upon the death of his wife on Christmas day, 1825, removed to Tennessee, and shortly afterwards died, leaving his son, Lawrence, to the guardianship of his distinguished brother, John Branch. The boy was brought back to North Carolina and was with his uncle in Washington during his career as a member of Congress and a cabinet official. Upon the disruption of President Jackson's cabinet in 1831, young Branch returned with his uncle to Enfield, where he entered a preparatory school and was ready for college by the time he was fifteen.

In 1835, he entered the University of North Carolina. The next year, however, he matriculated at Princeton, was graduated from that institution in 1838, and delivered the English salutatory. He studied law in Tennessee, obtained license, and began to practice in Florida before he was twenty-one years of age. In 1841, when the Seminole War began, he enlisted and was aid to General Reid. In 1848, he returned to his native State and located in Raleigh for the practice of law. Here his rise was rapid, for, in 1852, he was presidential elector on the Pierce and King ticket and member of Congress in 1854.

In 1852, he became President of the Raleigh and Gaston Railroad Company and served two years when he re-

MAIN STREET, ROANOKE RAPIDS, N. C.

signed to become a member of Congress from the Raleigh district. In this latter capacity, he served with ability until 1861 when he resigned because he saw that North Carolina was about to secede from the union. Upon his retirement from Congress, President Buchanan tendered him the portfolio of Secretary of the Treasury, but he declined it for the same reason that he gave up his seat in Congress.

Returning to Raleigh, in April, 1861, he, at once, joined the Raleigh Rifles as a private. He was made Quartermaster-General the same month and elevated to the position of Paymaster-General on May 20. In September, the same year, he resigned that position to accept the commission of Colonel in the Thirty-Third Regiment, a position that would give him more active duties in the field, which was more in keeping with his tastes.

In January, 1862, Colonel Branch was commissioned by President Jefferson Davis Brigadier-General and stationed at Newbern for the protection of that city and to safeguard eastern North Carolina. Branch had five thousand men, under his command, but the city was attacked in March, the same year, by 15,000 Federals and Branch was obliged to evacuate his fortifications and retreat to Kinston. Being relieved of his separate command, General Branch was given a brigade in the army of Northern Virginia, and was in the battle of Hanover Court House, where, on account of signal bravery and distinguished services, he was praised by General Lee.

General Branch was conspicuous for his gallantry in the Battles of the Seven Days, Cedar Run, Second Bull Run, Fairfax Court House, Harpers Ferry, and Antietam. At the latter place, while standing with some officers, near the firing line, he was shot through the head and fell into the arms of Major Joseph A. Engelhead, and died almost immediately. The remains were brought to Raleigh for burial.

General Branch married Nancy Haywood Blount, daughter of General W. A. Blount, and left four children, as follows: William A. B. Branch, an officer in the War between the States, and, from 1891 to 1895, member of Congress from the First Congressional district. The daughters were Susan, who married Robert H. Jones; Nannie, married Armistead Jones; Josephine married Kerr Craig of Salisbury.

XXIII

EDWARD CONIGLAND.

Edward Conigland was born in the county of Donigal, Ireland, April 22, 1819. He was the fifth son of Dr. Patrick and Margaret Brison Conigland. His father was a skilled physician, and gave his sons the best educational advantages the times afforded. Dr. Conigland's death, however, occurred when Edward was but fourteen years of age; and his mother, owing to financial losses, emigrated, with her children, to America, arriving in New York, October 26, 1834.

Like many another young Irishman, coming to this country, Edward found that life in the New World was not one of ease. He was, therefore, glad to do any kind of work that offered itself to keep the wolf from the door, and had but little opportunity to pursue his classical studies he had begun in Ireland. He was diligent enough, however, to bend his energies to the acquisition of knowledge and the improvement of his mind in whatever way chance offered. Through the mediation of an influential friend, he was elected to membership in the Metropolitan Debating Association, which had been established by young men of cultivated tastes and literary aspirations for mutual improvement, one of the exclusive social organizations in New York City. On several occasions, when the public was admitted to the debates, the talent displayed by young Conigland, both as a writer and a speaker, was much complimented in the New York Journal.

In 1844, having studied law in New York and being a

good mathematician and linguist, he came to Halifax County and taught school in the home of Isaac Falkland for a year or two. During his career as a teacher, he continued his study of law; and, in 1846, procured license to practice in the Courts of North Carolina, establishing an office in the town of Halifax.

Like most young lawyers, he came into lucrative practice slowly, having what is known as the "starving period" for several years. His talent and industry, however, ultimately put him in the first rank of his profession. His services were desired and employed in many counties in the State. Two of the most celebrated legal cases, in which he was engaged, were the impeachment trial of Governor Holden and the Johnston Will Case. In the former, he was counsel for the defense and used all the tremendous force of his brilliant intellect to save the accused Governor from conviction; but to no avail.

In 1865, he was one of the delegates from Halifax County to the Constitutional Convention in Raleigh. The stand he took in that convention gained for him the approval and high regard of the people of the State. He had not been a soldier in the War between the States because of his defective hearing, but he showed, in his speeches and his votes in that body that he was a patriotic North Carolinian.

Forming a partnership, for the practice of law, in 1875, with the late Robert O. Burton, he continued the work of his profession with increasing success until his tragic death in December, 1877, brought his career to a close. On December 4, that year, he was returning home from one of his farms near Halifax, walking on the railroad track, and in a few minutes would have been with his family, when he was run down and killed instantly by a freight train.

Edward Conigland was married three times, first to Eliza Tillery, of Halifax County; second, to Mary Wyatt Ezell, of Jackson, N. C., and third, to Emily Long, of Northampton County. None of his descendants now reside in the county.

XXIV

JUNIUS DANIEL.

In many respects, the most distinguished soldier that Halifax County has produced was Junius Daniel, the subject of this sketch. He was the youngest son and the last surviving issue of John R. J. Daniel, who was distinguished as Attorney-General and member of Congress for a long time. He was born in the town of Halifax on the 27th day of June, 1828, and, at the age of three, met with the loss of an admirable mother.

His youth was passed in a quiet and an uneventful manner in the elementary schools of his native town. When about fifteen years of age, he was sent to the excellent academy of J. M. Lovejoy, of Raleigh, and remained in that school until 1846. While in that institution, he was spoken of as "admirably made, muscular, a quick eye, and as determined a spirit as ever animated a body." His record in the Lovejoy Academy was admirable.

In 1846, under the appointment of President Polk he entered the Military Academy at West Point. After a highly creditable and honorable career as a student, both in deportment and scholarship, he was graduated therefrom in 1851. While in school there and during some maneuvers on the drill ground with the artillery corps, a heavy gun was thrown on him, injuring his spine, which affected his health for several years.

After graduation, he was ordered to Newport, Ky., as assistant quartermaster; but in the fall of 1852, he was sent, in charge of a detachment of soldiers, to New Mexico, and was stationed at Fort Albuquerque where he remained five years. While in this service, some refractory soldiers entered into a conspiracy to kill him and attacked him in his quarters. When set upon, Daniel drew his sword, which, however, was shattered at the first thrust and fell from his hand. Although disarmed, he, by his powerful strength, kept his assailants at bay until the attention of the guard was attracted, and he was rescued.

In 1857, he resigned his commission in the service of the United States government, at the solicitation of his father, and began a career as an agriculturist in Louisiana. This occupation was not altogether according to his tastes, and he was not reluctant to give it up at the first favorable opportunity, which was not long in coming. He was, according to a report, a good farmer, showing great adaptability to a career that he was compelled to force himself to like.

He married, in October, 1860, Ellen, an accomplished daughter of Colonel John J. Long, of Northampton County. He returned to Louisiana, and was engaged vigorously in working his large plantation when the first gun was fired at Sumter and a continent became engulfed in war.

When Lincoln called for troops to crush the South, the State of Louisiana offered Daniel a commission in the service of that State. He, however, preferred to serve with the troops of North Carolina and hastened home. Arriving in Halifax, he tendered his services to Governor Ellis, and was immediately accepted. He was shortly afterwards elected Colonel of the Fourth Regiment, but later of the Fourteenth, which he accepted and remained the commanding officer until the period of enlistment expired. He was then tendered command of the Forty-Third and the Forty-Fifth regiments, which had enlisted for the period of the war. About the same time, he was offered by Governor Clark the command of the Second North Carolina Cavalry. He accepted the command of the Forty-Fifth.

Soon thereafter, Colonel Daniel was ordered by General Holmes to lead the four regiments then in Raleigh to Goldsboro and there organize them into a brigade. This was done so efficiently that General Holmes recommended Daniel to the authorities at Richmond for appointment as brigadier-general. The Confederate government, however, had been too liberal in appointments, and had already commissioned more brigadiers than there were brigades to command. So Daniel found himself a brigadier without a commission and had to give place to one who had a commission but no command. He then organized another brigade, only to see it assigned to another. Later, he was called upon to organize a third, and this he retained command of as senior colonel for nearly twelve months.

During this period, he was serving under the different departmental officers, all of whom urged his promotion, but to no avail. In June, 1862, he was ordered to Petersburg, and, with the brigade, joined General Lee's army before the Seven Days' Battles, but took no active part therein.

In October, 1862, the long delayed commission as a brigadier-general was received. His brigade was composed of the following regiments: The Thirty-Second, commanded by Cowan; the Forty-Third, by Kenan, wounded and captured at Gettysburg; the Forty-Fifth, first by Morehead, who died at Martinsburg, Va., in January, 1863, then by Boyd, who was wounded and captured at Gettysburg, exchanged and killed at Spottsylvania; the Fifty-Third, by Owen, killed at Winchester; and the Second North Carolina Battalion, by Lieutenant-Colonel Andrews, killed at Gettysburg. What a melancholy record!

General Daniel spent the fall of 1862, with his brigade, at Drury's Bluff. In December, he was ordered to North Carolina, under the command of General D. H. Hill to repel a diversion of Foster in favor of Burnside at Fredericksburg, Va. Shortly after the Battle of Chancellorsville, he was transferred to Lee's army, Rode's division, Ewell's Corps during the Pennsylvania campaign which followed.

At Carlisle, Pa., General Ewell conferred a great honor upon General Daniel and his brigade. After reaching

BUILDERS OF THE COUNTY 199

that place, General Ewell made a speech to Rode's division, complimenting them upon the successes of the march, their military bearing, and soldierly conduct. Then turning to Daniel's brigade, recently attached to the division, he said: "You have shown yourselves so obedient to all orders, so sturdy and regular on the march and so well disciplined, that I will intrust to you the bearing of the 'Corps flag,' confident that its honor could never suffer while in the keeping of such troops."

This was a proud moment for General Daniel and the highest compliment that could have been conferred on his troops. The older brigades murmured at this preference, but the flag was valiantly borne in many hard fought battles. General Ramseur said that he coveted that flag and that he never saw troops move with more precision on parade than the troops who bore it when ordered to change their position under the full fire of the enemy. This tribute came from an honored rival and could not have been meant for mere pleasantry.

The action of General Daniel at Gettysburg and the troops under his command won for him the highest esteem among his fellow soldiers of whatever rank. The senior captain of the Forty-Third Regiment, Cary Whitaker, who commanded the regiment after Kenan was shot down and who afterwards sealed his patriotism with his blood, is reported to have said that General Lee thus accosted General Daniel after the battle: "General Daniel, your troops behaved admirably and they were admirably handled."

General Daniel made an admirable report of the battle of Gettysburg, which is of sufficient interest to reproduce, at least, a portion of it:

"I cannot, in justice to the officers and men of my command, close this portion of my report without recording my honest conviction that the conduct of the troops, who participated in this engagement, will furnish brighter examples of patient endurance than were ever exhibited before. Entering the fight in the first day at about one P.

200 HISTORY OF HALIFAX COUNTY

M. and hotly engaged until four P. M., during which time they constantly drove before them a superior force of the enemy, losing nearly one-third of their number and many valuable officers; exposed during the second day to a galling fire of artillery from which they suffered much, they moved at night in a line of battle on the enemy's strong positions, after which, with less than two hours' rest and having made a fatiguing night march, they reported to General Johnson and entered the fight again at four A. M. on the third day and were not withdrawn until between three and four in the afternoon, then skirmishers remaining engaged until nearly twelve at night, and this whole time being constantly exposed to, and suffering from, the enemy's fire. Shortly after twelve, they were required to repeat the march of the preceding night and occupy the positions from which they had driven the enemy on the first day. Nor was there exhibited by any portion of the command during the three days in which they were engaged any disposition to shrink from the duties before them or any indication of that despondency with which men similarly exposed are so often affected."

The next engagement, in which Daniel's brigade took part, was at Spottsylvania Court House, May 11, 1864. During a desperate charge of the Federals, the Confederate lines were broken and the enemy was rapidly advancing, when Daniel's brigade, which had been on the reserve line up to that time was brought into action, and, being led by General Daniel in a gallant charge, checked the advance of the Federals and converted a defeat into a victory. On the next morning, at the "Horseshoe Bend," near Spottsylvania Court House, General Daniel fought his last battle. General Edward Johnson's division had been surprised early in the morning and most of it captured or killed. General Daniel was leading his brigade to recapture the works when he was struck in the abdomen by a minie ball. He was carried in a litter to the hospital about one mile in the rear and kept under the influence of opiates until the next day when he died. His

ONE OF THE GOOD ROADS, HALIFAX COUNTY, N. C.

BUILDERS OF THE COUNTY 201

last thought was of his wife in her distant home unable to reach him.

His remains were brought to Halifax and interred in the old churchyard, overlooking the blue hills of Northampton. The grave is unmarked even by a stone, and, after the present generation has passed away, may be entirely lost to memory.

XXV

FRANCIS M. PARKER.

Francis Marion Parker was born in Nash County, September 21, 1827. His father, Theophilus Parker, was a thrifty merchant and farmer. The son had the privilege of country life, and enjoyed the wholesome opportunity of being reared on a prosperous farm.

He was educated at the well known Lovejoy Academy in Raleigh, where he had the opportunity of being under the tutelage of learned and competent instructors. Receiving a liberal education at this institution, he returned to his father's farm and took up the duties of a planter. A few years later, he married Sallie T. Philips, of Edgecombe County, and, having purchased a farm near Enfield, made his home there.

Here he was living with his family when the War between the States began in 1861. Even before the State seceded Parker had already made preparation for the war. In April, he assisted in organizing the Enfield Blues and became the Second Lieutenant of the company. In May, his company was assigned to the First North Carolina Regiment, which afterwards came to be called the Bethel Regiment, and, in the latter part of the month, was ordered to Virginia to assist in repelling the threatened Federal advance from Fort Monroe.

At Bethel, on June 10th, Parker received his first baptism of fire and distinguished himself with signal gallantry. On August 31, 1861, he became Captain of the Enfield Blues, but held that position only about six weeks when he was offered and accepted the commission of Colonel of the Thirtieth Regiment of North Carolina volunteers, which position he held until he was wounded and forced to retire from the service.

Colonel Parker was in the thickest of the Seven Days' Battles around Richmond, where his regiment performed heroic service. He was also in the battles of Seven Pines, South Mountain, Antietam, Fredericksburg, Chancellorsville, Gettysburg, Wilderness, and Spottsylvania. He was severely wounded at the last mentioned conflict and was obliged to retire from active service. In all these great struggles, more than the average soldier was expected to experience, Colonel Parker showed a patriotic devotion of the highest type and rare military skill.

After the close of the war, Colonel Parker retired to his country estate, where he spent the remainder of his life. He died January 18, 1905.

XXVI

SPIER WHITAKER.

Two distinguished sons of Halifax County have borne the name of Spier Whitaker. The first of the name was born in 1798, became prominent in politics in the early forties, was Attorney-General of North Carolina four years, 1842-46, and, after his term of office expired, removed with his family to Iowa, and died in his adopted State after the close of the War between the States.

Spier Whitaker, son of the one just mentioned, was born in Enfield, March 15, 1841. At an early age he entered the school of Major Samuel Hughes in Orange County, where he was prepared for college. In the fall of 1857, he matriculated at the University of North Carolina, and would have received his diploma in June, 1861, if he had remained until then; but the war clouds began to gather in increasing blackness, and young Whitaker, along with others, left college in April and volunteered as a

BUILDERS OF THE COUNTY

private in a company being raised by Captain Richard J. Ashe.

His company was assigned to the Bethel Regiment. He was in the Battle of Bethel and was in the maneuvers around Yorktown until his company was ordered to Newbern the latter part of the year and attached to the command of General L. O'B. Branch for the defense of Eastern North Carolina.

He was in the thickest of the fight at Newbern, and fell into the hands of the enemy as a prisoner of war. After being held four months, he was exchanged and at once resumed his position in the ranks. He was made second lieutenant, and, with his company, joined Lee's army just before the first invasion of Maryland. He was in the memorable Battle of Antietam and the most of the terrible struggles of 1863 and 1864. At Appomattox, he sheathed his sword and went to his father's home in Iowa.

Young Whitaker, however, was not satisfied with life in the West, and, after studying law under the tutelage of his father, returned to North Carolina in the fall of 1866 and located at Enfield. He became solicitor in 1867, a position he filled with splendid ability for several years. He was elected to the State Senate in 1881, and, in 1882, removed to Raleigh to form a law partnership with John Gatling.

In 1888 he was chairman of the State Democratic Executive Committee and conducted a masterly campaign that year. The next year, he was appointed by Governor Fowle to the position of Superior Court Judge and was elected for the unexpired term in 1890. He retired from the judgeship in 1894, and resumed the practice of law in Raleigh. In 1898, the Spanish-American war having broken out, he volunteered his services and was appointed and commissioned Major by President McKinley. He, however, did not see active service, for the war ended before the North Carolina troops were called to the front.

Major Whitaker returned to Raleigh in 1899 and again resumed the practice of his profession. He died in the capital city, July 11, 1901.

XXVII

WALTER N. ALLEN.

Walter N. Allen was born March 1, 1834, near Littleton. He was the oldest son of James V. Allen and his wife, Eliza Mason Johnson, and a great grandson of James Allen, who was Colonel of the Halifax regiment of minute men during the closing months of the Revolutionary War. His grandfather, John Allen, was also a soldier of the Revolution, being yet in his teens when commissioned a second lieutenant and entrusted with the important duty of carrying from Philadelphia to Newbern $2485.50 in gold to pay off the soldiers of the Continental line.

After receiving an elementary education in the schools of his neighborhood, Walter Allen, more generally known by his middle name of Norman, entered Lake Forest College, where he studied for two years. Leaving Lake Forest, he matriculated at the University of North Carolina in the school of law and continued his studies for two years longer. In 1856, he secured his license to practice law and was admitted to the bar in Halifax.

In 1857, he went to Kansas, locating in Jefferson County. In that new country, he quickly became prominent. In 1858, he was appointed county attorney and the next year was elected to the same position at the polls. In 1863, he was appointed clerk of the district court of Jefferson County by William McDowell, Judge of the First Judicial District of Kansas. In 1865, he was elected to the Kansas House of Representatives as the member from Jefferson County. While a member of that body, he was active in opposing the proposition to appropriate 500,000 acres of the public lands to the railroad company then traversing the county, taking the ground that these lands were held in trust by the State for the support of the public schools.

In 1867, Allen was elected clerk of the court. During his term of office, he came into violent conflict with the Board of County Commissioners. The proposition was submitted to the voters of the county to issue bonds to the amount of $300,000, in equal proportions, to the Atchison, Topeka, and Santa Fe and the Atchison, Oskaloosa, and Lawrence railroads. The election was held and the commissioners declared the bond issue carried, ordering Allen, as Clerk of the Court, to make the entry in the books of the county, subscribing to the stock of these railroads to the amount of $300,000. Allen refused to make the entry, and the commissioners instituted legal proceedings against him to oust him from office. In the end, he was dismissed from office and imprisoned.

These proceedings brought about a revulsion on the part of the people and an injunction was gotten out restraining the commissioners from issuing the bonds or subscribing to the stock of the railroads. Allen was released from jail and promptly became one of the most popular and influential men in that part of the State. He entered strenuously into the campaign to remove the commissioners from office and to put in a board opposed to the bond issue. He took the stump, and, in a series of brilliant speeches, completely routed the bond advocates and carried the county against the railroad domination of its politics.

From the beginning, Jefferson County was heavily Republican; but Allen, who was a staunch Democrat, was able to secure a majority vote whenever he came before the people and made a personal canvass. Because of political conditions in Kansas, which was always overwhelmingly Republican, he failed to realize his ambitions. Consequently he turned his attention to agriculture and lived upon his estate near the city of Topeka, giving his talents to the development of agricultural interests of Kansas.

In 1882, he purchased the Topeka Democrat, the leading Democratic paper of the State and became managing editor. The same year he purchased the Topeka State Journal, a Greenback organ, and united it with the Democrat, becoming editor-in-chief of the consolidated papers. For a number of years, he, as editor of the principal Democratic paper in the State, exerted an influence in party councils that was almost paramount.

About 1890, Allen turned his attention to the organization of the farmers of the Mississippi Valley into a union for protection against the grain and meat speculators. He succeeded in getting an immense number of farmers together in St. Louis and was elected the first president of the organization. He spent his remaining years in the Herculean task of perfecting this union and in making it a mighty instrument for good to the farmers of the west.

After going to Kansas, Norman Allen made two visits to his birthplace, once during the war between the States and again in 1885. He died Feb. 5, 1905. He left one son, Pope Walker Allen, who resides in Topeka, Kansas.

XXVIII

THOMAS L. EMRY.

Among the captains of industry of Halifax County, the name of Thomas L. Emry is prominent. He was conspicuous, during the closing years of the nineteenth century and the beginning of the twentieth, in some of the most notable industrial enterprises of the eastern part of North Carolina. The story of his life is interesting and inspiring.

Thomas L. Emry was born in Petersburg, Va., December 18, 1842, and was left an orphan at the age of six years. For eleven years the fatherless and penniless boy lived an unknown life in the city of his birth, acquiring such an education as the schools of that day could give him and his limited opportunities would permit.

In 1859, Tom Emry, as he was generally called, left Petersburg and came to Halifax to live, engaging in the business of a tinner, at which he worked for more than a year. Some of the work he did during that time, is still in existence in some portions of the county. As a tinner, however, his career was short.

BUILDERS OF THE COUNTY

When South Carolina seceded from the Union in December, 1860, Tom Emry, then a mere boy of eighteen, hastened to the Palmetto State and volunteered his services for the period of the war. He was attached to the Sixth Regiment of South Carolina volunteers and was present at the bombardment and capture of Fort Sumter, April 12, 1861. In July, the same year, his regiment was ordered to Virginia and reached the battlefield of Bull Run on the afternoon of July 22 in time to witness the complete defeat and precipitous retreat of the Union Army.

In the fall of 1861, he was transferred, at his request, from the Sixth Regiment of South Carolina troops to the Twelfth North Carolina Regiment, and rejoined the Halifax Light Infantry, of which he had been a member before going to South Carolina. With this regiment and company he remained during his active participation in the war and until he was wounded and had to retire from the service.

Tom Emry was a gallant soldier. He was in the Seven Days' Battles around Richmond, and, on the last day at Malvern Hill, won the admiration of his comrades and the praise of his Colonel and brigade commander by his heroic conduct in action. The following is an extract from the report of Colonel B. O. Wade relative to his gallant behavior:

"It is gratifying to know that the bravery of some was without precedent. The noble daring of private T. L. Emry won the admiration of all his command, he having seized the flag and rushed through a shower of bullets to the brow of the hill and there stood defiantly waving it in the enemy's face until it and staff were completely riddled with bullets."

On account of wounds received in battle, he became incapacitated for heavy duties, and, for the remainder of the war, was placed on detail for less arduous work. He thus passed through the remaining portion of the war without special mention.

Returning to Halifax, at the close of the war, he engaged in mercantile business and soon established himself as one of the commercial factors of the county. In 1869, he located in Weldon, and, at once, took a leading position in the industrial development of the town. For nearly twenty years, he was Mayor of Weldon, President of the Roanoke and Tar River Agricultural Society, for over fifteen years, and until the day of his death one of Weldon's most enterprising citizens.

In 1886, Major Emry, as he was now generally known, was elected a member of the Board of County Commissioners and served in that capacity for two years. In 1888, he was nominated by the Democratic party for the Senate of North Carolina, and was elected in November of that year, overcoming the heavy Republican majority in the county. He served only one term, declining to be drawn deeply into politics to the neglect of his business.

Major Emry's greatest distinction, however, was not as a soldier or a political leader, but as an industrial organizer and promoter. Some years after coming to Weldon to live, he became interested in the development of the immense water power of the Roanoke river. With an eye to the great value of that power and with the purpose of its ultimate utility, he purchased a tract of land near what was known as the "Great Falls," about five miles up the river from Weldon, and began active preparation for harnessing the tremendous energy that was running to waste.

About 1892, by his untiring zeal, enterprise, and perseverance, he succeeded in interesting several capitalists in the possibilities of utilizing the more than 50,000 horse power then unharnessed. A corporation, consisting of Charles Cohen and James M. Mullen, of Petersburg, Va.; John L. Patterson and S. F. Patterson, of Winston-Salem; W. S. Parker, of Henderson; and W. M. Hobliston, of Richmond, Va., together with Major Emry, was formed in 1895, and work was begun in the building of dams across the river and the construction of mills. The great enterprise was, therefore, fairly launched and Roanoke Rapids became an actuality.

COURT HOUSE, HALIFAX, N. C.

One of Major Emry's associates in the development of "Great Falls" as a manufacturing point thus speaks of him: "To Major Thomas L. Emry belongs the honor of discovering the advantages of this place as a manufacturing site. He built the first power plant ever erected here. When he began it, I doubt if he knew where the next pay roll was coming from. He was a man of indomitable energy, however, and finished it."

Major Emry lived to see the fruition of his dreams, a great manufacturing centre on a site chosen by himself. His name is associated with the magic city, and he will be remembered as one of the greatest potentialities in its development and growth. He died September 8, 1910.

XXIX

RICHARD H. SMITH.

Previous to the war between the States, agriculture was almost the only industry of importance in Halifax County. The agriculturist, or planter, as the large farmer of that day was called, was generally a man of influence and note in his community. As tilling the soil was the occupation upon which the welfare of the county chiefly depended, the man who brought wealth to his community in that way was a benefactor.

Richard H. Smith was one of the influential planters, among a number of such men in the lower part of the county, during the decades immediately preceding the Civil War. Born near Scotland Neck, May 10, 1812, he grew up on the farm of his father, William R. Smith, imbibing the strength, character, and spirit of the well-bred country boy of that period. At the age of five, he was sent to school at the Vine Hill Academy in Scotland Neck. When twelve years old he entered the school of W. E. Webb at Hyde Park in the Littleton section of the county, and remained there three years.

There is no record of his work as a student either at Vine

Hill or at Hyde Park; but as he was a model boy, it can well be inferred that he made good marks and won the respect and confidence of his teachers and class-mates. After spending a year at Oxford, he matriculated at the University of North Carolina in the fall of 1828, receiving his diploma of graduation in 1832.

In the spring of 1833 he went to Warrenton, N. C., and began the study of law under Edward Hall, an attorney of that town. After finishing his course and before applying for license to practice, he was married, December 4, 1834, to Sally Hall, daughter of Judge John Hall. Abandoning the practice of law, he turned his attention to agriculture, and, assuming the burden of management, he soon became an agriculturalist of recognized ability. Well educated and endowed with natural talents of a high order, he early became a leader among the farmers of the county.

He was not a politician by nature and refused to seek political preferment. In 1848, however, he was persuaded by his fellow citizens to become a candidate for the house of Commons on the ticket with William L. Long. Andrew Joyner, a veteran of the War of 1812, was the candidate on the same ticket for the senate. At the polls the ticket received a majority vote, and "Dick" Smith, as he was familiarly called, began his public career. As a legislator, he incurred unpopularity because he voted for the charter of the North Carolina Railroad, and, in the election of 1850, he was defeated. He was, however, renominated in 1852 and elected, and also again in 1854.

Retiring from politics at the end of his term in 1855, he devoted his energies to his farming interests, and amassed a fortune that was considerable for that day. Although out of politics, he took an active interest in the great questions then agitating the country, chief among them that of slavery, which seemed destined to disrupt the Union. He was an ardent supporter of States Rights and a strict constructionist, and, with other Southern men, viewed the unreasonable acts of the radical element

BUILDERS OF THE COUNTY 211

in the North with alarm. There seemed no chance for a peaceful settlement of the dispute between the North and the South, but Richard H. Smith was a union man and labored for peace until all hope of a solution of the trouble had passed.

In January, 1861, the General Assembly, by an act, submitted to the people the question of the call of a convention to consider the matter of secession, and, at the same time, called for the election of delegates to the convention if it should be called by vote of the people. Richard H. Smith was one of the candidates of the opponents of the convention and was elected, but the call for the convention was defeated. In May, however, of the same year, another convention was called by a majority vote of the people, and Richard H. Smith and Charles J. Gee were sent as the delegates from Halifax County. The country was in a state of excitement. Sumter had fallen and President Lincoln had called upon North Carolina and other Southern States for troops to wage war upon the Southern Confederacy. The war had actually begun. So when the convention met in Raleigh, May 20, there was no union sentiment among the members. All were for immediate secession. By a unanimous vote the ordinance was passed, the Halifax representatives being among the most ardent advocates of the step.

During the war that followed, "Dick" Smith remained at his home near Scotland Neck, his age excluding him from active participation in military service. He was, however, a diligent student of affairs as they transpired, and, at the end, saw and felt the crash with composure. The beginning of the war found him a man of wealth. The end revealed him almost financially bankrupt.

Perhaps the most eminent service Richard H. Smith performed was what he did as a churchman. He was one of the organizers of Trinity Parish and a vestryman for more than fifty years. For fifty-nine years he was a delegate from his church to the Diocesan Convention, and in October, 1865, was a delegate to the General Convention of the Episcopal Church, which met that year in Philadelphia. One of the great questions before the ecclesiastical body was the reunion of the northern and southern branches of the Church. Along with other southern members, Richard H. Smith's voice was raised in behalf of reconciliation. He gained the ear of the convention and the two bodies voted to forget the past and to bury all differences.

When the Roanoke and Tar River Agricultural Society was organized a few years after the close of the Civil War, Richard H. Smith was chosen its first president. Largely by his efforts and the efficiency of the secretaries of the Fair Association, the successful series of fairs, which had a great influence upon the activities of the county, was held for a number of years at Weldon.

He died March 3, 1893, at his home near Scotland Neck.

XXX

GEORGE GREEN LYNCH.

As a trusted employee of the Postoffice Departments of both the Confederacy and the United States, George Green Lynch had the unusual distinction of having been personally commended by both governments for meritorious services. His was a career notable and conspicuous for patriotic self-sacrifice and devotion to duty.

Born near Whitakers, Edgecombe County, November 28, 1817, he grew up on his father's farm and early developed the sturdy character of integrity for which he was so well known in later life. Taught only in the primitive schools of that day, his education was not as profound as would be supposed from the record of the excellent service which he afterwards rendered. He was, however, a close student of that which was most worth while, and became, as years passed, a man of strong personality and more than average intelligence.

About 1840, George Lynch entered the service of the

BUILDERS OF THE COUNTY 213

United States Government as Route Agent of the Postoffice Department, and, in a few years, was made Special Agent of the same division of the government. He held the latter position, when the Confederate Government was organized at Montgomery, Ala., in February, 1861. Without waiting to see what course North Carolina was going to take in the crisis, but, believing that the state was going to secede from the Union, he tendered his resignation to the department in Washington, March 1, 1861. In answer to his letter of resignation, he received the following communication:

"G. G. Lynch, Esq., of North Carolina, has been in the service of this Department as Route Agent and Special Agent for the long period of sixteen years and upwards, and has always distinguished himself by the most constant and untiring devotion to the public interests.

"From our knowledge of him both personally and officially, we cheerfully, and, as an act of justice, testify our high appreciation of his services, and regret that circumstances impel him to resign his office.

(Signed) HORATIO KING,
Postmaster-General

(Signed) A. N. ZEVERLY,
3rd Assistant P. M. G."

July 1, 1861, he was tendered and accepted the position of Special Agent of the Postoffice Department of the Confederate Government under Postmaster-General John H. Reagan, which position he held until the downfall of the Confederacy.

During the period of his connection with the Confederate Government, he was trusted with many dangerous and important missions. His field of operations was the entire South and portions of the West, through which he traveled, establishing postoffices and making collections for the government. At one time, he personally conveyed from Augusta, Ga., to Wilmington, N. C., $50,000 in gold, for which he was highly complimented by General Reagan in a letter written October 30, 1863.

At another time, he was sent to West Virginia to establish mail communication between the army of General Floyd, who was in command of that department, and the country to the east and south. Later, he was commissioned by General Reagan to establish postal service in such parts of Missouri as were in possession of the Confederacy. For three months he was engaged in this arduous task while his family knew not whether he was alive or dead.

So successful, however, was he in carrying out the orders of his superiors that he was offered by President Jefferson Davis the position of Assistant Postmaster-General with headquarters west of the Mississippi River, which, however, he declined. He continued his strenuous duties in a subordinate position until defeat settled upon the arms of the Confederacy in April, 1865. After Lee's surrender, he returned to his home out of employment but still vigorous and optimistic.

The next year he was made General Agent of the Wilmington and Weldon Railroad Company with headquarters at Weldon and was continuously in its employment until his death, December 28, 1886. During this time, he was a trusted employee and personal friend of some of the financiers, who were then laying plans for the great Atlantic Coast Line Railroad Company. Judge Lynch, as he was then familiarly known, may be considered as one of the factors, though in a modest way, of the formation of that standard railroad of the South.

Judge Lynch was married February 19, 1846, to Emma Whitaker, from which union now survive six children, Mrs. Margaret Pierce, George G. Lynch, Adolphus B. Lynch, Mrs. F. S. Overton, Mrs. L. B. Tillery, and Mrs. B. W. Arrington.

XXXI

THOMAS N. HILL.

Halifax County has been noted in the past, as well as in the present, for its able jurists. Some of the most profound students of the law have lived and practiced at the Halifax bar, and have shed lustre upon the name of the County.

Among the legal lights of the latter part of the nineteenth century, the name of Thomas N. Hill is conspicuous. He was the second son of Whitmel John Hill and Lavinia Dorothy Barnes Hill, and was born March 12, 1838, near Hill's Cross Roads in the Scotland Neck section of Halifax County, the neighborhood still retaining its name from the Hill family.

After preparatory study at Vine Hill Academy in Scotland Neck and at the Warrenton High School, he entered the Freshman Class at the State University in 1853, and was graduated with distinction in June 1857, receiving the bachelor's degree. Later the master's degree was conferred upon him by his alma mater. Some of his classmates were Robert Bingham, superintendent of the Bingham Military School at Asheville; A. C. Avery, of Morganton, for years a Superior Court and a Supreme Court Judge; Thomas S. Kenan, Attorney-General, and later Clerk of the Supreme Court; John W. Graham, for a long time one of the most eminent lawyers of the State; and Thaddeus Belsher, founder of the University of Columbus and Carrollton College in Mississippi.

Leaving college, he attended for two years Judge Pearson's Law School and became grounded in the principles of common law. In December, 1858, he was licensed to practice in the County Courts, and, the next year, received license to practice in the Superior Courts of the State. In 1860, he opened a law office in Halifax, but later the same year changed his location to Scotland Neck.

In politics, he was a Whig and a Union man. During the

fall and winter of 1860-61, when troublous times arose, he opposed secession and argued strenuously for the union as it existed. When, however, the State seceded, May 20, 1861, and war was inevitable, he enlisted as a private in the Scotland Neck Mounted Riflemen, afterwards Company G of the Third North Carolina Cavalry. He was a soldier for about a year, for in May, 1862, while in the army, he was elected Solicitor for Halifax County. Returning home, he took up his new duties and continued in office until 1866 when he declined re-election. He was immediately appointed Clerk and Master in Equity by Judge Fowle, who was on the Superior Court Bench at that time. He resigned this office in 1867, and devoted his energies to the practice of his profession.

As an office lawyer, Tom Hill, as he was familiarly known, had few superiors among his contemporaries. He was often appointed Referee, and, in that auxiliary court, his knowledge of law and his power of analysis were at their best in the investigation and determination of difficult questions both of law and fact. His report as Referee in the case of Badger vs. Daniel, in Volume 79 of the North Carolina State Reports, is an illustration of his careful preparation. He had an extensive practice in the courts of Halifax, Northampton, Warren, Bertie, Martin, and Hertford counties, in the Supreme Court at Raleigh, and in the United States Circuit and District Courts.

For more than forty-five years, he had as his opponents or associates, in the trial of cases, some of the ablest lawyers in the State. Among them may be mentioned John Gatling, Fabius H. Busbee, Joseph B. Batchelor, and John W. Hinsdale, of the Raleigh bar; William W. Peebles, Robert B. Peebles, Matt. W. Ransom, Thomas W. Mason, and W. C. Bowen, of the Northampton bar; Henry A. Gilliam, of Edgecombe; James E. Moore, of Martin; William D. Pruden, of Chowan; B. B. Winborne, of Hertford; William A. Jenkins, of Warren; Edward Conigland, Robert O. Burton, William H. Kitchin, Spier Whitaker, William H. Day, John A. Moore, William A. Dunn, Claude Kitchin,

BUILDERS OF THE COUNTY 217

Edward L. Travis, James M. Mullen, Walter Clark, and Walter E. Daniel, of the Halifax bar.

In 1877, upon the creation of the Inferior Courts, he was elected Chairman of the Halifax County Inferior Court Board of Justices and continued as the presiding officer of that Court until it was abolished by act of the General Assembly some years later. As presiding judicial officer, Judge Hill was fair and impartial in his decisions, and retained the highest respect and confidence of his associates.

January 1, 1878, he located in Halifax for the second time, and shortly thereafter, he became a candidate before the Democratic State Convention for the nomination for the position of Associate Justice of the Supreme Court. The following notice of his candidacy is taken from the Raleigh News in its issue of June 6, 1878:

"Mr. Thomas N. Hill, a gentleman prominently spoken of in connection with a place on the Supreme Court Bench, is in the city; but if he ever finds the office or the office finds him, it will have to seek him, for he appears to be entirely too modest and unassuming for the practical business of political electioneering, but it is said by those who know him that a very high order of merit is concealed about his person and that he has few superiors in the law."

When the convention met, Judge Hill received a large vote, but was defeated by the venerable Judge W. N. H. Smith, of Hertford County. In 1888, he was again a candidate and was defeated by James E. Shepherd, of Beaufort County, who was elected and was afterwards elevated to the Chief Justiceship. It appears, therefore, how narrowly Judge Hill failed of being signally honored by his fellow citizens.

In 1902, he was importuned to become a candidate before the Democratic State Convention for the nomination of Chief Justice of the Supreme Court against the then incumbent, Judge Walter Clark, another distinguished jurist of Halifax County. Judge Hill, however, declined to be a candidate before the convention, but afterwards announced his candidacy as an independent, "subject, however," as he explained, "to such action as may be taken by any State Convention composed of Democrats that may assemble hereafter for the purpose of making a nomination in opposition to Judge Clark." Shortly after his announcement, the Republican State Convention met and passed the following resolution:

"Resolved, that, whereas the Republican party desiring the elevation to the Bench of the best fitted lawyer of the State, regardless of party affiliations, the candidacy of the Hon. Thomas N. Hill, of Halifax, for Chief Justice of North Carolina, is hereby endorsed, and, we, the Republicans of the State, in convention assembled, do earnestly recommend him to the people of the State for this high office."

Although his candidacy was urged by a campaign committee with headquarters at Greensboro, and a thorough canvass made, he failed of election. This was his last appearance before the public, for he died July 24, 1904, at his home in the town of Halifax. He was a communicant of the Episcopal Church, a member of the Masonic Fraternity, the State Bar Association, the American Bar Association, and the Sons of the Revolution.

He was twice married, first to Eliza Evans Hall, June 4, 1861, who died October 25, 1884, from which union there were ten children, four sons and six daughters; second to Mary Amis Long, daughter of Nicholas Long, of Weldon, on March 1, 1887, who died October 12, 1901, without issue.

XXXII

PETER EVANS SMITH.

Peter Evans Smith, son of William Ruffin Smith and Susan Evans Smith, was born in Edgecombe County, January 20, 1829, and, like most boys of that day, was reared on a farm. He was named for his maternal grandfather,

BUILDERS OF THE COUNTY

who lived near Old Sparta in Edgecombe County. He was the oldest of thirteen children.

When old enough to attend school, he was sent to the Vine Hill Male Academy in Scotland Neck; but later, he was thoroughly prepared for college at the famous William Bingham School in Orange County. In September, 1846, he matriculated at the University of North Carolina. It is said that he was so well prepared that he did not have to study as much as other freshmen; but while his class-mates were struggling over their lessons for next day, Peter Smith was sitting under the Davis Poplar playing the flute or violin, or out elsewhere taking daguerrotypes. On the day of graduation, however, he stood among the best in his class and received his diploma.

At the age of twenty-five, he married Rebecca Whitmel Hill, daughter of Whitmel J. Hill; and, although he had no fondness for the life of a farmer, he was given a farm by his father, settled upon it, and became an agriculturist. He was a born mechanic, but did not have the opportunity, in early life, to give attention to his developing genius along that line. For some years, he followed the life of a planter, but finally gave up his farming interests and turned his attention entirely to shop work.

As a mechanic and inventor, he is probably best known. He was the first man in the county to introduce the use of the planing mill. He invented the method of shrinking tires; an electric buoy, similar to the kind now used in New York harbor; a drill for boring holes through iron rails, which was stolen by some Federal raiders during the Civil War and patented afterward; a cotton planter, which was among the first of that useful implement on the farm; and others of a minor nature. He was a railroad builder of considerable note, was one of the principal contractors in the construction of the Kinston branch of the Wilmington and Weldon Railroad, and of the Norfolk and Carolina.

During the Civil War, Peter Smith was no slacker. His mechanical genius caused his services to be in demand in other departments more important than in the ranks. A notable example of the work he did during that time is the construction of the Confederate Ram *Albemarle* at Edwards' Ferry near Scotland Neck. Gilbert Elliott, of Elizabeth City, had the contract for building the boat; but Peter Smith was the chief builder. Much of the credit for the success of that wonderful piece of mechanism is due him.

After the Civil War, he lived quietly and unpretentiously at his home in Scotland Neck, working at his trade as a mechanic. He had his shops in "Old Clarksville" and in addition to his regular work in that line, he mended clocks, watches, locks, and guns for his neighbors free of charge. His genius, which, in more populous centers, might have brought him fame and fortune, was expended unsparingly in the interests of his friends almost without pay.

XXXIII
ROBERT O. BURTON, D. D.

Among the men intimately connected with the rise and progress of Methodism in Halifax County, the name of Robert O. Burton stands preeminent. For more than fifty years, he labored as an itinerant minister in the Roanoke section of North Carolina, most of the time in destitute localities, where the people heard him gladly. The story of his life is an almost complete account of the beginning of the Methodist Church in this portion of the State.

Robert Oswald Burton was born in Campbell County, Virginia, June 30, 1811. His father planned for him a military career and fashioned his education with that in mind. As soon as he was prepared, he was sent to the West Point Military Academy to take up his studies there; but the young soldier, although a brilliant student, did not complete the course. Feeling that he was called to preach the gospel, he resigned the West Point Cadetship, after two years, and returned home.

BUILDERS OF THE COUNTY 221

Shortly after giving up his prospects of a military career, he joined the Virginia Conference, in 1833, which met that year in Petersburg, and was ordained deacon the same year and elder in 1837. He was sent in the former year, as an itinerant preacher, to that portion of the Virginia Conference included in North Carolina with headquarters at Weldon. This was the beginning of his connection with Halifax County, a relation which continued to the day of his death.

When the North Carolina Conference was organized in 1837, he became a member of that body and retained his membership for more than fifty years. During all those years, he was one of the most prominent members and wielded an influence which was felt throughout the state. He filled some of the most important pastorates in the Conference and was several times Presiding Elder.

On March 29, 1842, he was married to Elizabeth Joyner, daughter of Colonel Andrew Joyner of Weldon, and built his home, Wyandoke, near Poplar Grove, the home of his father-in-law, a few miles from town, near the present city of Roanoke Rapids. Throughout all the years of his ministry, even in other counties, he held this house as an anchorage to which he returned, an experience that few Methodist preachers have. Here he reared a family of nine children.

The extent of his work can be best judged from the list of charges that he had at different times:

In 1834, Junior preacher on Amelia circuit; 1835, Granville circuit; 1836, Greensboro; 1837, Salisbury; 1838-42, Agent of Randolph-Macon College; 1843, P. E. of Washington District; 1846, Henderson Circuit; 1847-48, Raleigh Station; 1849-50, Roanoke Circuit; 1851-54, Roanoke Circuit; 1855-58, P. E. Raleigh District; 1858, transferred to the Virginia Conference; 1859-62, P. E. Petersburg District; 1863, Greenville Circuit; 1864, Military encampment at Garysburg; 1865, Greenville Circuit; 1866-68, Union Circuit; 1869, Supt. of Colored work; 1870, transferred to North Carolina Conference; 1871-3,

Supt. Colored work; 1874-76, Roanoke Circuit; 1877, Littleton Circuit; 1878, Henderson Circuit; 1879-80, Roanoke Circuit; 1881, Edgecombe Circuit; 1882-83, P. E. Wilmington District; 1884, P. E. Greensboro District; 1885-88, Warrenton Circuit; 1889, Ridgeway Circuit.

As a pulpit orator, he had few equals in the North Carolina Conference. His language was impassioned and forceful, and he rarely ever spoke without leaving a profound impression upon his hearers. His influence in the Conference was almost unlimited. Whenever Dr. Burton spoke, the audience gave immediate attention.

Dr. Burton was not a politician in the sense of seeking advantage for himself. He never made an effort to advance his own interests in the Episcopacy of his church. Several times his name was prominently mentioned in connection with the bishopric, but he declined to put forth any effort to obtain it. His principal ambition was to serve, and, if he could do that in an humble position better than in an exalted one, he was content. Whatever honors, therefore, came to him were unsought and wholly deserved.

Dr. Burton was a man of intense religious convictions, convincingly in earnest when trying to persuade, and dignified in both speech and demeanor. While all that was in his general character, he was not slow to see the point of a joke, or to appreciate real shafts of wit. The following paragraph is taken from an appreciative sketch of him printed a few years ago in the Roanoke News.

"There was a humorous side to Dr. Burton's character and many are the quaint stories told of him by those who knew him well. One of these is that upon an occasion when he was dining away from home, having helped a lady quite plentifully, from a dish he was serving, with more candor than good breeding she remarked, 'I didn't want a cart load.' Dr. Burton did not reply, but, biding his time, he soon saw that she had eaten all on her plate, and then said to her, 'Sister, back your cart up and I'll load it again.' "

BUILDERS OF THE COUNTY

One of the most dramatic incidents in his career occurred at the annual Conference in Greensboro in 1889. The motion was made to put the name of R. O. Burton on the superannuated list. Immediately Dr. Burton took the floor in his own behalf and combatted the motion, declaring that he was able to do the work of the pastorate and that he wanted to die with his armor on. He made one of the greatest speeches of his life and succeeded in getting the Conference to place his name on the supernumerary list instead. He was thus allowed in his old age and failing health to continue in the ministry though with light work.

Dr. Burton was married twice. His second wife was Mary Olivia Pearson. His first marriage was blessed with an offspring of four sons, his second of three sons and two daughters, all of whom reached maturity. Having reached his four score years by reason of his strength, he breathed his last December 17, 1891, at his home near Weldon.

XXXIV

ROBERT O. BURTON, JR.

Among the able lawyers that Halifax County has produced, Robert O. Burton, Jr., ranks high. Although he died at an age before most men attain their greatest successes, he can be classed with those who have reflected honor upon the county and state.

He was the fourth son of Dr. Robert O. Burton, a distinguished Methodist minister, and Elizabeth Joyner Burton, daughter of Colonel Andrew Joyner, a veteran of this War of 1812 and for a long time senator from Halifax County. Born January 9, 1852, he was a mere lad at the time of the Civil War and experienced the hardships of that period and grew to manhood during Reconstruction Days. Who can tell but that the privations of those days taught him lessons that contributed no little to the sturdy character he afterwards developed?

Of his boyhood days, one of his earliest friends, a

school-mate, has the following to say: "His early years were spent like other boys of his neighborhood with the distinction of being a favorite at all times among his comrades and school-fellows. At the old school taught by Mr. (afterwards Dr.) Archer, it was this writer's privilege to share this comradeship. Was a game of 'prisoners base' proposed? 'Bob Burton' was the one boy clamored for on both sides. Was a less bright boy troubled with the solving of what seemed to him intricate problems in percentage, or partial payments? Bob Burton was the friend to stand between him and Mr. Archer's rod, while he, too, sometimes felt the persuasive eloquence of this same rod. His nature was calm, cool, thoughtful, and deliberate, and he was at all times ready to help the needy, defend the weak, and exact justice for his childhood friends."

Early in life, Robert Burton felt himself called to the practice of law. Unwilling, however, to enter this learned profession without being fully equipped, as a boy, he began to canvass the situation to secure the funds needed for the completion of a college course. The disasters of the war and reconstruction days left the boy, along with others, almost penniless. His father's income, now reduced, and his mother's fortune, now swept away, added nothing to his prospects. His opportunity to complete his academic education seemed indeed slight.

Determined, however, to go to college, the nineteen year old boy taught school for a year near Ridgeway, N. C., and practiced the most rigid economy in order to save money. He boarded that year in the home of Thomas Carroll, whose daughter he afterwards married. His work as a teacher was as conscientiously done as his larger labors afterwards as a lawyer were accomplished.

Finishing the school year as a teacher, he prepared to enter college in the fall of 1872. He matriculated at Randolph-Macon and was a close student for about two years. He did not take a degree, but his work was so well done that he won the respect and confidence of the faculty and student body. It is said that as a student he was methodi-

MAIN STREET, LITTLETON, N. C.

BUILDERS OF THE COUNTY

cal and systematic. When prevailed upon by his fellow students to play ball with them, he would promise to play only for a certain length of time, and when it was out, he would quit and go back to his studies. No one was more conscientious in his work than he.

Leaving college in 1873, he taught school again for a year in order to pay some college debts. While teaching he read law privately, and, in 1874, received his license and located in the town of Halifax. There he formed a partnership with Edward Conigland, which continued until the tragic death of the latter in 1877. For fifteen years, he practiced at the bar of Halifax and was one of the leading barristers in that historic town. He fought many legal battles during that time, and in all of them, he won fairly or lost because his adversary had the better cause.

In 1889, in search of a broader field, he moved to Richmond, Va., and remained about a year. Returning to North Carolina, he located in Raleigh, and, for nine years was one of the leading attorneys of the capital city. Endowed with two natural gifts, a strong mind and unwearied diligence, Robert Burton built up a wide practice, which began to be lucrative and exacting. Speaking of his success, the News and Observer made the following remark:

"Mr. Burton's most notable victory at the bar was when he won the difficult and celebrated case of State vs. Wilmington and Weldon Railroad. By the terms of its charter, that railroad claimed and exercised exemption from taxation. The Supreme Court of the United States had affirmed their right to exemption in a case that went up before it built any branches. After it had built numerous branches and had come to be one of the best paying railroads in the whole country, the State felt that, even if the exemption on the main line could hold, the road could not go on building numerous branch lines and feeders without subjecting such property to taxation. There was much agitation of the matter between 1888 and 1891, during the administration of Governor Fowle. After an investigation of the matter, Governor Fowle and State Treasurer Bain determined to test the right of the claimed exemption, and Mr. Burton, Mr. Ryan, and perhaps other attorneys were retained to represent the State. Mr. Burton entered into this difficult case with all his zeal, giving almost his whole time to a study of the question. Most of the lawyers thought that the exemption was unlimited and perpetual, and that nothing could be done which would subject that property to taxation. The difficulties were many. But Mr. Burton's ability and genius were able to overcome them. He made a test case that was tried when Judge Connor was on the Superior Court Bench. Judge Connor decided that Mr. Burton's contention was sound and he had won first blood. The case was one of such great importance that Judge Connor rendered his decision in an ably written opinion. The railroad appealed to the Supreme Court. Mr. Burton's argument there was one of the ablest that has been heard in the chamber of the State's highest court. The court affirmed Judge Connor. The opinion of the court was delivered by Justice Clark. The opinions of Judge Connor and Justice Clark, sustaining the contention made for the State by Mr. Burton, made it so clear that the exemption could not long stand that at the next session of the Legislature a compromise was effected by which the railroad surrendered all claim to exemption from taxation. It is the most important case that has been decided in North Carolina in a quarter of a century, and his success in that case gave Mr. Burton wide reputation and rank with the first lawyers of the State."

That case established his reputation in North Carolina and, thereafter, his success was assured. Some years afterward, the Wilmington and Weldon Railroad Company, having recognized his ability in the great legal battle against them, secured his services to represent them at the State capitol; and, true to his instincts as a lawyer, he accepted the trust, thus becoming the defender of the Corporation that he had so ardently fought a few years before, a distinct compliment to his ability and integrity.

The last legal battle in which he appeared was the celebrated case of Gattis vs. Kilgo, which was tried in Oxford the latter part of November, 1900. His speech on that occasion for the defendant was one of the best ever delivered in the Granville Courthouse. He went home and took his bed with a raging fever. He died December 27, 1900.

Robert O. Burton was a lawyer. He was devoted to his profession, and avoided politics. May 29, 1878, he was married to Mary Carroll, who survived him.

XXXV

WILLIAM T. SHAW, JR.

One of the young men that Halifax County sent to the Great European War and who came not back again was William T. Shaw, Jr., who was killed in action in the Second Battle of the Marne, July 16, 1918. The record of his brief life deserves a place in the annals of the county.

William Shaw, son of Mr. and Mrs. W. T. Shaw, of Weldon, was born June 21, 1892. His early life was spent under ideal influences, developing in him those high traits of character that distinguished him throughout his brief life. As a pupil in school, he easily led his classes and was regarded by teachers and class-mates as a boy of superior mold.

He was fond of athletics, and was usually leader of the boys on the playground. In all his school life, both on class and on the athletic field, he was the champion of fair play. William Shaw's word went a long way in the decision of questions of right or wrong among his play-fellows.

Before completing the course at the Weldon High School, he was sent to the College of Agriculture and Mechanic Arts, Raleigh, N. C., for the purpose of studying textile industry. There, as he had done in the preparatory school, he led his classes, graduating with honor in 1914. While in college, he was made captain of one of the companies of the cadet battalion, and ranked high as a soldier and a disciplinarian. In a competitive drill, his company easily won the prize as the best trained men in college.

Leaving college in 1914, he accepted work in one of the cotton mills in Danville, Va., where he remained a year. Returning to Weldon in 1915, he was made Superintendent of one of the mills of the Weldon Manufacturing Company, and continued in that capacity until August, 1917, when he volunteered for service in the Great War. He entered the Officers' Training Camp at Fort Oglethorpe, Ga., for three months' intensive drill for a commission in the United States army. In November, he was commissioned captain, an honor bestowed upon few.

Upon winning this high honor at the Training Camp, William Shaw was assigned to the Fifty-First Regiment of Infantry and ordered to report for duty at Fort Oglethorpe early in December, 1917. His duties there for four months brought him in contact with some of the best drilled men in the United States Army, and in every trial of skill, Shaw was a match for the best.

Early in May, 1918, William Shaw's regiment received orders for overseas duty and entrained for Hoboken. There he was detained for several weeks, but finally embarkation orders came and he joined his company in France about the last of May. After a month's training behind the lines, his regiment was ordered to the front about the time the Germans made their last great drive in July. Arriving upon the battle front, these fresh American troops, anxious for a trial of strength with the famous Prussian guards, were thrown into the thickest of the fight and brought the advance of the enemy to a standstill. A few days later when the time came for the great counter attack of the allies, Captain Shaw led the charge upon the hitherto invincible Prussians and forced them to give ground; but in that victorious advance, Shaw received a mortal wound, dying in the arms of victory.

BUILDERS OF THE COUNTY 229

William Shaw was a hero and a patriot. When great pressure was brought to bear upon him to remain in the productive occupation he was in and take deferred classification in the draft, he replied that it was his duty to go and fight for the cause of humanity and justice. When his mother endeavored to persuade him to remain at home until there was a more urgent call, he said, "It is my duty to go, and, mother, it is your duty as a Christian to bid me go." Thus did he see his duty clearly, and seeing it he dared to perform it.

OTHERS WHO HAVE WROUGHT.

To give a biographical sketch of all the men who have left their impress upon the County and State would take these pages far beyond the original purpose, and yet there are others whose lives and deeds are like "Apples of gold in pictures of silver". Only a brief mention of them can now be made because of the difficulties in getting possession of the facts. Perhaps some Boswell will be induced to do the delving that is necessary to discover the hidden gems, and will some time bring them to the light.

Abner Nash, who, afterwards, became Governor of the State, lived in the county many years. He was, for several times, a member of the General Assembly, part of the time representing the town of Halifax and at other times the County. He owned at one time immense tracts of land on the Roanoke river, but he later sold his belongings and moved to Hillsboro.

Rev. Thomas Burgess was a pioneer Episcopal minister, who was among the first religious teachers to work in the borders of the present county. He was one of the few ministers of the Church of England in North Carolina in the middle of the eighteenth century. His field was the parish of Edgecombe, which later became the County of Halifax. He was for years rector of the Episcopal Church in the town of Halifax.

William E. Webb was an educator of ability and a man of considerable influence in the town of Halifax during the first quarter of the eighteenth century. In addition to being a teacher and Principal of Union Academy, he was for three terms a representative from the county in the General Assembly.

John Campbell was for some years editor of the Halifax Minerva, a weekly newspaper published in the town of Halifax about 1830. He later quit the newspaper work and came to Weldon to live, became a railroad employe, organized the first lodge of Odd Fellows in North Carolina, and later, became the first Grand Master of the Grand Jurisdiction of North Carolina.

William H. Kitchin was one of the Democratic warhorses of the period following the Civil War. Leading a forlorn hope in 1878, he accepted the nomination for Congress, and, by adroit political maneuvering, divided the opposition to him into two hostile camps and was elected by a plurality vote. His influence in politics was felt in the State for a number of years, and he was considered one of the best stump speakers in Eastern North Carolina. His two eminent sons, Will and Claude, are still adding honor to the County of Halifax.

Rev. Thomas G. Lowe was, during the period following the Civil War, a distinguished minister of the Methodist Church. He was an eloquent speaker and was known all over the State as one of the best equipped preachers of the Methodist denomination. He lived in the town of Halifax.

William A. Dunn, for a number of years following the Civil War, was a prominent lawyer of Scotland Neck. He had a large practice, and, for a long time, was a leader socially, economically, and commercially of his section of the county.

John A. Collins was a prominent physician of Enfield, and a political leader for almost a generation. Small of body but with a big heart and brain, he wielded a large influence in the affairs of the county until his death in 1916.

William H. Day was a lawyer of considerable ability of Weldon during Reconstruction Days, and for years afterward. He was one of the best criminal lawyers of his day. In later life he moved to Raleigh and was prominent at the bar of that city when he died.

W. T. Whitfield, who was born near Weldon, made his home in that place in 1834 when a boy fourteen years old and was a factor in the upbuilding of the place for seventy-six years, dying at the age of ninety. For thirty-five years, he was the agent of the Southern Express Company in Weldon. He was a prominent Odd Fellow, and did much in building up that brotherhood in North Carolina.

And these lived and wrought and "slept with their fathers", and their works do follow them.

THE END.

INDEX

ALBEMARLE, the ironclad ram used by the Confederates in the Civil War, 116-120.
Allen, Elisha, 90
Allen, Hamlin, 90.
Allen, James, 53, 57.
Allen, John, 46, 47.
Allen, Walter N., sketch of, 204,-206.
Alston, William, 25, 28.
Alston, Willis, 31, 34, 37, 40, 43, 68, 105; sketch of, 168.
Alston, Willis, Jr., 69; sketch of, 169, 170.
Ashe, John B., 7, 68, 69, 95, 103; sketch of, 151-153.

BAKER, Blake, representative of Halifax County in Colonial Assembly, 16, 17.
Baker, L. S., 121.
Barrow, Jacob, 42.
Bertie precinct, organized in 1722, 6; Halifax County included in, 7; new precinct formed from, called Edgecombe precinct, 7.
Blount, William, 65.
Bradford, John, 25, 28, 31, 33, 40, 41; sketch of, 172, 173.
Branch, John, 53, 54, 68, 72, 77, 99, 105, 144; sketch of, 177-181.
Branch, L. O'B., 75, 121; sketch of, 192-194.
Burgess, Rev. Thomas, 229.
Burke, Thomas, 32.
Burton, Hutchings G., 103; curious story connected with his death, 140; sketch of, 181-183.
Burton, Rev. Robert O., sketch of, 220-223.
Burton, Robert O, Jr., sketch of, 223-227.
Bynum, Jesse A., 99, 103; rivalry between, and Robert Potter, 186-188.

CAMPBELL, John, 81, 230.
Campbell, John K., 90.
Caswell, Richard, 40, 43, 45, 65.

Champion, John, 37, 41.
Chowan, river, 6.
Clarendon County, 9.
Clark, David C., 121.
Collins, John A., 230.
Colonial Assembly, list of representatives to, from Borough and County of Halifax, 21.
Committee of Safety appointed, 25; met in Halifax, Dec. 21, 1774, 26.
Conigland, Edward, sketch of, 194, 195.
Constitutional Convention and Congress, 40-43.
Cox, P., 37.
Cox, W. R., 121.
Crawley, David, 33.
Crowell family, 136-138.

DANIEL, John R. J., 99; sketch of, 185, 186.
Daniel, Joseph J., 72, 99, 103; sketch of, 183-185.
Daniel, Junius, 121; sketch of, 196-201.
Davie, William R., 63, 65, 68, 69, 103, 144; sketch of, 156-162.
Davis, James, 42.
Davis, Orondates, 53, 68, 105; sketch of, 171, 172.
Dawson, Henry, 37, 42.
Day, William, 43.
Day, William H., 231.
Dewey, Stephen, first representative of town of Halifax in Colonial Assembly, 16, 17.
Drew, William, 72, 103.
Dunn, William A., 230.

EATON, Thomas, 35, 43.
Edgecombe precinct organized in 1732, 7; long contest over, 7, 11; became Edgecombe County in 1738, 8; divided into two parishes, of which Edgecombe Parish became Halifax County, 8.
Elliott, Gilbert, constructer of the

234 INDEX

Confederate ram *Albemarle*, 116; description of the vessel by, quoted, 116–119.
Emery, Thomas L., sketch of, 206–209.
Enfield, oldest town in Halifax County, 11, 12; made county seat of Edgecombe County in 1745, 11, 12; seat of district court of Edgecombe, Northampton, and Granville, 12.
Enfield Academy, 77.

FARMWELL Grove Academy, 77.
Freemasonry in Halifax, 92–98.

GEDDY, John, 25, 27, 43.
Glasgow, James, 40, 43.
Green, James, 31, 40.
Green, James, Jr., secretary of Provincial Congress at Halifax, April 4, 1776, 31.

HALIFAX County, formed in 1758 from part of Edgecombe precinct, 7, 14; settled as early as 1732, 11; population in 1758 nearly 3000, 14; Halifax selected as county seat, 15; resolutions passed by freeholders of, August 22, 1774, 23, 24; spirit of independence in, pronounced, 30, 31; its part in the Revolutionary War, 31–61; and the national constitution, 65, 66; influential in Federal Congress, 69; roster of two companies of volunteers in war of 1812 from, 70, 71; visit of Lafayette to, 73, 74; schools in, 76–79; newspapers in, 80, 81; coming of railroads, 87; cultivation of fruits popular industry, 87; in the Mexican War, 100; in the State Legislature, 103–105; in the Civil War, 107–127; reconstruction days in, 128–131; list of state representatives, 1891–1917, 132; active part of county in the World War, 134; members of National House of Representatives from, 144; State officers from, 144, 145.
Halifax, town, chosen as county seat of Halifax County, 15; occupied by the British, 57; celebrates surrender of Cornwallis, 62; Visit of Washington to, and his description of, in his Diary, 66, 67; for many years after the Revolution political centre of State, 80; list of representatives in the State Legislature, 102; historic homes in, 141, 142.
Hamilton, John, 28, 34; sketch of, 38, 39.
Harnett, Cornelius, 28, 32, 37, 40, 43.
Haynes, Thomas, 25.
Haywood, Egbert, 25, 28, 33, 40, 53, 68.
Haywood, John, 68; sketch of, 165–167.
Haywood, William, 43.
Hewes, Joseph, 34, 37, 41.
Hill, Thomas N., sketch of, 215–218.
Hodge, Abraham, 81; sketch of, 176, 177.
Hogan, James, 25, 27, 31, 34, 40, 41, 42, 52; sketch of, 162–164.
Hooper, William, 34, 37, 41.

INDIANS, various tribes in Halifax County before the coming of the whites, 3; cultivation of soil by, rude, 4; peaceable relations with whites, 4; disappeared by 1720, 5.
Ivedell, James, 66.
Irwin, Henry, 28.

JOHNSTON, Samuel, president of Provincial Congress at Halifax, April 4, 1776, 31.
Jones, Albritton, 42.
Jones, Allen, 32, 33, 53, 56, 57, 61.
Jones, John Paul, 48–51; sketch of, 173–176.
Jones, Thomas, 32, 42, 43.
Jones, Willie, 25, 26, 27, 31, 34, 37, 40, 41, 42, 45, 53, 62, 65, 67, 68, 95; sketch of, 153–156.
Joyner, Andrew, 88, 91; sketch of, 190–192.

KEHUKEE Creek, settlement on, in 1742, 12; oldest Baptist church in North Carolina at, 12.
Kinchin, M., 32.
Kitchin, Claude, 133, 134.
Kitchin, W. H., 133, 230.

LA VALLIE Female Academy, 78.
Leech, Joseph, 43.
London, David, 92.

INDEX

Long, Nicholas, 25, 27, 34, 41, 57, 68; sketch of, 170, 171.
Long, William Lunsford, 90.
Lynch, George Green, 212-214.
Lowe, Rev. Thomas, G., 230.

McCulloch, Benjamin, 34, 40, 68, 80.
McCullough, Alexander, representative of Halifax County in Colonial Assembly, 16, 17.
Martin, Alexander, 65, 105.
Miller, Andrew, Merchant of Halifax, boycotted for refusing to sign Resolutions of the Association, 26; property confiscated in 1779, 27.
Milner, James, 27.
Montford, Joseph, 16, 21, 26, 27, 92, 94, 95, 96, 97.
Montford, Henry, 42, 53, 68.
Montford, Joseph, 92, 94, 95, 96, 97, 143; sketch of, 149-151.
Moore, B. F., 99, 105; sketch of, 188-190.
Moore, James, story of a privateer's adventures by, 138, 139.
Munday, Caleb, 37.

Nash, Abner, 22, 32, 41, 56, 57, 229.
Nash, Francis, 27.
Newspapers in Halifax, 80, 81.
Noblin, William, 37, 42.
North Carolina, early settlers of, from Virginia, 9.

Parker, Francis M., sketch of, 201, 202.
Parsons, James M., 37.
Pearce, Josiah, 41.
Penn, John, 34, 37, 105.
Peterson, E. K., 90.
Potter, Robert, 103; rivalry between, and Jesse A. Bynum, 186-188.
Provincial Congress at Halifax, 25, 27; authorizes enrollment of minute men, 27, 28; organizes Provincial Council, 28; important steps in favor of independence of the colonies, 31-35.
Provincial Council of Safety, at Halifax, 36, 37, 40.

Quarles, Peter, 68.
Quit-rents, trouble over, 18-20.

Regulators, in Orange County, 22, 23.
Religion, progress of, in Halifax, 82-84.
Rice, Nathaniel, 7.
Roanoke Navigation Company, opening of Canal by, 88.
Roanoke, river, 3; called "Morotuck" by the Indians, 7.
Royal White Hart Lodge, 92-98.

Scotland Neck Female Academy, 78.
Scurlock Thomas, 54.
Sevier, John, 41.
Shaw, William T., Jr., sketch of, 227-229.
Simmons, James, 90.
Smith, Peter Evans, sketch of, 218-220.
Smith, Richard H., sketch of, 209-212.
Spaight, Richard Dobbs, 65.
Starkey, Edward, 43.
Sumner, David, 25, 27, 28, 31, 34.
Sumner, Jethro, 28.
Sumner, Josiah, 34.

Tories, very few in Halifax County, 26, 28.
Tyron, William, governor of Province in 1765, 22; calls on counties for troops to fight Regulators, 23.
Tuscaroras, Indians who inhabited Halifax County before the coming of the whites, 3.

Union Academy, 77.

Vine Hill Academy, 77.

Webb, John, 27, 28, 32, 34, 37, 68.
Webb, William E., 77, 230.
Weldon, Samuel, 25, 34, 40, 41, 43; sketch of, 165.
Weldon, William, 53, 54.
Wheaton, John, 43.
Whitaker, John, 53.
Whitaker, Matthew C., 68, 107.
Whitaker, Spier, 105; sketch of, 202, 203.
Whitefield, W. T., 231.
Willis, Augustine, 53.
Williams, Joseph John, 25, 31, 35.
Williamson, Hugh, 65.
Wilmington & Weldon Railroad, opened in 1840, 89.

www.ingramcontent.com/pod-product-compliance
Lightning Source LLC
Chambersburg PA
CBHW060554230426
43670CB00011B/1823